« *Exclusive Conversations* »

« *Exclusive Conversations* »

The Art of Interaction in Seventeenth-Century France

ELIZABETH C. GOLDSMITH

upp   *University of Pennsylvania Press · Philadelphia · 1988*

Copyright © 1988 by the University of Pennsylvania Press
All rights reserved
Printed in the United States of America

Library of Congress Cataloging-in-Publication Data
Goldsmith, Elizabeth C.
   Exclusive conversations: the art of interaction in seventeenth-century France / Elizabeth C. Goldsmith.
      p.   cm.
   Bibliography: p.
   Includes index.
   ISBN 0-8122-8102-0
   1. French literature—17th century—History and criticism.
2. Conversation in literature.   3. Social interaction in literature.
4. Courtesy in literature.   5. France—Social life and customs—17th
century.   6. France—Court and courtiers—History—17th century.
7. Salons—France—History—17th century.   I. Title.
PQ249.G64   1988
840'.9'355—dc19

87-30788
CIP

Designed by Adrianne Onderdonk Dudden

Contents

Acknowledgments

This book would not have been possible without the participation of friends, colleagues, and institutions. A Summer-Term Research Support Grant from Boston University in 1980 gave me the time to develop my initial formulation of the project, and a grant from the American Philosophical Society in 1982 funded some indispensable research at the Bibliothèque Nationale in Paris. A Folger Library Fellowship in 1985 allowed me to spend a summer working with the collections there and to profit from discussions with other Folger readers and librarians. I am also grateful for the patient assistance provided by the staff of the Houghton Library and the Department of Rare Books and Manuscripts of the Boston Public Library.

Parts of chapters two and three appeared in *Papers on French Seventeenth-Century Literature* (XIII, 24) and *French Forum* (VIII, 3), respectively. They are reprinted here by permission.

I wish to thank Nelly Furman, Jeff Kline, Phil Lewis, and Alain

Seznec for their encouragement and assistance in obtaining the above-mentioned grants. Finally, my greatest debt is to Art Goldsmith, whose criticisms and sometimes tough advice have been as important to the completion of this book as his good humor and utterly partisan support.

« *Exclusive Conversations* »

Introduction

From Castiglione to Miss Manners, courtesy literature has always told readers how to interact in social situations. In seventeenth-century France, social deportment was the key, not only to success, but to acquiring a personal identity. For members of court society the representation of self was always a highly social event, and styles of social interaction were matters of serious political and philosophical speculation. Elite culture during the reign of Louis XIV was based, perhaps more than at any other moment in European history, on ritualized interaction. The art of social existence encompassed an elaborate repertoire of skills, the most important of these being conversation.

This book examines the changes in the theory and practice of conversational interaction during the second half of the seventeenth century, changes that occurred in the wake of what used to be called "the decline of the nobility," and what historians more recently have described as the cultural transformation of a nobility into an aristocracy—a change in the definition of what constituted elite status.[1] My use of the term interaction is based on Erving Goffman's studies of "focused interaction," or the mutual dealings that occur when individuals agree to sustain for a time a single focus of attention.[2] The word "conversation," though, has a more specific historical meaning in this study. In the seventeenth century the verb "converser" retained its latin sense of "to frequent"or "live with," and the noun "conversation" conveyed a sense of place that it no longer has today. Conversation created its own social space with carefully marked boundaries; to "be somebody" one had to be "in the best conversations."[3] Conversation was an artifact as much as an activity, and it was through conversation that all other cultural forms were assigned or denied a place in "le monde." In the classical written portrait, the best compliment one could pay one's subjects was to praise their conversation; no skill was more important for enhancing one's social status. The successful self-promotion of a Vincent Voiture would become emblematic of how conversational skills could replace and even supersede the more traditional qualifications for privilege and favor.

In different ways, all of the writers studied here viewed their own texts as conversations. My point of departure in Chapter 1 is a body of material—for the most part the most frequently reprinted conduct books and collections of model conversations and letters—discussing conversation as the principal activity or skill necessary for social survival. These works present their readers with scenarios for interaction and motives for learning them. I view these manuals chronologically, showing how they record important changes in the way people were taught to interact, changes that reflect an expansion of the realm of sociability codes to include private conversation and the conduct of intimacy.

Against this background of some thirty normative texts, I look at the works of four writers who had close ties to both the Versailles court and the Paris salons. These authors' lives as well as their works illustrate different responses to the problem of fashioning verbal models for the enactment of new social relationships. Scudéry, Sévigné and Bussy-Rabutin were as famous in their own day for their mastery of the art of conversation as they were for their writing. All three worked to realize the aesthetic ideal of salon culture: to write as they spoke, and to make of writing an extension of worldly talk. Others describe them, and they describe themselves, as obsessive speakers. In her model con- versations Madeleine de Scudéry sets up an economy of interaction with verbal excess as its central principle. Madame de Sévigné and Bussy-Rabutin, when cut off from the verbal contacts that sustain them, reconstruct their social selves through correspondences which they fashion as conversations.

Scudéry--
verbal excess-
principle

Chapter 2 studies ideal interaction as envisioned by Madeleine de Scudéry in her ten volumes of written conversations. These books are rarely studied separately from her novels, and until recently Scudéry scholars have assumed that all of the conversations were excerpted from them, whereas in fact many were written for the new collection. Her conversations function in this study as an example of the code of sociability in its purest enactment, within and against which the other writers evolve their own versions of interaction.

Scudéry's code
of sociability --
pure enactment

Chapters 3 and 4 look at different adaptations of conversation in the correspondences of the two most admired letter writers of their time, Madame de Sévigné and Bussy-Rabutin. Bussy-Rabutin's personal ex- perience of exile, and the rhetorical techniques he uses to reassert con- trol over it, reflect some broader political changes that were being set in motion under Louis XIV. Sévigné's letters display a more complex and changing definition of her public and private selves. Unlike her cousin Bussy, she has occasion to feel that the norms of sociability are not always appropriate for communicating intimacy. This is particu- larly visible in her letters to her daughter, whose move to Provence in 1671 marked the beginning of a long and passionate correspondence.

Chapter 5 studies the writings of Edme Boursault, an author who is little known today but who was extremely popular in his time. The unifying thread in his very disparate assortment of works is his fasci- nation with the phenomenon of publicity, and the ways in which this peculiar blend of information, gossip and courtly flattery could be used as both an artistic and political tool. By the standards of seventeenth- century elite culture, Boursault was an outsider, a professional writer who neither belonged nor apparently aspired to the "parasitic bour- geoisie," Erich Auerbach's term for the non-noble members of "la cour et la ville."[4] A middle-class writer who worked for pay, he was excep- tionally sensitive to changing styles of behavior and verbal interaction. Boursault's representations of sociability reveal how aristocratic codes of conduct were being modified by a more heterogeneous public to accommodate new ideas about what a meaningful and authentic conversation was supposed to be.

*   *   *

In the salons and court of seventeenth-century France, rules of social conduct were refined and adapted to the demands of courtly politics. Ambitious courtiers, wanting to exploit the increasing opportunities for members of the noblesse de robe and the commercial classes at the court of Louis XIV, learned to use courtesy codes in refashioning their social selves. No one seeking to enhance his or her social status would have underestimated the potential of etiquette as a political tool. That *politesse* could be used as an instrument of power was demonstrated daily in the increasingly codified interaction at court, and in the elaborate deference rituals surrounding the person of the king. Paradoxically, at a time when traditional signs of social status were becoming less rigid, the norms for behavior in polite society were becoming more hierarchical.[5]

The proliferation of conduct manuals, collections of model conversations and letters, and other prescriptive texts on proper social behavior during the seventeenth century in France was largely a response to the demands of a growing public eager to learn the art of sociability. "Il serait inutile de dire combien la société est nécessaire aux hommes," writes La Rochefoucauld, "tous la désirent et tous la cherchent, mais peu se servent des moyens de la rendre agréable et de la faire durer."[6]

It was one thing to find oneself in good company, and quite another to know what to do when you got there. Conduct literature offered a growing number of readers a system of rules, methods, and techniques for making social interaction both agreeable and lasting. The courtesy book was a genre that had developed as a literary form in Renaissance Italy, where the art of civility was regarded as a branch of rhetorical theory.[7] The works of Renaissance Italian writers such as Castiglione, Guazzo and Della Casa reflected a new social mobility characterizing the fifteenth and sixteenth centuries in Italy. Personal effort was becoming a viable means of improving one's social standing. Noble birth, writes Castiglione, gives the courtier a great advantage, but it is a "matter for congratulating one's ancestors rather than oneself."[8] Other, acquirable qualities are more important for winning the rank of a good, if not perfect, courtier.

The strategies for acquiring the traits of a cultivated person were aimed at exclusion as much as inclusion. Renaissance courtesy literature had created a strategically vague definition of the perfect social self, asserting that the ideal courtier must have a "certain something" that could only be acknowledged by an elite public qualified to recognize this elusive virtue. Ease or naturalness, named "sprezzatura" by Castiglione, was the *sine qua non* of social success. "Sprezzatura" was the courtier's test, a test he knew he had passed when he received the approbation of the group he was imitating. It was essential that the courtier's techniques be impossible to define precisely, because only by remaining meticulously evasive about the requirements for admission to superior status were those who had it able to maintain the exclusivity of their group.

Renaissance courtesy theory in England focused more intently on the relationship between courtly behavior and private ambition, and it was this relationship that concerned seventeenth-century French writers of conduct books as well.[9] Cultural transformations caused by unprecedented social mobility turned everyone's attention to the techniques of personal image-making. The disruption and questioning of traditional status systems made ambitious people more aware of the symbolic systems at work in social interaction, and made privileged individuals more concerned with how to justify their status. In the culture of the ruling elite in France we see a phenomenon similar to what has been studied in the status systems in Elizabethan high society, where the symbolism of deportment and gesture came to compete with and sometimes dominate more practical motives for interaction.[10] In France, where elite culture was much more dominated by the court and crown than in England, the competition for status and prestige was more intense. Collective judgment and public opinion assumed tremendous importance in determining individual worth, as society's members looked for confirmation of their own moral status in daily interactive rituals. Cynical observers such as La Bruyère saw in the constant process of personal evaluation a system motivated solely by self-interest: "L'on dit à la cour du bien de quelqu'un pour deux raisons: la première, afin qu'il apprenne que nous disons du bien de lui; la seconde, afin qu'il en dise de nous."[11]

art of talk/
conversation

Whatever one's motives for learning it, the art of talk was the most important of the courtly skills. This is true for the Italian Renaissance courtier as well as his descendant, the habitué of Paris salons. Castiglione writes that it was the evening conversations that made the court of Urbino superior to all others, and Guazzo describes conversation as the most natural expression of civilized man: "conversation is not only profitable, but moreover necessary to the perfection of man, who must confess that he is like the bee which cannot live alone."[12] While their Italian predecessors had said that conversational skill was the natural foundation for the formation of the courtier, French courtesy literature gave it a more transcendant role in determining the worth of a person in society. The French classical ideal of *honnêteté* gave particular emphasis to the *honnête homme*'s manner of interaction in conversation and letter-writing. In the theorizing about *honnête* behavior we find Renaissance definitions of sociability refashioned in response to new social pressures.

salon:
exclusive space
for nurturing
elite culture

The most important modification of Renaissance notions of courtesy in France was the extension of its space to what we now call the salon, and what was known in the seventeenth century as the *alcôve* or *ruelle*. The salon emerged in the first half of the seventeenth century as a new, exclusive space for the nurturing of elite culture. By the end of the previous century the traditional occupation for the nobility in France, the profession of arms, was widely viewed as an inadequate and limiting basis for the justification of elite status. Treatises on the philosophical and moral foundations of the nobility turned to the Italian model of a nobility of birth buttressed by learning and personal culture.[13] The abbé de Pure's comment on a special, superior place reserved for the *précieuse* emphasizes the challenge to traditional signs of status that salon culture posed:

> quand on entre dans une ruelle, comme les duchesses ont leur rang dans le cercle, ainsi la précieuse a le sien; et si la belle place est fortuitement occupée par quelque personne de condition, vous voyez le chagrin dans toute la ruelle, comme une profanation d'un autel qui était destiné à la précieuse.[14]

When the Marquise de Rambouillet had her city residence redesigned in the first decade of the seventeenth century, she gave architectural proportions to a new concept of exclusivity. Unlike the salons

of predecessors such as Marguerite de Valois, her *chambre bleue* was
carefully conceived as separate from the court society of the Louvre
and other royal residences. Contemporary accounts delightedly report
her aversion to court ceremonial, and Tallemant suggests that the purpose of her infrequent visits to the antechambers of the Louvre was to
amuse herself with observing how refreshingly different her own idea
of "divertissement" was:

> Elle disait qu'elle n'y trouvait rien de plaisant, que de voir comme
> on se pressait pour y entrer, et que quelquefois il lui est arrivé de
> se mettre en une chambre pour se divertir du méchant ordre qu'il y
> a pour ces choses-là en France. Ce n'est pas qu'elle n'aimât le diver-
> tissement, mais c'était en particulier.[15]

While most of the habitués of both court and salon preferred to pass
freely between both places, the social milieu of the salon was increasingly viewed as the more hospitable environment for perfect sociability.
"Le monde," the seventeenth-century designation for elite society, suggests a notion of restricted exclusivity that is at the same time all-
encompassing, it encloses everything (of any importance) within its
boundaries. Pure writes that from within the confines of a *ruelle* or
alcove it is also possible to see everything that is outside more clearly:
"On voit, mais clairement, dans une ruelle, le mouvement de toute la
terre; et trois ou quatre précieuses, débiteront dans un après-midi tout
ce que le soleil peut avoir vu dans ses divers tours de différentes sai-
sons" (I, 67). Salon culture proposed to redefine the criteria for inclusion and exclusion, and create a "grand monde purifié," as Chapelain
called the Rambouillet circle.[16] The normative literature of conduct, a
literature that was most prolific during the reigns of Louis XIII and
Louis XIV, documents these efforts to systematize the ways in which
members of society interact.

*   *   *

The French nobility suffered severe challenges to its traditionally accepted social functions and privileges during the late sixteenth
and early seventeenth centuries. Ellery Schalk has described the "prise
de conscience" of the noble classes in the last decades of the sixteenth
century, in the wake of social disruptions caused by the wars of reli-
gion.[17] A wave of anti-noble feeling directed against the excesses of the

military nobles was accompanied by members of the nobility them-selves questioning the adequacy of their traditional military function as a justification for privilege. By the 1650's a more modern view of no-bility, based on birth but also giving an entirely new emphasis to edu-cation, personal cultivation, and techniques for social interaction had replaced the medieval code of valor. At the same time, as members of the middle class grew in wealth and power, they also aspired to this new style of life that was neither characteristically bourgeois nor tra-ditionally noble. To "live nobly" was to eschew both the petty greed of the merchant and the barbaric behavior of the old *noblesse d'épée*.[18] Dur-ing the seventeenth century, as state institutions became increasingly centralized, there were efforts to reestablish traditional status systems while taking into account the more sophisticated norms of social behav-ior that had been cultivated by the newly educated middle classes. Prominent families, who in the last decades of the sixteenth century had been able to get away with calling themselves noble, under the regime of Richelieu were summoned to register proof of their claim. Yet at the same time royal bureaucrats were learning to use codes of etiquette and civility as a means of creating systems of privilege that undermined the traditional social hierarchy.

The most important of the new catalogue of courtesies were rules having to do with speech and gesture. Richelieu was so effective in his manipulation of courtesy to control speech that insolence and breaches of *politesse* came to be regarded as crimes against the state.[19] The tyran-nical conduct codes at Versailles were to carry this method of control-ling speech to its most rigid extreme until the 1680's when in an effort to create a salon to escape his own court, the king began constructing new residences where a select group of courtiers could flee the oppres-sive ceremonial of Versailles.

At the beginning of the seventeenth century in France, the very idea of a noble class defined by its cultural sophistication was new; but in the long run, challenges to traditional ways of justifying privilege probably helped to prolong rather than weaken the dominance of noble culture.[20] Political and social policies under Richelieu and Mazarin forced a broadened definition of aristocratic identity, which at the same time assured the survival and enrichment of the cultural ideology of the nobility. Progressive social formations such as the salon, which led the way in admitting non-noble members to the social elite, at the same time insured that a newly defined noble culture continued to thrive. Salons acted as a kind of social laboratory, where nobles and non-nobles alike proposed to discover new definitions of what it meant to be "naturally" superior.[21] Faced with the evident loss of their exclusive claim to power and privilege, members of the *noblesse d'epée* mustered elaborate defensive justifications to sustain the superiority of the aristocratic image. One of the most important results of this intellectual effort was the concept of the *honnête homme*, a modification of the perfect courtier, who promoted a new definition of noble conduct, rejecting the ancient connection of noble virtue and military valor. Domna Stanton's study of *honnêteté* and nineteenth-century dandyism has shown how both were essentially aesthetic artifacts designed to sustain an aristocratic view of social identity.[22] While the seventeenth-century nobility was losing its exclusive claim to political and economic superiority, its existence as a cultural artifact was both strengthened and modified.

The Principle of Exclusivity

In an essay on the nobility as a prototypical elite society, the social theorist Georg Simmel has examined some of the aesthetic principles underlying the concept of status.[23] Social interaction within all exclusive groups is typically heavily motivated by considerations of style, and the nobility has historically provided a continuous example of the view that a social circle can be an artistic structure. By maintaining as its primary criterion for admittance a mark of status granted by birth, the traditional aristocracy claims for itself a uniquely insular form, in which each part is granted meaning by the whole, and which ritually displays to the world its utter self-sufficiency. The nobility sustains its aesthetic attraction precisely because of the clarity and totality of its closure. For it is not just the individual who is attractive, although the individual display of superior care and cultivation of the body and social forms has historically been an important element in the fascination that a noble can exert over outsiders. More important, it is the "collective image" of the nobility that makes it a powerful cultural artifact, dependent, writes Simmel, "on the aesthetically satisfying form of autonomy and insularity, of the solidarity of parts—all of which are analogues to the work of art" (p.209).

Exclusive groups counterbalance their collective sense of superiority with the conviction that they themselves are a community of equals.[24] Communication among the members of the group must be based on the principle of reciprocity, with each speaker contributing to the equanimity of the circle as a whole. Interaction within exclusive groups always works to create the impression that there is no ultimate end outside the social process itself. The sociability impulse destroys idiosyncracy in order to guarantee perfect balance among members of the group. Simmel writes that the court society of the *ancien régime* exemplifies an extreme form of "pure" sociability, a system of codes whose radical closure was a response to the fact that individual opportunities for status and glory were being significantly reduced. At such moments in the history of the aristocracy, he remarks, "the substance itself becomes form, and the meaning of life is no more than the preservation of specific status honors and of good demeanor—as finally occurred in the nobility of the *ancien régime*" (p.209).

When we look at seventeenth-century discussions about proper social conduct, we see that an important requirement is that individual participants present themselves in balanced *relation* to others, and that it is only the group support provided by this ambiance of mutual generosity that gives value to the contribution of any single member. The pleasure of conversation, writes La Rochefoucauld, is often destroyed by one individual demanding gratification at another's expense. "Il faut éviter de contester sur des choses indifférentes, faire rarement des questions inutiles, ne laisser jamais croire qu'on prétend avoir plus de raison que les autres, et céder aisément l'avantage de décider."[25] In this system the self exists primarily because of the place it occupies and the role it plays within the group. Because the presentation of self is so carefully orchestrated, there is little concern with individuals as isolated or lonely beings; individual selves seem to come into existence as they enter the group.

Erving Goffman's studies of ritual presentations of the self in today's world is another rich resource that can help us understand the ritualization of interaction in the society of Louis XIV. Goffman writes that in certain social situations, codes of conduct can become the most important measure of individual worth: "An environment, in terms of the ceremonial component of activity, is a place where it is easy or difficult to play the ritual game of having a self. Where ceremonial practices are thoroughly institutionalized it would appear easy to be a person. Where they are not established, it would appear difficult to be a person."[26] During the seventeenth century in France, ceremonial practices of social interaction were catalogued, examined, and restruc- tured. Above all, they were talked about, and it was through the filter of conversation that new ideas about *la vie civile* came into being.

Social anthropology also provides a useful vocabulary for studying the functions of conversation. The concept of potlatch applies to an essential feature of seventeenth-century courtesy, namely, that success- ful interaction must be conducted according to the principle of pure reciprocity, not exchange, of gift-giving, not trade. The classical ideal of civility, it would seem, depends on a kind of perpetual verbal pot- latch within a circumscribed social circle. Social contact is a kind of constant circulation of verbal gifts. Marcel Mauss's description of an American Indian tribe operating with a considerable surplus of goods sounds like a description of the Versailles court. There is one season, he writes, when "they are in a perpetual state of effervescence":

> The social life becomes intense in the extreme . . . This life consists of continual movement. There are constant visits . . . There is feast upon feast, some of long duration. On the occasion of a marriage, on various ritual occasions, and on social advancement, there is reckless consumption of everything which has been amassed with great industry from some of the richest coasts of the world during the course of summer and autumn. Even private life passes in this manner . . .[27]

The organizing principle behind this kind of "agitation without dis- order" (Madame de Lafayette's famous phrase describing the dynamic of court society) is reciprocity, or rather, reciprocity in one of its ex- treme forms. Marshall Sahlins writes of the two poles of reciprocity— the pure gift and self-interested seizure—and of "generalized recipro- city," which combines the aristocratic ideal of sociability with the prin- ciple of potlatch. In generalized reciprocity, individual members of a group "give" freely. Their gifts are either material possessions or more abstract kinds of contributions to collective life, such as hospitality, ceremonial gestures, or speech. No payment is demanded in return, and in fact all mention of a counter-obligation is scrupulously avoided. This does not mean that there is none, but it is crucial to the success of the interaction that no reckoning is ever overtly made. There must be a sustained pretense that the resources being offered are abundant, even unlimited.[28] La Rouchefoucauld writes of ideal interaction in much the same terms, maintaining that contributions must seem to be freely given: "Il faut contribuer, autant qu'on le peut, au divertissement des personnes avec qui on veut vivre; mais il ne faut pas être toujours chargé du soin d'y contribuer" (pp. 186–87). What is important in conversation is that all participants allow the form and flow of talk to continue without paying too much attention to what is being said or weighing too carefully the value of each contribution: "on doit entrer indifféremment sur tous les sujets agréables qui se présentent, et ne faire jamais voir qu'on veut entraîner la conversation sur ce qu'on a envie de dire" (p. 193). Curiously, this radically civilized version of sociable interaction seems more analogous to the social structures characterizing primitive cultures than to those of contemporary society.

The Territory of Conversation

Social philosophers of the *ancien régime* thought sociable talk was the activity that both sustained and created the reality of "le monde." Conversation was the best indicator of the worth of an individual or of an entire group, enabling members of society to both measure and construct their personal status. Polite dialogue was the best form for giving an aesthetic dimension to sociability. Like the laws of etiquette which can construct a closed system of self-referentiality, the aristocratic ideal of conversation saw it as generating its own self-sufficient content. Sociable conversation, which focuses on the play of relations it establishes between individuals rather than on the references it carries to the world outside the circle, must also maintain a careful balance between members of the group. It is essential that personality traits always be shaped and displayed in relation to the other speakers. As La Rochefoucauld remarks, too much expressed difference destroys the necessary *illusion* of unanimity.[29] Neither the individual participants nor the specific content of their speech can be given more weight than the play of conversation as form.

This systematic emphasis on form over substance in the conduct of sociable dialogue carries with it certain risks. Members of the group must be careful to exclude rhetorical expressions which draw attention to, rather than disguise, relations of power within the social circle. In a study of the disruptive power of flattery in the discourse of classical civility, Jean Starobinski has analyzed the "narcissisme de groupe" characterizing the doctrine of *honnêteté*. Like Simmel, Starobinski emphasizes the importance of a perfectly balanced system of group interaction in salon culture. "L'idéal de l'honnêteté," he writes, "c'est la réciprocité parfaite, . . . Le commerce qui s'engage ainsi est celui du même avec le même; la différence est réduite au point de n'être plus génératrice de conflit mais de jeu . . ."[30] Consequently, he observes, the most potentially disruptive forces for *honnête* conversation are situations which reveal the real differences existing between members of the group, if only by expressing the specificity of an individual experience or personality. This can happen, for example, when flattery draws too much attention to differences in status, or when the play of coquettish conversation is menaced by an aggressive display of passion.

When the illusion of reciprocity can no longer be easily maintained, interaction becomes more focused on individual needs. Such disruptions constitute a substitution of personal interest for mutual pleasure in social interaction. As La Rochefoucauld comments, "Ce qui fait que si peu de personnes sont agréables dans la conversation, c'est que chacun songe plus à ce qu'il veut dire qu'à ce que les autres disent" (p. 191). But the intrusion of private self-interest into the world of sociable living seems to have been increasingly difficult to repress during the course of the seventeenth century. This development, as we shall see, is documented in conduct manuals from the end of the century that allow much more room for individual expression in their discussions of ideal conversation. Changes in ideas about how sociable communication should work coincide with a shifting distribution of wealth and power within the larger social group to which members of court and salon culture belonged. In the evolution of seventeenth-century codes of interaction we see reflected the changing position of the French aristocracy and the reorganization of social hierarchies in the first modern state.[31]

NOTES

1. See for example François Billacois, "La Crise de la noblesse européenne (1550–1650)," *Revue d'histoire moderne et contemporaine* 23 (1976), pp. 258–77; and

14   *Introduction*

Ellery Schalk, *From Valor to Pedigree: Ideas of Nobility in Sixteenth- and Seventeenth-Century France* (Princeton, N.J.: Princeton University Press, 1986).

2. *Encounters* (Indianapolis: Bobbs Merrill, 1961), p.7.

3. Furetière's 1690 dictionary defines *conversation:* "entretien familier qu'on a avec des amis dans les visites, dans les promenades . . . se dit dans le même sens des assemblées de plusieurs personnes savantes et polies."

4. Erich Auerbach, *Scenes From the Drama of European Literature* (New York: Meridian Books, 1959), p.167.

5. See Norbert Elias, *The Court Society* (New York: Pantheon, 1983), pp. 78–116, for a discussion of some social functions of this increasingly ceremonialized etiquette system. He focuses on early eighteenth-century court society as described by Saint-Simon. By this time aristocrats were given few a priori advantages over middle-class courtiers in the competition for favor at court. Elias's discussion of the desperate status-consumption ethos of this society is suggestive of how the constant "motivation by rank, honor and prestige" applies also to the exchange of visits, dinners, and talk (pp. 64–68).

6. *Maximes*, ed. J. Truchet (Paris: Garnier, 1967), p.185.

7. See Quentin Skinner, *The Foundations of Modern Political Thought* (Cambridge: Cambridge University Press, 1978), pp. 28–35.

8. *The Book of the Courtier* (Middlesex: Penguin), p.56.

9. Frank Whigham has studied the symbolic systems of Elizabethan conduct literature in *Ambition and Privilege: The Social Tropes of Elizabethan Courtesy Theory* (Palo Alto, Ca.: Stanford University Press, 1984).

10. Whigham, "Interpretation at Court: Courtesy and the Performer-Audience Dialectic," *New Literary History* XIV (1983), pp. 628–29.

11. *Les Caractères* (Paris: Garnier), p.232.

12. Cited in John Lievsay, *Stefano Guazzo and the English Renaissance* (Durham: University of North Carolina, 1961), p.15.

13. Schalk's study of changing definitions of nobility in early modern France includes a useful synthesis of recent historical research on the subject. *From Valor to Pedigree*, see especially chapters 6 and 8.

14. *La Précieuse ou le mystère des ruelles* (Paris: Droz, 1938), I, p.67.

15. *Historiettes* (Paris: J. Techener, 1854), II, p. 486.

16. Cited in Maurice Magendie, *La Politesse mondaine et les théories de l'honnêteté en France au dix-septième siècle* (1925; rpt. Genève: Slatkine, 1970), p.124.

17. *From Valor to Pedigree*, ch. 4.

18. George Huppert has analyzed the ideological and cultural formations of this new "gentry" class in *Les Bourgeois Gentilhommes: An Essay on the Definition of Elites in Renaissance France* (Chicago: University of Chicago Press, 1977).

19. See Orest Ranum's essay, "Courtesy, Absolutism, and the Rise of the French State, 1630–1660," *Journal of Modern History* 52 (1980), pp. 426–51. In this regard, the violence of the Fronde can be viewed as "an escalation of insolence into popular revolts and civil war" (p.442).

20. Schalk comments that the idea that conversation was the principle skill a young nobleman should learn "would have horrified most of the moralist nobles of the sixteenth century" (p.132). In a recent study of the nobility in Normandy during the sixteenth and seventeenth centuries, James Wood has shown how noble reactions to social mobility helped to preserve rather than

undermine the position of the class as a whole. *The Nobility of the 'Election' of Bayeux, 1463–1666* (Princeton, N.J.: Princeton University Press, 1980).

21. Carolyn Lougee's study of the class status of salon habitués has shown that salon society, "by accommodating into the aristocratic elite those who benefitted from the emergence of non-feudal fortunes, parried the threat those fortunes posed to the traditional aristocracy itself." *Le Paradis des femmes: Women, Salons, and Social Stratification in Seventeenth-Century France* (Princeton, N.J.: Princeton University Press, 1976), p.212.

22. Domna C. Stanton, *The Aristocrat as Art* (New York: Columbia University Press, 1980).

23. *On Individuality and Social Forms* (Chicago: University of Chicago Press, 1971), pp.199–213.

24. Simmel speaks of "pure" sociability: "Inasmuch as it is abstracted from sociation through art or play, sociability thus calls for the purest, most transparent, and most casually appealing kind of interaction, *that among equals.*" P. A. Lawrence, ed., *Georg Simmel* (Sunbury-on-Thames: Nelson, 1976), p.86.

25. *Maximes*, p.191.

26. *Interaction Ritual* (Chicago: Aldine, 1967), p.91.

27. *The Gift* (New York: W. W. Norton, 1967), pp.32–33.

28. *Stone-Age Economics* (Chicago: Aldine-Atherton, Inc., 1972), 191–96.

29. "Comme il est malaisé que plusieurs personnes puissent avoir les mêmes intérêts, il est nécessaire au moins, pour la douceur de la société, qu'ils n'en aient pas de contraires. On doit aller au-devant de ce qui peut plaire à ses amis, chercher les moyens de leur être utile, leur épargner des chagrins, leur faire voir qu'on les partage avec eux quand on ne peut les détourner . . ." (p.188).

30. "Sur la flatterie," *Nouvelle revue de la psychanalyse* 4 (1971), pp. 132, 134.

31. The most comprehensive history of seventeenth-century theories of civility in France before 1660 is Magendie, *La Politesse mondaine*. Two more recent studies analyzing the aesthetics of the *honnête homme* are, Jean-Pierre Dens, *L'Honnête homme et la critique du goût: esthétique et société au 17e siècle* (Lexington: French Forum, 1981), and Stanton, *The Aristocrat as Art*. For summary discussions of the place of conversation within the social system of *honnêteté* see Dens, "L'Art de la conversation au 17e siècle," *Lettres romanes* 27 (1973), pp. 215–24, and Stanton, pp. 139–46.

« 1 »

Seventeenth-Century Guides to Interaction

Nicolas Pasquier's *Le Gentilhomme* is a useful point of departure, for it was written early in the century and relies on traditional definitions of status relations, yet at the same time displays an unabashed confidence in the effectiveness of some new social climbing techniques. Published in 1611, this book of manners presents a list of qualities that young noblemen must strive to attain. *Le Gentilhomme* is divided into four books, the first two being general remarks on conduct, the third an extended discussion of military strategy and the warrior's code of honor, and the fourth on proper behavior in the presence of the prince. Pasquier's itemization of noble virtues is closely derived from the traditional code of a warrior nobility—with an emphasis on military prowess and valor—and he bases his image of "le gentilhomme" on the nobility's historic role as a knightly class.[1] In fact, Pasquier seems to see potential hostilities lurking behind the facade of every social interaction. Much of the section on *entregent* discusses conflictual situations and the proper means of resolving disputes: (". . . les

qualités des injures, l'état qu'il faut faire du démenti, qu'il ne faut offenser, le sujet des combats et querelles, l'origine des seconds, avec un
discours des duels . . .").[2] As a gentleman's principle concern in society
is with his reputation, he must know how to respond with restraint to
threatening situations, and Pasquier's enumeration of the highest social
virtues conveys this fundamental self-discipline: "Modestie," "Foi,"
"Vaillance," "Tempérance," "Justice," "Prudence," "Oisiveté et travail,"
"Sobriété," "Libéralité" (pp. 76–102).

In the conduct of conversation, metaphors of combat also prevail.
Social climbing is a kind of military campaign, for which the gentleman
trains by learning defensive and offensive tactics. He is advised to use
his words sparingly and only when necessary—like weapons: "Sa parole soit modérée, rare et chiche, afin de ne lui faire point perdre sa
trempe pour trop la mettre en oeuvre: qu'il fasse plutôt paraître la nécessité de parler que la volonté . . . car une parole jetée à la légère ne
se peut retenir non plus que la flèche décochée" (p. 69). He must surround himself as much as possible with people he wants as allies. By
imitating them and winning them to his cause, the gentleman will come
to resemble these members of the "compagnie des bons" (p. 42). His
campaign will be won when he is securely accepted into the circle of
those whose behavior he has been imitating. By identifying himself
with the elite, the gentleman will be protected from the dangers of
médisance: "Quand il procédera en sa conversation de cette grâce, nul
ne pourra mal parler de lui . . ." (p. 72).

In his survey of seventeenth-century conversation theory, Christoph Strosetski has noted that the use of the word "conversation" to
mean simply a group of people or "assemblée" was common in the first
part of the century.[3] This is certainly the way that Pasquier uses it. In
his manual, "conversation" is synonymous with "compagnie", and to
learn about conversation techniques is to learn how to surround oneself
with certain people. One is judged by the company one keeps: "Ainsi
la conversation de ceux avec lesquels il fréquente d'ordinaire, donne
jugement certain de l'assiette de son âme, si elle tend au bien ou au mal
. . ." (p. 42). Pasquier does not assign a specific section of his book to
the art of conversation, but places it under the rubric "parler." What is
important is the quality of the people one is with, not the manner in
which one interacts with them. Pasquier's guide reflects the relatively
fluid definition of elite status that characterized the late sixteenth and

early seventeenth centuries; the label "gentilhomme" is something one can come to deserve by means of careful social maneuvering, but a maneuvering that often sounds like a transposition of military discipline to the social arena. To enter the most exclusive status group, the social climber must learn how to make his actions conform to those of the group, until he is accepted as the inevitable result of a kind of natural law:

> . . . la raison veut que ceux qui par une longueur de temps hantent les uns avec les autres, ayent par une conformité de moeurs les âmes, les coeurs, et les volontés étroitement enchaînés et liés ensemblement: et la nature nous apprend que volontiers toute chose s'unit avec son semblable   (p.42).

Nicholas Faret's *L'Honnête homme ou l'art de plaire à la cour,* first printed in 1630, was the most popular conduct guide of the century. Closely modeled after Castiglione, Faret's book clearly addresses itself to the aspiring courtier, and its purpose, as the title indicates, is to teach its readers how to succeed at court. But Faret's title gives a new name to the model courtier, and in his text Pasquier's "gentilhomme" refers only to those who are noble by birth.[4] Like Pasquier, Faret acknowledges that "les armes" is the classic gentleman's profession, but his idea of social relations is not structured around metaphors of combat; in fact, Faret discusses military prowess only as an accomplishment that might enhance one's already established status as a *gentilhomme* on the road to *honnêteté.*[5] Faret attacks the fanfaronnerie" to which he says most men fall prey in their impatient desire for the approval of other *honnêtes gens.* Too much attention is given, he says, to quarrels and confrontations; as a consequence, sociability is still dominated by the rhetoric of combat.

> Plusieurs de nos vaillants s'imagineraient ne l'être point, s'ils ne faisaient mille grimaces et mille contenances farouches . . . Tous leurs discours sont d'éclaircissements, de procédés, et de combats, et qui retrancherait de leur entretien les termes d'assaut et d'escrime, je crois qu'ils seraient réduits, pour leur plus sublime science, *aux compliments de la langue française.* Leur fanfaronnerie est même montée jusqu'à ce degré de brutalité, que de mépriser la conversation des femmes, qui est l'un des plus doux est des plus honnêtes amusements de la vie   (p.15).[6]

By rejecting military metaphors for social interaction, Faret facilitates the participation of women in a new definition of elite sociability. Indeed, Pasquier's reader was never advised, as Faret's is repeatedly, to seek the company of women. By the middle of the century, prescriptive literature on *honnêteté* was citing conversation with cultivated women as the most exacting means of achieving a social education. Feminine conversation, writes Faret, is "the most difficult and the most delicate," for women have less tolerance than men for "mistakes" in interaction. The ultimate "théâtre de la conversation des femmes" is Anne of Austria's circle, but the discerning courtier should also consider leaving the court to attend other salons: "Il faut donc descendre à la ville et regarder qui sont celles d'entre les dames de condition que l'on estime les plus honnêtes femmes, et chez qui se font les plus belles assemblées, et s'il se peut, se mettre dans leur intrigue . . ." (p.90).[7]

In a book addressed to male readers, Faret's emphasis on the value of conversing with women inspired others to write conduct books teaching women how to converse. In the decade following the appearance of Faret's work, three important works on female *honnêteté* were published and reprinted: Du Bosc's *L'Honnête femme* (1633–36), followed by two manuals by Grenaille, *L'Honnête fille* (1639–40) and *L'Honnête veuve* (1640). Du Bosc, an ecclesiastic, is especially concerned with mediating between the conflicting value systems of worldly sociability and Christian virtue, but he argues passionately for the need for women to be educated in conversational rhetoric and the social skills of polite society. We are not living, he says opening his section on conversation, in a world where innocence and simplicity are highly regarded, and women must learn how to mask their speech if only to protect their virtue. A woman's good reputation is based on her intellect as well as her virtue, and the forum where one gains and protects one's reputation is in conversation:

> le principal but de la conversation est de se mettre dans la créance d'avoir de l'esprit et du jugement: c'est pour cette raison qu'on a besoin d'autre chose que de bonne humeur, et qu'il faut pour le moins avoir autant d'adresse que de vertu. . . . il n'est pas assez d'être vertueuse, . . . il faut persuader . . .[8]

Grenaille echoes Du Bosc's arguments in his precepts for *l'honnête fille*, encouraging girls to cultivate "la délicatesse de l'esprit" if only to

courtier, who is always aware that the purpose of his social accomplishments is to make of himself a model for the prince. Conversation among Méré's *honnêtes gens* has become utterly self-contained.[15] The space occupied by "le grande monde," defined with such careful indeterminacy by Méré, is much more vast than the clearly circumscribed court, but at the same time it is more exclusive. In order to sustain a vision of civility and personal accomplishment that is radically elite, the space in which it is enacted can no longer be the court, frequented now by "all kinds of people." More precisely, Méré considers the rules of sociability to be no longer observable in the overtly competitive atmosphere of court interaction. It is no longer enough to propose, as Faret had, a list of precepts to help the reader "qui se veut rendre agréable dans la cour" (p. 6). In fact, Méré's *honnête homme* seems to be fleeing the turbulence of court interaction and seeking a milieu which is completely separate from it. While Faret had opened his treatise with warnings of the dangers of court life, he nonetheless viewed it as a territory occupied by the best as well as the worst of "le monde." Méré, on the other hand, states flatly that true *honnêtes gens* must leave the court to find ideal conversation.

> Pour ce qui est des Maisons Royales, les entretiens en sont fort interrrompus; on y va moins pour discourir, que pour se montrer . . . Aussi la plupart qui ne s'y rendent que pour leur interêt particulier, me semblent plutôt de facheux négotiateurs que des gens de bonne compagnie   (p.122).

Méré's definition of conversation is similar to that of Madeleine de Scudéry, who made important contributions to the literature of conduct in her novels and in a vast collection of conversations partially excerpted from her fiction and published between 1680 and 1692. She also insists on a loose, evasive definition of ideal conversation, stating *Scudéry* instead that there are many forms of dialogue that *cannot* be properly called by that name:

> Lorsque les hommes ne parlent précisément que pour la nécessité de leurs affaires, cela ne peut pas s'appeler ainsi . . . un plaideur qui parle de son procès à ses juges, un marchand qui négocie avec un autre, un général d'armée qui donne des ordres, . . . tout cela n'est pas ce qu'on doit appeler conversation.[16]

All of her counterexamples are of individuals of unequal status engaging in dialogue with a practical end, two situations which she found incompatible with ideal sociability.

Both Méré and Scudéry also tried to promulgate a new notion of sociable exchange that would reject any similarity to the scholastic idea of "dialogue." Other theoreticians of social conduct viewed sociability as simply a sub-genre of traditional rhetoric, and organized their rules for conversation and letter exchange accordingly. René Bary, who in 1653 wrote an important treatise on modern rhetoric, decided in 1664 to publish a book on conversation. He had been unwilling to print the book, he says, until pressure from his friends, particularly his female acquaintances, persuaded him of the usefulness of such a work.[17] The book is comprised of 100 conversations in the form of short dialogues, in which all interlocutors contribute to the exchange in regular alternation. The main purpose of his collection, he says, is moral instruction.[18]

Bary's idea of moral instruction could hardly be further from the notion of conversation as presented by Scudéry or Méré. Their idea of *honnête* conversation is closer to what Kenneth Burke calls "pure persuasion," which "involves the saying of something not for an extraverbal advantage to be got by the saying, but because of a satisfaction intrinsic to the saying."[19] While both the scholastic and the more worldly models of interaction can be detected in conduct books published throughout the second half of the century, the scholastic model was gradually replaced by a looser concept of sociability.[20] This was accompanied by an increasingly negative attitude toward the usefulness of any sort of "rules" at all in the conduct of conversation.

François de Callières's two conversation books, published in 1690 and 1693, illustrate this development. In *Des Mots à la mode* (1690), he presents the reader with a transcription of a salon conversation, "une fameuse conversation qui se fit il n'y a pas longtemps chez une femme de qualité."[21] While Courtin had been concerned with expanding the system of differentiation to include all social interaction, Callières argues that such a scientific view of status distinctions has been rendered inoperable. The speakers in Callières's conversations observe that everyone now borrows each other's manners, gestures, and, especially, styles of speech, so that conversation is often nothing more than a rampant verbal display. It is impossible to participate in a group discussion that is not riddled with neologisms, vulgar turns of phrase, and ostentatious forms of address—all improperly used. The art of social interaction, it would seem, has been lost to an obsessive concern with titles and other verbal signs of privilege. The acquisitive discourse of the bourgeoisie has made dangerous incursions into the social life of the elite. The most pernicious example of this that is put forward is the bourgeois usurpation of noble titles, but Callières notes that members of the aristocracy also abuse their titles by parading them immodestly: "Je voudrais encore que les gens de qualité apprissent à se corriger d'un défaut très grand . . . qui est de prôner sans cesse leur rang et leur naissance à ceux qui ne la leur contestent pas" (p.139). What has been lost, the company eventually agrees, is a "sens commun" that would put a stop to these abuses of language (p.20).

While the speakers in Scudéry's and Méré's conversations seem to feel that the boundaries of their model world are secure, discussions of polite interaction in books purporting to teach the uninitiated were becoming more skeptical. Morvan de Bellegarde, while calling *politesse* "un précis de toutes les vertus morales," warns that most people who seem to have acquired these virtues in fact have only "borrowed" their appearance:

> Bien des gens passent pour polis, qui n'ont que l'écorce de la politesse: ils se cachent, mais sous des dehors empruntés qui éblouissent . . . Il ne faut donc pas faire un grand fonds sur cette politesse purement extérieure, qui ne consiste que dans de certaines manières composées . . . il faut qu'elle ait ses racines dans le coeur, et qu'elle soit fondée sur de véritables sentiments.[22]

In a second volume of conversations published three years after his first one, Callières presents the same group of speakers, this time reflecting on lessons learned since their earlier conversation. They return to the idea of "common sense", proposing that it is the only principle that may be able to effectively exclude from conversation "les façons de parler bourgeois."[23] Callières compares this sort of speech to counterfeit money, " . . . la fausse monnaie qui s'était introduite dans le commerce des jeunes gens, mais qui est décriée, et qui n'a plus de cours parmi ceux qui parlent bien" (p.2). The new mission of polite society, he says, is to prevent any further weakening of this system of verbal commerce by refusing to honor the false coin of bourgeois speech, which has value only for those who are unable to recognize it as counterfeit. At the end of this conversation the hostess reads a letter she has just received, saying it will provide the best example of the kind of discourse the group is trying to be rid of. After critiquing it word by word, they rewrite it in a more suitable style, and in the end agree that they have succeeded in doing justice to the thoughts that had been hidden and distorted in the first version by the misuse of langugage. The key to their process of reconstruction, however, was the complete absence of rules. By following their "common sense," the company claims, they were able to purge the text of its false rhetorical display and restore its message in a simple style exemplifying "politesse":

> Autrefois . . . on examinait avec soin les conditions de ceux à qui on écrivait; on s'en formait divers degrés auxquels on écrivait différemment . . . La civilité a augmenté parmi nous à mesure que la politesse s'y est introduite, et c'est cette politesse qui a établi sagement la mode d'écrire en billet, où on supprime toutes sortes de souscriptions et de cérémonies dans les lettres . . .   (p.227–29).

The business of civility here seems to be simply a process of verifying credentials. In their discussion of both speech and writing, the members of the group set out to distinguish authentic from inauthentic discourse, the authentic speakers being those who have so thoroughly digested the rules of "politesse" that they can now pretend to abandon them.

Written Conversation: The Epistolary Manuals

The choice of a letter test to illustrate the principle of "politesse" in verbal communication reflects a widespread interest in epistolary writing, an interest that was rapidly increasing at the end of the seventeenth century. In fact, epistolary manuals became at least as important as conduct books in providing readers with models for verbal communication in society. Reflecting an increasing interest in the letter as a practical means of communication and as an art form, epistolary manuals studied chronologically also document significant changes in thinking about how language functions in conversation, both written and spoken.[24]

French epistolary manuals of the seventeenth century define letter correspondence as a written equivalent of polite conversation. Richelet begins his introduction to a collection of exemplary letters with a remark on the writer's need to cultivate the illusion of this equivalence: "Lorsqu'on veut faire une lettre, il faut bien se persuader, qu'écrire et parler à un absent, c'est la même chose . . ."[25] The principal objective of both letter and conversation is to construct a balanced verbal dialogue, with each interlocutor "giving" and "taking" in equal measure. Above all, the good letter writer, like the good conversationalist, always has the interlocutor in mind. The most important consideration in composing a letter, writes Paul Jacob, is the person you are addressing: "L'essai d'une bonne lettre ou d'un bon discours est de bien connaître les personnes à qui on écrit, et leur préparer toujours ce qui leur est plus propre."[26]

Yet, while the authors of letter manuals seem to agree that letter exchange is a representation of conversation, they also cite differences between speech and writing that make any total equivalence impossible. The objective of making a letter *seem* like speech, and the resulting problems posed to epistolary writers and readers, is a common topic of conduct literature. Count Ludovico's definition of writing in *The Book of the Courtier* is echoed in many of the later French conduct books:

> . . . writing is none other than a kind of speech which remains in being after it has been uttered, the representation, as it were, or rather the very life of our words . . . writing preserves the words and submits them to the judgment of the reader, who has the time to give them his considered attention.[27]

Letter exchange imitates conversation, but the written word cannot easily "escape" the reader, as speech can the listener. Written dialogue is forced into a kind of orderly economy, and the "politesse" of letter conversation can be more closely scrutinized for evidence of those "véritables sentiments" whose reality Bellegarde finds so difficult to confirm. Vaumorière says that conversation "nous accoutument insensiblement à nous exprimer avec facilité," but when it comes to writing, he reluctantly admits otherwise: ". . . que l'on ne flatte point, il faut écrire plus exactement qu'on ne parle. Nous devons considérer que les yeux sont plus fidèles que les oreilles. Ce que nous voyons sur le papier, demeure exposé à notre critique, et la plupart des choses que l'on nous dit se dérobent à nos reflexions."[28]

The earliest French *secrétaires* were written for the education of young princes and aspiring courtiers; Etienne du Tronchet's *Lettres missives et familières* (1569), is the first of this type. They are typically divided into two sections, general precepts for the letter writer and illustrative examples of various types of letters. The readers are invited to copy the models in order to learn, and, as the manuals are usually written by court secretaries who have been asked to write letters for others, the proven value of a letter is often noted by the author, as in this preface by François de Rosset: "Si tu es versé aux affaires de la cour, tu y pourras remarquer la qualité de ceux qui parlent aux lettres, qui ne portent aucun nom sur le front, et que j'ai presque toutes faites par le commandement ou à la prière des personnes illustres, qui s'en sont servies en divers sujets."[29] Echoing Pasquier's precepts for learning how to speak in courtly circles, the early authors of model letter collections emphasize that the best way to learn to write is by imitating. In a collection of his own letters which he offers to readers instead of a list of rules, Jean de Lannel suggests how individual readers of model texts thus become linked to one another; "Ceux qui sauront bien vous imiter, se rendront incontinent dignes d'être eux-mêmes imitées."[30]

Letter dialogue, like conversation, depends on each interlocutor working to sustain a balanced exchange. This means that the writer must pattern the text of a letter after the correspondent's discourse. As Puget de la Serre writes, it is important to respond to a letter point by point, so as to make your "lettre de réponse" a mirror image of the message it is answering.[31] In deciding what to say and how to say it, the letter writer must always be guided by the addressee. Thus one of the most important qualities of a good letter writer is the ability to change, to use different voices according to the situation and the person being addressed. As Paul Jacob states in *Le Parfait secrétaire:* "Le plus expédient est de faire de sa plume ce que faisait Protée de sa personne, la changeant en toutes les formes possibles, à la diversifier selon la nécessité du sujet, et la qualité de la personne . . ."[32] Accordingly, Jacob divides his model letters into sub-genres defined by the occasion ("Lettres de consolation, de conjouissance, d'étrennes," etc.), and also provides a model response for each type, with accompanying "préceptes" for both letter and response.

Both Jacob and Puget de La Serre model their precepts for epistolary discourse on classical rhetoric. Puget de La Serre states that a letter should be divided into three parts, analogous to the Ciceronean parts of speech.[33] Whether writing a dedicatory epistle or a love letter, the writer's purpose is to persuade, to "enter" the interlocutor's mind: "La perfection de l'éloquence consistant à faire entrer des vérités dans l'esprit humain, et les y rendre maîtresses absolues de toutes les affections, soit par amour, soit par plaisir, soit à vive force de persuasion" (Jacob, p. 35). Jacob is quick to warn, however, against the degeneration of sociable rhetoric into abject flattery, which he describes as a formidable threat to true civility; "C'est le vrai visage de la cour, aussi bien que du siècle, et que les hommes ne devraient point recevoir puisqu'il renverse et confond toutes les marques de l'amitié et de la société civile par ses charmes trompeurs qui empêchent le discernement" (pp. 37–38).

The art of persuasion is to be used in written conversation only as a means of assuring the illusion of reciprocity, of dialogue as a balanced exchange of gifts. Of all the occasions for letter writing discussed by Jacob, the exchange of news is the one he views as "le premier et le plus agréable" (p. 160), for it is in the "lettre de nouvelles" that one can most clearly see written dialogue as an exchange of gifts, and epistolary rhetoric as the art of giving what is desired, and of making desirable what is given:

> . . . si celui à qui nous envoyons des nouvelles nous les a demandées, on dira que c'est avec ardeur que nous désirons lui satisfaire, lui proposant la chose en telle sorte que son esprit soit toujours en suspens et en attente . . . s'il n'en a fait aucune demande, nous l'en rendrons désireux par quelque insinuation   (pp. 162–64).

In many of the epistolary manuals written after 1670, the definitions of letter communication are different than those presented in earlier texts. Ortigue de Vaumorière, writing in 1688, remarks that a letter is structured like an oration, and should be divided into parts accordingly, but he goes on to say: "Après avoir dit que l'on peut garder cet ordre, j'ajoute qu'il vaut mieux y renoncer que de le faire paraître. Rien ne doit sentir la contrainte ni l'affectation dans une lettre, tout y doit avoir l'air de liberté qui règne dans l'entretien ordinaire."[34] Jean Léonor de Grimarest's 1709 manual abandons the analogy with oratory completely; in his preface he attacks his precursors for neglecting the importance of sentiment:

> . . . on a pris les lettres pour des ouvrages d'esprit et d'éloquence; on leur a donné des parties distingués, comme à un discours oratoire: et l'on n'a pas fait reflexion que la nature doit y paraître à découvert, et dégagée de tout ornement étranger . . . ils ont négligé les sentiments et ils doivent dominer dans une lettre.[35]

While letter writing continues to be considered an expression of civility, and the skilled writer of them someone who has mastered sociability, certain types of letters, such as the "lettre de compliment," are now thought artificial and thus unworthy of polite society. La Fevrerie remarks: "Quelle ridicule et bizarre civilité, que celle des compliments! Il entre encore de la ruse et de l'artifice dans cette sorte de combat, et je ne m'étonne pas si les hommes francs et sincères sont si peu propres, et regardent nos compliments comme un ouvrage de la politique, comme un effet de la corruption du siècle, comme la peste de la société civile."[36] Terms like "sincère," "franc," "simple," are now given more importance in discussions of the qualities essential to letter dialogue. La Fevrerie writes that these traits are the only ones necessary for a reader to adequately judge a love letter, which cannot be appreciated by anyone but the person to whom it is addressed:

> Il est dangereux de les intercepter, et de les communiquer à qui que ce soit qu'aux intéressés, qui en connaissent l'importance. Le don de pénétrer et de bien goûter ces lettres n'appartient pas aux esprits fiers et superbes, mais aux âmes simples, pures, et sincères, à qui l'amour communique toutes les délices   (pp. 37–38).

In learning how to write any type of letter one must avoid copying letters presented as models. Whereas the earlier manuals had recommended that readers learn by imitating, the later ones warn against this.[37] Puget de La Serre's manual consisted almost entirely of model letters to be studied and adapted to the reader's needs. The authenticity of the models, moreover, was not an issue; though his collection includes both fictional and real letters, we are not told which is which.[38] The model letters presented in manuals later in the century tend to be highly specific, that is, written for more precise occasions than those found in earlier manuals, so that they would not be easily copied. While Jacob's manual had divided letters into general sub-genres and added an appropriate response for each model, Vaumorière's models have long titles referring to a distinct occasion (e.g. "Reproche à un homme de la cour, au sujet de l'indifférence qu'il a pour ses amis, depuis qu'il est élevé à une grande dignité."). Grimarest emphasizes that the number of occasions for letter dialogue is limitless, and cannot be adequately systematized (p. 58).

The underlying change in attitudes toward sociable dialogue in all of these later modifications is new emphasis on the personal, on a discourse marked by the traits of the individual writer and reader.[39] Letters, writes La Fevrerie, "n'ont point de règles précises et certaines . . ." (p. 19–20). This, he says, is because they are true images of their writer and must communicate the uniqueness of the writer's situation (p. 20). Richelet, in his collection entitled *Les Plus belles lettres des meilleurs auteurs français*, adds introductory biographical notes to the individual texts, many of which had been printed before in other epistolary manuals. Presented in this way, the letters are not simply models of style, but also tell the story of their authors' lives.[40]

With this new emphasis on the expression of private sentiment and personal circumstances in letter dialogue, it is not surprising that increased attention is given to the love letter as a new form of authentic communication. For La Fevrerie, the love letter is the purest form of the genre, resulting from the desire of one person to reveal her or his most private thoughts to another:

> Je crois même que l'Amour a été le premier inventeur des lettres . . . La grande affaire a toujours été celle du coeur. L'amour qui a d'abord uni les hommes, ne leur donna point de plus grand désirs que ceux de se voir et de se communiquer, lorsqu'ils étaient séparés par une cruelle absence   (p. 30–31).

Changes made by Richelet in successive editions of his letter collection reveal this interest in new styles of sentimental communication. As in the case of many of the later manuals and epistolary collections, Richelet's third edition, published in 1705, multiplies the number of letter categories and includes more references to specific people and situations. The longest new section he calls "lettres passionnées." All but one of the letters in this section are written by women, and included are several letters taken from *Lettres portugaises*. Richelet provides prefatory remarks "sur la manière de faire les lettres passionnées," stressing the point that the purpose of a passionate letter is to elicit compassion from the reader. To that end, one must learn to "make the heart speak" (p. 86).

Descriptions of the love letter genre always warn, though, that this is one rhetorical art that cannot be taught. The love letter is the form least ruled by convention. Grimarest exempts it from other rules of epistolary style, and Du Plaisir writes that a "lettre passionnée" expresses the lover's true thoughts more clearly than speech: "On ne garde point de règle dans les lettres passionnées; la véhémence, l'inégalité, les doutes, les tumultes, tout y a place; et de même qu'ailleurs on écrit comme on parle, ici on écrit comme l'on pense."[41] Writers who may have otherwise mastered the epistolary art are often unable to produce a good love letter. Méré, noting that even Voiture did not write any memorable love letters, says "il n'y a point de sujet qui souffre moins les fausses beautés" (I, 58). He concludes that Voiture's love letters were insincere. The love letter is a kind of litmus test of textual purity, it is considered to be the only epistolary form in which the writer's feelings cannot be disguised.

A love letter, then, cannot be imitated; to learn to write one it is only necessary to be sincere. This is why, for La Fevrerie, there are no good love letters in novels. A fictional love letter is automatically inferior:

> on ne trouvera pas à prendre depuis *L'Astrée* jusqu'à *La Princesse de Clèves*, de lettres excellentes . . . toutes les lettres en sont médiocres, et la raison est, que ces sortes de lettres ne sont pas originales. Ce sont des fantaisies . . . Ces auteurs n'ont écrit ni pour Cyrus, ni pour Clélie, ni pour eux, mais seulement pour le public . . .   (pp. 36–37).

For La Fevrerie, a letter, like its author, can never be pleasing to everyone; it is vain for a letter writer to seek the approval of a general audience; "D'ailleurs comme nos manières ne plaisent pas à tout le monde, il est impossible que les lettres qui en sont pleines, aient une approbation générale" (pp. 21–22). On the other hand, a purportedly "real" letter correspondence, written with no view to publication, would have much to teach any reader interested in the sincere expression of human emotions. The conventional frame of an epistolary novel, beginning with the publication of *Lettres portugaises* and *Lettres de Babet* in 1669, will cater to this reader's taste for "true" letter dialogue, published only by accident, in circumstances beyond the writer's control.

The question of control over what one is writing is central to the production as well as the publication of love letters at this time. What is valorized in the style of a "lettre passionée" is an esthetic of excess, a form of expression exceeding the limits of prescribed behavior, particularly when the letter is written by a woman. It is not surprising, then, to find Richelet presenting anonymous letters by women as examples of the best passionate letters, for simply writing such a letter in the first place is proof of a female author's loss of self-control. This fundamental transgression that a love letter written by a woman was thought to represent could result in the displacement of feminine discourse from the controlled economy of sociability to a much larger and more dangerous public marketplace.[42]

The new interest in epistolary exchange as an expression of the writer's unique self stands in obvious contrast to earlier definitions of both written and spoken dialogue as an interlocking system of mutual obligation, wherein imitation was the principle of conduct enabling individuals to learn how to interact. This shift in the normative codes for social interaction was accompanied by several changes in the society at large. The literature of sociable living was read by a much more diverse audience at the end of the century than at the beginning, and it was increasingly difficult to sustain the illusion of "le monde" as a circle of equals.[43] The growing power of the state was eroding aristocratic privileges, while the increasing wealth of the bourgeoisie was giving it access to marks of status which had previously been granted only to the nobility. As we saw in Callières's conversation book it was impossible to exclude specific signs of one's individual status on "the outside" from the discourse of "insiders" in salon culture. With the rules of entry and exit, of inclusion and exclusion becoming increasingly diffuse, the ideology of sociability was gradually being replaced by a new ideal of sincerity.

In a recent study of the letter book as a literary institution from the Renaissance to the end of the eighteenth century, Janet Altman discusses the neglect of the personal and private realm in seventeenth-century texts, viewing it as a massive represssion of the self brought about by the politics of absolutism.[44] It is certainly true, as we have seen, that changes in prescribed norms for epistolary interaction during this period were linked to transformations in the political and cultural functions of elite society. But it is important to keep in mind that prescriptive writings about epistolary style were closely related to the broader literature of conduct and conversation, and *honnêteté* cannot be viewed as simply a method of disguising the private self, motivated by censorship and other forms of political control imposed from above. Strategies of refinement and limitation advised by seventeenth-century guides to interaction reflect the idea that the most gratifying form of self-representation is in fact neither private nor intimate, and can be achieved only by a systematic grooming of individual interests to bring them in harmony with those of a narrowly defined public.

Norbert Elias, in his study of the history of manners, has remarked that sincerity is the ideology of outsiders, originally emerging in European culture as a "specific trait of the middle class person in contrast to the worldling or courtier."[45] As a new standard for ideal interaction, sincerity also subverted the aristocratic ideal of sociability. More often than not, sincere speech was thought to disrupt the perfect equanimity of a social encounter. When Méré says his *honnête homme* should be sincere he does not consider this attribute to be the transcendent measure of authentic communication, as La Fevrerie does. Méré's *homme sincère* is essentially an *homme naturel*, a consummately sociable individual who knows how to project a consistent self-image. Even in the conduct of love, spontaneous declarations are considered both inappropriate and ineffective, to be rejected in favor of a more reasoned "art de plaire."[46] Méré would agree with La Rochefoucauld who warns that too much personal revelation is destructive of social relations, sometimes cruel, and always pointless.[47]

In what came to be considered its purest expression—the love letter—sincerity was thought to be signified by disorder, unconditional adulation, and a total lack of self-control, all forms of conduct that were unacceptable in the sorts of sociable encounters described by Méré or Scudéry. Personal confession can function as a principle of conversation only according to a system whereby participants take turns exchanging intimacies, in a kind of market process that values the substance of what is said much more than the process of saying it. The model of generalized reciprocity does not fit this kind of conversation, in fact the social relationships suggested by this new notion of ideal interaction are much more familiar in today's world. Richard Sennett has written of the "the fall of public man" associated with the rise of the bourgeoisie after the French Revolution, and the new belief in the social value of private, individual character. He describes an "ideology of intimacy" that began in the eighteenth century and survives today, a belief that "social relationships of all kinds are real, believable and authentic the closer they approach the inner psychological concerns of each person."[48] But by the end of the reign of Louis XIV, writings on social interaction were already promoting a rhetoric of self-revelation that was radically opposed to the worldly ideals of a La Rochefoucauld or Madeleine de Scudéry. In the next chapter we will look more closely at what the most popular of the early writers on conversation had thought "la société" should be.

NOTES

1. George Huppert, in his book *Les Bourgeois Gentilhommes: An Essay on the Definition of Elites in Renaissance France* (Chicago: University of Chicago Press, 1977), remarks that Pasquier discusses the profession of arms in an aside, "2 pages in a book which runs to 359!" (p.45). In fact, Pasquier devotes nearly the entire third part of *Le Gentilhomme* (over 100 pages) to the role of military life. More importantly, though, for our purposes, there is a battle ethic that seems to permeate Pasquier's discussion of every interactive situation in which the *gentilhomme* finds himself involved.

2. *Le Gentilhomme* (Paris: Jean Petit-Pas, 1611) [p. ii] (n.pag.).

3. *Rhétorique de la conversation: Sa dimension littéraire et linguistique dans la société française du dix-septième siècle* (Paris, Seattle, Tübingen: Papers on French Seventeenth-Century Literature/Biblio 17, 1984), p.22. Strosetski's study provides a useful inventory of theoretical writings on conversation. For the most part he is not concerned as I am here, with any particular chronological development, nor does he address the connections between the rhetoric of conversation and writings on epistolary interaction.

4. For an analysis of the evolution of the word *honnête* as a signifier of privilege, see Donna C. Stanton, *The Aristocrat as Art: A Study of the Honnête Homme and the Dandy in Seventeenth- and Nineteenth-Century French Literature* (New York: Columbia University Press, 1980), pp.13–30.

5. Translating Castiglione, Faret writes that arms are the means by which the nobility "s'acquiert . . . se doit conserver," but he immediately adds a warning against the dangers of aggressive behavior in society: "ceux qui joignent la malice à la valeur, sont ordinairement redoutés et haïs comme des

bêtes farouches, parce qu'ayant le pouvoir de faire du mal, ils en ont aussi la volonté . . ." *L'Honnête homme ou l'art de plaire à la cour* (Paris: P.U.F., 1925), pp. 12–13.

6. Military service, one of the traditional justifications for the nobleman's special exemption from the taille, was by the end of the sixteenth century no longer an exclusively aristocractic function. In *Le Gentilhomme* and elsewhere, Nicolas Pasquier argued for a return to the old system of the military as an aristocratic privilege, while Faret, writing twenty years later, is concerned with designating other social functions as marks of elite status. See Davis Bitton, *The French Nobility in Crisis, 1560–1640* (Stanford: Stanford University Press, 1969), pp.27–41, and Ellery Schalk, *From Valor to Pedigree: Ideas of Nobility in 16th- and 17th-Century France* (Princeton, N.J.: Princeton University Press, 1986), pp. 139–40.

7. Pasquier's index does not include the words *amour, galant*, or even *femme*, which were to become paramount in later definitions of civility and exemplary interaction.

8. *L'Honnête femme* (Paris: Jean Cochart, 1662 [4th edition]), pp. 30, 67.

9. *L'Honnête fille* (Paris: Jean Paslé, 1639), ch. 1. For a lengthier discussion of the conduct manuals of the 1630's and 40's designed for female readers see Ian MacLean, *Woman Triumphant: Feminism in French Literature 1610–1652* (Oxford: Clarendon Press, 1977), pp. 123–35.

10. Antoine de Courtin, *Nouveau traité de la civilité qui se pratique en France* (Paris, 1671), p.6.

11. "Avis au lecteur," n. pag.

12. The description of self-masking as an unpleasant but necessary aspect of verbal interaction is echoed in many early conduct books, e.g. Du Bosc's *Honnête Femme* (Paris: Claude Prudhomme, 1639):

> . . . puisque nous sommes dans un siècle d'artifice, où il semble que les paroles qu'on a inventées pour exprimer les pensées, ne servent plus qu'à les cacher de bonne grâce, il faut confesser que l'innocence même a besoin de masque, ou de voile aussi bien que les visages, et que ce n'est pas une moindre imprudence de montrer son coeur à découvert . . . que de marcher tous nus entre les ennemis armés . . .   (p.52).

Jacques de Caillère warns his readers against letting down their guard, saying that confessing one's inner thoughts to a friend is "une marque d'imprudence plutôt qu'un témoignage d'amitié." He advises "retenue": "Cette façon de vivre me semble d'autant plus raisonnable, qu'elle assure nos interêts sans offenser ceux de nos amis. La prudence n'est pas contraire à la franchise, elle ne l'est qu'à la légerté . . ." *La fortune des gens de qualité et des gentilhommes particuliers, enseignant l'art de vivre à la cour* . . . (Paris: Etienne Loyson, 1661), ch. 8.

13. Magendie notes this contrast, pp.384–85.

14. Méré, *Oeuvres complètes* (Paris: Editions Fernand Roches, 1930) II, p.102.

15. John Lyons has brought out the textual workings of Méré's present-centered, self-fulfilling theory of *honnêteté* in "Being and Meaning: The example of *Honnête* Text," *PFSCL* 17 (1982), pp. 153–72.

16. *Conversations sur divers sujets* (Paris: Louis Billaine, 1680), I, p.2.

17. *L'Esprit de cour ou les conversations galantes, divisées en cent dialogues* (Bruxelles: Balthazar Vivien, 1664), p.2.

18. Other rhetoricians wrote books that attempted to broaden the definition of rhetoric to accomodate the new, anti-scholastic bias of polite society. Templery de Leven emphasizes in his preface that he is interested in instructing a female audience: "l'auteur l'ayant dédiée à une dame, afin de retrancher les termes ennuyeux de l'école, et accomoder son style à la portée des gens qui ont le moins de teinture de la rhétorique . . ." *La Rhétorique française, très propre aux gens qui veulent apprendre à parler at à écrire avec politesse* (Paris: Martin Jouvenal, 1698). See also P. Lamy, *De l'Art de parler* (Paris: André Pralard, 1676), in which he traces a "natural" evolution of rhetoric, and André Renaud, *Manière de parler la langue française* (Lyon: Claude Rey, 1697), a more ambitious cataloguing of conversational styles that praises Scudéry, Méré, and Bouhours "qui ont donné au public de parfaits modèles des plus belles conversations" (p.143).

19. *A Rhetoric of Motives* (New York: Prentice-Hall, 1950), p.269.

20. Strosetski's study of the rhetoric of conversation in the second half of the seventeenth century focuses on those connections between normative writing about conversational style and theories of speech in the works of rhetoricians and grammarians. He sees in the promotion of the "style simple" at the end of the century a parallel with the esthetic of negligence, or the "dissimulatio artis" of rhetorical theory (pp. 48–61).

21. François de Callières, *Des Mots à la mode* (Paris, 1690), p.2.

22. *Reflexions sur la politesse des moeurs, avec des maximes pour la société civile* (Amsterdam: Henri Desbordes, 1699), pp. 1–6.

23. *Du Bon et du mauvais usage dans les manières de s'exprimer* (Paris: Claude Barbin, 1693), p.192.

24. Four recent studies have discussed the evolution of standards of taste in the seventeenth-century letter: Bernard Beugnot, "Style ou styles épistolaires?" *RHLF* 78 (1978), pp. 929–57; Roger Duchêne, *Madame de Sévigné et la lettre d'amour* (Paris: Bordas, 1970), pp. 21–114; Alain Viala, "La Genèse des formes épistolaires en français," *Revue de littérature comparée* 55 (1981), pp. 168–83; and Janet Altman, "The Letter Book as a Literary Institution, 1539–1789: Toward a Cultural History of Published Correspondences in France," *Yale French Studies* 71 (1986), pp. 17–62.

25. *Les Plus belles lettres françaises . . .* (The Hague: Guillaume de Voys, 1708), p.4.

26. *Le Parfait secrétaire* (Paris, 1656), p.22.

27. Baldasar Castiglione, *The Book of the Courtier* (Baltimore: Penguin, 1967), p.71.

28. *Lettres sur toutes sortes de sujets . . .* (Paris, 1689), pp.3–4.

29. François de Rosset, *Lettres amoureuses et morales des beaux esprits de ce temps* (Paris, 1618), n. pag.

30. Jean de Lannel, *Lettres* (Paris: T. Du Bray, 1625), p.17.

31. Jean Puget de la Serre, *Le Secretaire à la mode* (Amsterdam: L. Elzevier, 1663), deuxième partie, n. pag.

32. Paul Jacob, *Le Parfait Secrétaire* (Paris, 1646), p.41.

33. Puget de la Serre, deuxième partie; Jacob, p. 304.

34. Ortigue de Vaumorière, *Lettres sur toutes sortes de sujets . . .* (Paris, 1690), p.16.

35. Jean Léonor de Grimarest, *Traité sur la manière d'écrire des lettres et sur le cérémonial . . .* (Paris: J. Estienne, 1709), pp. 5–6.

36. La Fevrerie, "Du style épistolaire," Extraordinaire du *Mercure galant*, juillet 1683, pp. 25–26.

37. See for example Vaumorière, ch. IV; Grimarest, p.22.

38. Viala has also noted this feature of Puget de la Serre's text (p.176).

39. In a study of changes in reader attitudes toward published letter correspondences, Roger Duchêne notes that readers were increasingly asked to view letters as confessional texts, expressing the writer's true self: "Le Lecteur de lettres," *RHLF* 78 (1978), pp. 977–90. The increasing attention to "natural style" in conversation manuals parallels this development in the epistolary manuals. Strosetski remarks on a proliferation of descriptive terms to define conversation styles at the end of the century, reflecting the new idea that there were potentially as many rhetorical styles as there were people (p. 51).

40. Pierre Richelet, *Les Plus belles lettres . . .* (Lyon: Benoit Bailly, 1689).

41. Du Plaisir, *Sentiments sur les lettres et sur l'histoire . . .* (Genève: Droz, 1975), p. 32.

42. Janet Altman has noted that in the seventeenth century the publication of *Lettres portugaises* at once consecrated women's epistolary writing in the public marketplace and limited that writing to their erotic response to men. "The Letter Book as a Literary Institution," p. 45.

43. Whereas at the end of the sixteenth century the *noblesse d'épée* still dominated the groups of courtiers closest to the king, during the seventeenth century both court and salon society became increasingly heterogeneous. See Bitton, pp. 42–43, and Lougee, pp. 113–70.

44. See "The Letter Book as a Literary Institution."

45. Norbert Elias, *The Civilizing Process* (1939; rpt. New York: Urizen Books, 1978), p. 31.

46. See Louise K. Horowitz's discussion of Méré on love and its expression in *Love and Language: A Study of the Classical French Moralist Writers* (Columbus: Ohio State University Press, 1977), pp. 15–28.

47. "Comme on doit garder des distances pour voir les objets, il en faut garder aussi pour la société: chacun a son point de vue, d'où il veut être regardé; on a raison, le plus souvent, de ne vouloir pas être éclairé de trop près, et il n'y a presque point d'homme qui veuille, en toutes choses, se laisser voir tel qu'il est." *Maximes*, p.188.

48. *The Fall of Public Man* (New York: Knopf, 1977), p.259.

« 2 »

Excess and Euphoria in Madeleine de Scudéry's "Conversations"

Assessments of Madeleine de Scudéry's writing have always tended to take one of two extreme positions. Her two ten-volume novels, published between 1649 and 1650, were immensely popular, but even among her first readers, for whom leisure time was almost limitless, there were some who thought her texts were simply too long. Tallemant records one such opinion offered by Madame de Cornuel: "Dieu avait fait suer de l'encre à Mademoiselle de Scudéry, qui barbouillait tant de papier.[1] Her admirers retorted with equally hyperbolic statements. Ménage suggested that the inability to absorb Scudéry's epic work was a sign of a small mind: "ceux qui blâment la longueur font voir par ce jugement la petitesse de leur esprit, comme si on devait mépriser Homère et Virgile . . ."[2]

The number of enthusiastic readers of Scudéry's novels dwindled during the eighteenth century. Voltaire thought her portraits of contemporaries were interesting documents of the period, but eighteenth-century literary historians joined him in criticizing her "enormous novels."[3] The literary historian responsible for rescuing Mademoiselle de Scudéry from public indifference was Victor Cousin, who in 1858 published a "key" to *Le Grand Cyrus*, enabling readers to once again regard the novel as an intriguing testimony to seventeenth-century elite culture, disguised as myth and historial legend. The key, discovered by Cousin in an obscure early edition of *Le Grand Cyrus*, rendered Scudéry's work, he wrote, intelligible: ". . . en son temps le *Cyrus* était parfaitement compris des lecteurs d'élite auxquels il s'adressait de préférence; tandis qu'aujourd'hui et depuis très longtemps it est absolument inintelligible."[4] But even Cousin does not suggest that his readers take the time to actually read the novels; in fact, he recommends against it. Instead, he submits his own text as a substitute, and his own research as having saved his readers much work: "Pour nous du moins, notre mémoire n'est pas assez forte pour porter un pareil poids, et nous n'avons pu venir à bout d'embrasser l'ensemble et les diverses parties . . . que grâce à tout un travail que le lecteur ne se doit pas imposer . . . " (p.13). As an alternative to shouldering the full weight of the novels, Cousin recommends sampling the *Conversations*, consisting of excerpts from the longer works. In contrast to the intimidating volume of the novels, these shorter texts are conveniently parceled "petits chefs d'oeuvre de politesse et de bon goût" (p.14).

Sainte-Beuve gives a new twist to this preference for Scudéry's *Conversations* in his "causerie" on her work. If Scudéry the novelist is "extravagant," he says, the author of the conversations is a rationalist, constantly aware of the pedagogical function of her writing: ". . . on doit la considérer comme une des *institutrices* de la société, à ce moment de formation et de transition . . . Elle cherche et donne des raisons de tout . . . Jamais on n'a fait plus d'usage du mot *car*."[5] The *Conversations* continue to be viewed today as Scudéry's most approachable work, and as the best example of the pedagogical purpose of all her writing, which was to give its original readers, as Magendie writes, "a worldly education" by depicting an elaborate, idealized vision of aristocratic social life.[6] Modern readers, rebuffed by the excessive length of her novels, tend to ascribe their unreadability to the fact that today's reader does not have unlimited time. Scudéry's "pages interminables," writes one, "peuvent être bien goûtées par morceaux ou par épisodes, mais non pas de suite."[7]

The very existence of the *Conversations* suggests that Scudéry her-

self was preoccupied with the questions of readability and excess in her
novelistic writing. Published over a twelve-year period, between 1680
and 1692, the conversations include selections from her two novels, as
well as many new pieces written for the collection.[8] Many of her contemporaries agreed that they constituted the best of her work. Madame
de Sévigné, who had been an avid reader of the novels, nevertheless
remarked after reading the first volume of the conversations: "il est
impossible que cela ne soit bon, quand cela n'est point noyé dans son
grand roman."[9]

Scudéry's books of conversations not only extracted the best of her
novelistic writing and gave it a new form, they also made her writing
more accessible, and offered idealized social encounters as models to an
ever-widening audience. Even the physical size of the books seems to
signal their practical function. Following the fashion of the day, the
collections tended to decrease in size with each successive edition, so
that the later volumes are literally "pocket books," designed to be easily
carried in a dress or vest and consulted according to the whim of the
reader. The texts are made further accessible by tables of contents list-
ing a short descriptive title for each conversation. These titles enumerate the virtues and vices of social behavior: from the opening "de la
conversation" to "des plaisirs," "de la raillerie," "de la politesse," "de
l'air galant," "de l'hypocrisie," to her last conversation on "la reconnaissance."

Within the circumscribed structure of a "conversation," some of
those features of Scudéry's novels that her readers have traditionally
found excessive take on a new meaning. The lack of differentiation
between characters, which Magendie calls "a basic flaw" in the novels,[10] in the context of a conversation draws attention to the principle
of equality that for Scudéry is essential to sociable dialogue. Social
sameness is an important prerequisite for ideal interaction, as seventeenth-century conduct manuals stress. Scudéry's flagrantly imprecise
descriptions of place, which René Godenne calls "le signe d'une faiblesse du point de vue de l'organisation romanesque,"[11] in this frame-
work emphasize the power of each social encounter to locate the
speakers in a kind of moveable ideal landscape. Verbal excess has an
important function in Scudéry's economy of conversational exchange.
And the inconclusive structure of the novelistic narratives—their endless avoidance of closure—becomes an element in the code of civility,

the precept that dialogue must occur according to an ongoing exchange whose delicate balance must never be destroyed by the conclusive "winning out" of one speaker over another. Endings are problematic in these conversations, and usually are imposed simply when the company retires, or night falls.

In choosing to republish excerpts from her novels in the form of "conversations," Scudéry was also clearly resituating them in the conduct literature tradition. By 1680 the reading public was familiar with a number of texts in this genre, the most popular being courtesy manuals by Nicholas Faret and Antoine de Courtin, and Méré's collection of "Conversations." As we saw in Chapter 1, these writers presented to their readers techniques for living in polite society, for obtaining and retaining one's place in elite circles. The single most important activity of court society was conversation, and as such it was viewed as an art essential to the education of *honnêtes gens*. "Ce n'est pas une affaire à négliger," writes Méré, "car on passe les plus doux moments de la vie à s'entretenir."[12]

The social milieu of the salon, within which all of Madeleine de Scudéry's writing was generated, is a historical space that, like her writing, seems to lend itself to descriptive metaphors opposing large and small, grand and insignificant. The ideal of a radically restricted, enclosed space was crucial to the earliest manifestations of salon culture. Salons became an important locus of French elite culture in the first decades of the seventeenth century, when courtiers were becoming increasingly interested in learning the techniques of etiquette in the Italian tradition, while at the same time the status credentials of the royal entourage were no longer uniformly aristocratic. Salon life was thought to be sheltered from the distractions of courtly politics, while very much committed to cultivating ideal courtly behavior.

The Marquise de Rambouillet's prototypical salon, the *chambre bleue*, was conceived as a social territory distinctly different, smaller, and superior to the milieu of the court, both in its physical configuration and in the quality of its habitués. Tallemant's portrait of the Marquise de Rambouillet includes a detailed description of the rooms in her *hôtel*, which, he says, she designed. Its interior combined architectural features facilitating movement between the rooms, thus creating a more unified interior space, with tall windows and doors offering the

NB: Clinte &
restricted salon space

occupants enlarged exterior perspectives. Subsequently, Tallemant tells us, the Rambouillet design was imitated by even the royal architects, a response to fashion which reiterates the social ascendancy of salon over court culture during the first half of the century (I, 443).

salon:
intimate +
grand
à la fois

In both physical space and ideological configuration, then, the salon was thought of as simultaneously intimate and grand, apart from the world yet able to encompass all that was best in it. This psychological territory of the seventeenth-century salon has been described as the privileged *locus* for perfect sociability: a tiny, exclusive space that, unlike either *la cour* or *la ville*, was "spiritually large enough to contain the ideal of *honnêteté*."[13] Rambouillet's *chambre bleue* generated numerous imitations throughout the seventeenth century, among the most famous Madeleine de Scudéry's salon. But as elite culture turned increasingly to Louis XIV's court as a staging ground for all social encounters, salon society came to be defined not so much by a concrete space as by its occupants' principal activity, conversation.

Salon habitués cultivated the idea that they constituted a kind of ideal elite, which could always close ranks and create a separate reality even when surrounded by the heterogeneous crowd of courtiers. They themselves were not, however, a uniformly aristocratic group. In fact, salons served the important historical function of extending polite culture to non-nobles. By asserting the principle of absolute equality within the confines of the *ruelle*, salon life helped break down traditional systems of social stratification, while also creating a new concept of elite solidarity based on certain kinds of personal accomplishment.[14] The ideology of sociability underlying salon culture, however, remained aristocratic in the sense that it cultivated the image of an exclusive group of superior beings. If salon habitués were increasingly bourgeois, the style of interaction they were learning was nonetheless directly descended from the courtly notions of polite conversation. As the principal expression of salon culture, ideal conversation was understood to be possible only if all participants were confident both of their equal standing within the group, and of their superiority to all who were outside it. The coterie of speakers had to be sure of the boundaries separating them from the rest of society, and at the same time they had to be able to comfortably contemplate that society. Ideal conversation had to seek this balance of closure and openness, of internal

social
stratification ↓

yet still:
image of an
exclusive
group or
superior
beings

equilibrium and external orientation. Like the physical design of the hôtel de Rambouillet, it had to permit both a smooth pattern of movement between the participants and a broad view of the outside world.

It was in the company frequenting the Scudéry salon that the art of conversation was thought to achieve its most perfect expression.[15] In her first volume of conversations, Scudéry's characters spend much time defining just what it means to conduct an exchange that has "le véritable air du monde." They describe the qualities of an ideal speaker, who must be able to discuss a strictly limited subject in an open and unconstrained style:

> . . . Car toutes ses expressions sont nobles et naturelles tout ensemble; elle ne cherche point ce qu'elle dit; il n'y a nulle contrainte en ses paroles; son discours est clair et facile; il y a un tour galant à ses manières de parler; nulle affectation au son de sa voix, beaucoup de liberté en ses actions; et un merveilleux rapport entre ses yeux et ses paroles, qui est une chose qui contribue à rendre le parler plus agréable   (*C* I, 241).[16]

While ideal speakers must appear to be expressing a loose, unpremeditated chain of thoughts, what in fact makes perfect conversation possible is their willingness to submit to the rule of the group: "la véritable politesse . . . c'est soumettre judicieusement sa raison au bel usage du monde . . ." (*CN* I, 126–7). This "bel usage du monde" requires that participants repress individual expressions of self in favor of the group dynamic, which is seen by Scudéry as a kind of ideal system of verbal reciprocity. Character traits which suggest a reluctance to participate in this system are the most abhorred. "L'ingratitude," for example, "renverse toutes les lois de la société, qui parmi des gens raisonnables ne devrait être autre chose qu'un commerce continuel de bons offices . . ." (*C* II, 418). The test of conversational skill is one's ability to restore the equanimity of polite dialogue whenever it is threatened by personal idiosyncracy: "Je veux enfin qu'on sache si bien l'art de détourner les choses qu'on puisse dire une galanterie à la plus sévère femme du monde; qu'on puisse conter une bagatelle à des gens graves et serieux, et qu'on puisse parler à propos de science à des ignorants si l'on y est forcé . . ." (*C*, 42).

Euphoric Conversation

The social theories of Georg Simmel and Erving Goffman can help elucidate some of the features of conversation as defined by Scudéry and her contemporaries. Simmel's definition of sociability is based, as we have seen, on the principle of balanced exchange. Sociable conversation is "talking as an end in itself," a discourse constantly working to minimize objective content. As an extreme example of this "falling off of the concrete life-content," he cites the court society of the *ancien régime*.[17]

More recently, Erving Goffman has used Simmel's definition of sociability as a point of departure for his own theory of "focused encounters." Arguing that Simmel's distinction between "sociable" and "serious" life is too sharply drawn, Goffman analyzes the "transformation rules" that determine the boundary between the outer world and a focused gathering.[18] When the main focus of attention in a gathering is talk, the capacity of the participants to create a world of their own is particularly intense. Conversation "is a little social system with its own boundary-maintaining tendencies; it is a little patch of commitment and loyalty with its own heroes and its own villains."[19] All focused encounters are sustained by the participants adhering to rules of "obligatory involvement" while minimizing spontaneous, individual reactions which undermine the ease of group interaction. But no social encounter can be said to fully exclude all externally based attributes from its inner dynamic. The barrier between an artificially created focused encounter and the external order is, Goffman notes, "more like a screen than like a solid wall" (*Encounters*, p.33). External properties are expressed within a sociable gathering according to the particular set of "transformation rules" to which the group adheres. In any given encounter there are ideal circumstances which can "bring actual involvements and obligatory ones into perfect congruence." These circumstances Goffman calls the encounter's "euphoria function" (p.44).

The speakers in Scudéry's conversations may be said to be committed to enhancing the euphoria function of each encounter, and they collectively formulate the transformation rules which help them realize this objective. All the conversations share structural features which the participants often explicitly discuss as essential to the conduct of sociable dialogue. Thus, while each conversation is a debate between

no
polarization

barrier
between them
+ rest of world

Goffman:
group
displacement
⇒ exclusion

members of the group on a specific topic, the differences of opinion are never allowed to polarize the company, and each point of view is carefully balanced against the others. The discussion may end with a judicious bargain being struck between the two members of the group who have taken opposite positions in the debate, as in "Contre ceux qui décrient le gouvernement": "Pisistrate s'engagea à ne parler plus d'affaires d'état à Cléorante: et Cléorante promit aussi à Pisistrate d'endurer qu'il lui dit d'elle et de lui, tout ce qu'il lui plaisait . . ." (*C*, I,270). All conversations begin with the members of the group moving to a location apart from the rest of society, usually a bucolic setting, such as a hidden "cabinet" on the grounds of a country estate. By situating their dialogues in locations defined primarily by their separateness, the group creates that barrier between itself and the rest of the world that is so essential to their image of themselves as an exemplary elite. In Goffman's terms, this group displacement helps to create "the membrane that encloses it, cutting it off from a field of properties that could be given weight" (p.79).

Having established themselves as collectively exceptional but individually equal, the speakers in Scudéry's conversations perceive their own group interactions as a standard by which the rest of society can be judged. Isolated from the "outside" world, the insiders observe it, to more precisely identify the behavior they wish to exclude from their own social interaction. This design is also apparent in the geographical locus of each conversation, which Scudéry typically describes in the opening paragraphs. The framing of the conversations is, in fact, so uniform as to assume a ritualistic aspect, as Godenne has remarked.[20] The conversations always occur in a private enclosure—a "chambre," "appartement," or "pavillon" of one of the company, for example— where the group often goes to seek shelter from a storm or simply from the inclemencies of the outside social world.[21] When a description of the architectural features of these spaces is included, it always describes two aspects: interior ornament and design (wall paintings, arrangement of furniture, the shape of a room) and the views afforded of the outside (through large windows or the open structure of a garden pavillon).

"De l'espérance," for example, opens with the group walking in a garden, seeking relief from the summer heat. They stop "dans un cabinet écarté, dont l'ombrage et la fraîcheur était fort agréables, et comme il se rencontra par hasard qu'il n'y avait qu'autant de sièges qu'il en fallait, la conversation n'y pouvait être interrompue . . ." (*M*, p. 3).

It seems crucial that the company should happen upon these ideal spots, which seem to be magically designed to "fit" the group, as does this "*cabinet écarté*," with just the right number of chairs. Otherwise the magic of the occasion would be ruined by overly obvious contrivance. Conversation begins when "chance" brings the right people together in the right place at the right time : "Le hasard ayant assemblé quatre personnes d'un grand mérite chez une Dame appellée Clarinte qui en avait infiniment . . ." (*NCM*, 247). The topic of the conversation can also seem to come up by chance, suggested by a feature of the setting. In the conversation on "les plaisirs," the group sits down in a blossoming orange grove and, remarking on the scents of different flowers, someone comments that agreeable odors, like other pleasures, lose their appeal when they are habitually experienced (*C* I, 48).

A conversation typically progresses in three stages. First, the separateness of the group is established, either by a description of the unique qualities of each member of the company, or by their installation in a protected, enclosed space, or both. There follows a kind of inventory of the subject at hand; each speaker contributes examples for all to discuss. Finally, after the increasingly centripetal movement of the discussion has led the company to a state of total self-absorbtion, the frame of reference again shifts to a broader perspective of the world outside the circle, but from the vantage point of an exclusive group that has freshly examined the qualities that make it superior to that world.

Approaching the problem of describing the meaning of the day's topic, the group typically finds it easier to specify what it is *not*. That is, in defining conversation, for example, they decide that "avant que de bien définir en quoi consiste principalement le charme et la beauté de la conversation, il faudrait que toutes les personnes qui composent la compagnie se souvinssent des conversations ennuyeuses qui les ont le plus importunées" (*C* I, 3). At the end of this exercise an exasperated Cilénie reviews the dozens of ungracious social exchanges that various members of the group had described. "Je suis bien embarassée de vous entendre tous parler comme vous faites," she says. "De quoi faut-il donc parler? Et de quoi faut-il que la conversation soit formée, pour être belle et raisonnable?" The answer she is given is simply that there are indeed few other *topics* of conversation, but they must be addressed in a different *manner:*

> Il faut que ce soit de tout ce que nous avons repris, répliqua agré-
> ablement Valérie, en souriant. Mais il faut qu'elle soit conduite par
> le jugement. Car enfin, quoique tous les gens dont nous avons parlé
> soient incommodes, je soutiens, . . . qu'on ne peut parler que de ce
> dont ils parlent, et qu'on en peut parler agréablement   (pp.34–37).

style &
Substance

The desirable ingredients of a *good* conversation, then, have to do with style, not substance, and are infinitely more difficult to illustrate than their negative counterparts. Pressed by the other members of the group to be more specific, Valérie can only list a series of attributes necessary to a good conversation; it must be "libre," "diversifiée," "na-turelle," "raisonnable," "adroite," "modeste," "galante," (pp.39–42). Fi-nally Amilcar interrupts her: "Enfin, . . . sans vous donner la peine de parler davantage de la conversation, pour en donner des lois, il ne faut qu'admirer la vôtre, et qu'agir comme vous" (p.43). Thus the definition of conversation ends with an extended exchange of this compliment between all members of the group, and the narrator concludes: "nous fîmes ensuite une conversation si galante et si enjouée, qu'elle dura presque jusqu'au soir, que cette belle troupe se sépara" (p.45).

This movement from a critical and highly specific description of what occurs "outside" the exclusive circle, to an approbatory but much more nuanced observation of the group's own inner dynamic, is typical of the structure of Scudéry's conversations. In this way her speakers inevitably end their conversations by turning inward and indulging in a kind of group narcissism, transforming the object of discussion from a reference to a reality outside into a contemplation of the inner world they have created in juxtaposition to it.

group
narcissism --
ref to reality
outside
becomes
contempl
of inner world

The conversation on "l'envie" illustrates this progression in a par-ticularly striking way. The company has travelled to a house where a number of paintings by famous artists are on display. Their purpose is to impress Ericlée with the force of "fables" and visual representations of moral lessons, while she insists that the most convincing examples come from history and contemporary events. After listening to Tima-gène explain an allegorical representation of *l'envie*, inspired by one of Ovid's *Metamorphoses*, Ericlée remarks that the company would learn more by simply talking about "l'envie en elle-même . . . je connais des envieux et des envieuses en grand nombre . . ." (*M*, p.46).

The ensuing conversation is a list of examples that each speaker has observed at court, and concludes with Timagène and Ericlée assuring each other that neither of them could ever be *envieux*. The last sentence describes the group's final gesture of recognition toward the object that had inspired their conversation: ". . . cette aimable troupe acheta le tableau de l'envie, le joua, et le hasard le donna à Timagène, qui en avait si bien parlé; mais il l'envoya le lendemain à Ericlée, qui fut contrainte de l'accepter par le jugement de la compagnie" (p.61). A concrete object, open to the public gaze, is thus made personal and absorbed into a narrower world by becoming an object in a private game, with a new meaning accorded to it by the players. The members of the group who had expressed opposite points of view are reconciled through a collectively sanctioned exchange of gifts, but more importantly, this whole process is a playful pedagogical exercise wherein the standard pose of one authority figure lecturing to the uninformed is rejected in favor of a kind of group indulgence in talk, until the subject of discussion is properly digested.

Indeed, Scudéry's notion of conversation may be regarded as an elaborate verbal game, but one whose "transformation rules" are very loose, and serve to describe each encounter's tie to the outside world, as much as they serve to break that tie. While the democratic world of her conversations is carefully isolated from the "real" world of power struggles, personal victories, and defeats, at the same time its separateness is defined precisely by its selective relationship to a wider reality. In Goffman's terms, the "membrane" separating a focused encounter from the world outside also filters in "components in the encounter's external milieu that will expand or contract the range of events with which the encounter deals" (p.66).

In the pieces she composed specifically for her conversation collections, Scudéry shows the most concern with the relationship of her small idealized circles to the locus of power "outside."[22] One of the conversations dealing explicitly with this is entitled "De l'ennui sans sujet." It was published for the first time in Scudéry's 1684 collection of *Conversations nouvelles*. The conversation begins with a description of one of the participants, who is plagued by boredom. Unlike the transitory feeling of disaffection occasionally experienced by her companions, Aminte's perpetual *ennui* is radical, transcending all other experiences. It separates her from the other members of the group, as she cannot bear to remain in any social gathering for long. Like the perpetually dissatisfied Alceste, Aminte is constantly on the move, "elle doit toujours changer de place." In fact, Clorélise remarks, "le seul moment de votre plaisir est celui où vous passez d'un lieu à un autre." But unlike Molière's character, Aminte wants desperately to be rid of her disorder.

The other speakers in this conversation at first underplay the seriousness of her ailment. By pointing out other "humeurs" similar to Aminte's, they try to place hers in a hierarchy of behaviors, to reassimilate her into the group by showing how she does, after all, resemble others. Her *ennui* is a feature of individual "tempérament"—alienating, yes, but only to the extent that all personal taste inevitably distinguishes one person from another: "sans cela tous les honnêtes gens aimeraient également tout ce qui mérite d'être aimé" (*CN* II, 459). It is soon obvious, however, that Aminte's *ennui*, being non-specific, "sans sujet," makes it impossible for her to be assimilated in any social circle. Such determined boredom, remarks Stenobée, does not deserve sympathy: "quand le divertissement qu'on cherche ne divertit point, il faut conclure qu'on porte l'ennui dans son propre coeur, et qu'il faudrait se fuir soi-même pour ne s'ennuyer jamais" (p.461).

Discouraged by their failure to coax Aminte into a more sociable frame of mind, the three friends try another tactic. They list all the activities, games, and diversions they can think of that should amuse "une dame d'esprit": "la lecture, des ouvrages d'or et de soie, la peinture, la musique . . . ," only to have Aminte respond point by point on why such things would not entertain her. Furthermore, Aminte insists, she is not able to control her responses; *ennui* overcomes her despite her efforts to be like the others. Thus her friends will not be able to cure this "maladie" by appealing to her rational faculties: "Je soutiens que l'ennui n'est pas volontaire, car je voudrais bien ne m'ennuyer point, mais, par malheur, je ne puis m'en empêcher" (p.474).

At this point the group decides that they are dealing with one of those people "who don't even love themselves." Exasperated, Clorélise tells Aminte: "Cet ennui universel . . . vous fait passer votre vie dans une inquiétude continuelle dont vous ne pouvez rendre bonne raison." True to form, Aminte decides to leave, and in her absence the others

continue to discuss her situation, now somewhat more harshly. Stenobée asserts that the rules of civility oblige a person such as Aminte to
repress *ennui*. Aminte's failure to maintain the appearance of being involved in a social encounter may ultimately destroy her capacity for
intimacy or love:

> il est très nécessaire d'éviter soigneusement cette sorte d'humeur,
> être toujours où l'on doit être, s'accomoder sagement aux gens
> qu'on voit, ne se faire point de plaisirs singuliers, ni d'ennui sans
> sujet, et penser sérieusement que l'instabilité de l'esprit pourrait
> bien se communiquer au coeur, ce qui est sans doute un des plus
> grands malheurs qui puisse arriver, puisque cela vous rend égale-
> ment incapable ni d'aimer ni d'être aimée   (p.478).

Aminte's dilemma illustrates a risk inherent in the indolent style of
life elsewhere described by Scudéry as a necessary condition for true
pleasure. In "De l'oisiveté et de l'ingratitude," a conversation taken
from *Clélie*, her characters extoll the virtues of unmitigated leisure: "le
repos est le but de toutes les actions des hommes . . . un galant homme
oisif est un philosophe, qui ne fait rien parce qu'il n'y a rien au monde
qui soit digne de l'occuper . . ." (*C* p.394). This kind of *oisiveté* is clearly
different from Aminte's state, which seems closer to the relentless *ennui*
described by Pascal:

> Ainsi s'écoule toute la vie, on cherche le repos en combattant
> quelques obstacles. Et si on les a surmontés, le repos devient insup-
> portable par l'ennui qu'il engendre. Il en faut sortir et mendier le
> tumulte. Car ou l'on pense aux misères que l'on a ou à celles qui
> nous menacent. Et quand on se verrait même à l'abri de toutes
> parts, l'ennui, de son autorité privé, ne laisserait pas de sortir du
> fond du coeur, ou il a des racines naturelles, et de remplir l'esprit
> de son vénin.[23]

Pascal/ divertissement

Like the Pascalian man, Aminte is in a perpetual state of agitation
in a futile effort to hit upon a *divertissement* that would relieve her boredom. While in Scudéry's earlier text Amilcar evokes *repos* as a delec-
table condition, it appears that for Aminte, cessation of movement
would only mean a plunge into despair.

But Pascal's abyss is not really to be found in Mademoiselle de Scudéry's social landscape, even by the vagrant Aminte. And in fact, the
company in "De l'ennui sans sujet" does finally succeed in evoking a

scenario that would engage the interest of their difficult companion, who is so stricken that even her own dreams bore her. What Aminte is suffering is closer to a personal humiliation, a failure to achieve that dominance over herself that for Scudéry is the necessary condition for self-love. In one of the conversations in Scudéry's last collection, another group of speakers, discussing the pleasures and dangers of "la paresse," concludes that "si le loisir est un bien, ce n'est pas pour ne rien faire, c'est seulement pour faire ce que l'on veut, et non pas pour s'anéantir par la paresse excessive" (*M* II,78).

It is her self-defeated posture that ultimately elicits scorn and impatience from Aminte's companions. Her *ennui* finally appears to Clorélise to suggest a kind of refusal to play the game of sociability, a violation of *politesse oblige:* "Quand je vois Aminte s'ennuyer sans raison en un lieu où je me divertis, elle m'impatiente de telle sorte que je voudrais qu'elle n'eût ni beauté, ni esprit, et que je ne l'aimasse pas" (p.474). At this point in the conversation Aminte's intransigent boredom is viewed by her companions as a threat to the success of the group interaction; they criticize her not only for her personal abdication of responsibility but for the effect her behavior has on others. Aminte does not or cannot observe what Erving Goffman calls the "fundamental requirement" of most conversational exchanges—that "the spontaneous involvement of the participants in an official focus of attention must be called forth and sustained."[24] In intimate and restricted spoken encounters like those portrayed in Scudéry's idealized conversations, supreme importance is given to this basic rule of conduct. Clorélise's impatience with her companion, and her wish that Aminte should no longer possess other attributes facilitating sociability—"beauté," "esprit"—show how the delicate illusion of a separate reality brought into being by these social encounters can be threatened by an individual's failure to participate to the proper degree.

Refocused Encounters

After a brief excursion away from the company of her friends, Aminte returns with Clindor, who has heard about a recent *fête* given by the king at Marly. Although he did not personally witness the event, the description he heard of it leads him to believe it would have dissipated Aminte's *ennui*. At this gathering, the king had presented his court with a new diversion. Displaying several rooms full of precious and exotic artifacts which had been acquired for him from all parts of the world, he invited his guests to amuse themselves by gambling with them. The display is orchestrated by the king's *oiselier*, or "marchand de la cour," who instructs four other *marchands* in how to present their array of *marchandises*. Clindor recites an impressive list of hundreds of objects that were offered to the guests to be used in their gaming. At first the players are inhibited by the variety and wealth of the items, so they play cautiously, fearful of losing: "Et comme cette abondance offrait aux yeux tant de choses différentes à choisir, la suspension fit qu'on ne joua pas d'abord avec empressement; les dames cherchaient à résoudre ce qu'elles voulaient jouer, à proportion de ce qu'elles voulient hasarder" (*CN* II, 492). But it slowly becomes apparent that this wealth has no monetary value; these *marchands* are asking no price ". . . comme ces quatre marchands ne s'expliquaient pas nettement sur le prix des choses, et se contentaient d'exhorter à jouer hardiment, on commença de soupçonner qu'il y avait de mystère; . . ." (p.494). And when the king himself begins to play, and to lose, the guests change their attitude: "Mais enfin le roi ayant joué le premier et perdu fort noblement, son exemple fut un commandement de jouer" (p. 493). At the end of the evening the players, who keep their winnings as physical reminders of the king's "liberalité," compare this *fête* to others, which, while equally grand, had left the guests with only a dream-like memory of them. At Marly, the king had magically transformed a familiar game into a diversion with heroic dimensions: "le jeu qui partout ailleurs n'est qu'un plaisir, et qui quelquefois même est un vice quand on y trompe, devient une vertu héroïque dans ce palais . . ." (p.497).

Aminte, of course, agrees that this game would indeed have relieved her *ennui*, and the company concludes with praise for Louis XIV: "la liberté ingénieuse du roi était l'âme de ce commerce héroïque. Le roi seul perdit tout ce que les autres gagnèrent, si toutefois on peut appeler perdre d'avoir le plaisir de donner sans vouloir même être remercié . . ." (pp.494–95).

The king's gesture is introduced as a *divertissement* which is effective first of all because it surprises the court, as something new, and at the same time it is compared to another situation in which Louis had used the tactic of surprise: "le roi surprit autant toute sa cour qu'il surprit autrefois la Franche-Compté, lorsqu'il partit à la fin du carnaval pour l'aller conquérir; . . ." (p.497). The "heroic" role attributed to the king at Marly is the posture of the conqueror; by making of himself the sole source of goods for the gambling party, he asserts his power over his subjects, specifically over a noble class which has been reduced to finding action, glory, and honor all within the confines of polite ceremonial and courtly gaming. The gambling party plays out the political relationship between king and court, while also transforming this relationship into a system of polite "commerce continuel de bons offices," from which no one ever really emerges a loser.

gambling

The gambler's attraction to gaming is usually thought to be based on the element of risk, and on the player's obsession with a possible gain. Pascal writes that the pleasure of gambling derives from the uncertainty of winning, which in turn excites the gambler's eagerness to win:

> Il faut qu'il s'y échauffe, et qu'il se pipe lui-même en s'imaginant qu'il serait heureux de gagner ce qu'il ne voudrait pas qu'on lui donna à condition de ne point jouer, afin qu'il se forme un sujet de passion et qu'il excite sur cela son désir, sa colère, sa crainte pour cet objet qu'il s'est formé comme les enfants qui s'effraient du visage qu'ils ont barbouillé.[25]

In this version of gambling the player's *ennui* can only be relieved by introducing the possibility of losing, and the gambler derives no pleasure from simply being given what he might have won. In his classification of games Roger Caillois notes that card games combine the two forces of *agôn* and *alea*, competition and chance, while Goffman views gambling as a form of "action-seeking" which in a leisure society means taking chances perceived as unavoidable.[26]

In her portrait of the ideal gambling party, though, Scudéry emphasizes that the special quality of this diversion, which made it singularly interesting to the perpetually bored Aminte, is precisely that the players are risking nothing. The participants only enter into the spirit of the game when they realize that there are no restrictions on what they can play. What is gambled, moreover, is not money, but a seemingly limitless quantity of exotic and foreign objects whose monetary value is, we are told, impossible for the guests to calculate. Thus the initial attempt of the ladies to "decide what they wanted to play according to what they wanted to risk," is rendered pointless. In this situation, it is impossible for the participants to experience the game as "action" in Goffman's sense; it is closer to ritual, but without the element of repetition and familiarity that is so crucial to ritualized group activity. The only player to actually risk losing anything is the king, and he transforms his material loss into a personal victory.

It is significant that Scudéry chooses, in this conversation on aristocratic disaffection, to evoke a gambling party as the one activity capable of curing courtly *ennui*. By 1684, when *Nouvelles conversations* was published, gambling was viewed by many members of the nobility as a sign of their demise as a power elite. The spectacle of the obsessive *joueur* consuming his wealth in one evening at the gambling table was not unfamiliar, and it became emblematic of some of the devastating effects of Louis XIV's fiscal policies on the personal fortunes of his courtiers. Artistic representations of gambling, particularly in the theater, stressed the destructive power that one individual's fascination with risk and money had for the fabric of social relations.[27] La Bruyère's well-known descriptions of the social dynamics of the gambling table make a particularly sharp contrast with Scudéry's utopian fantasy:

> Une tenue d'états, où les chambres assemblées pour une affaire très capitale, n'offrent point aux yeux rien de si grave et de si sérieux qu'une table de gens qui jouent un grand jeu: une triste sévérité règne sur leurs visages; implacables l'un pour l'autre, et irréconciliables ennemis pendant que la séance dure, ils ne reconnaissent plus ni liaisons, ni alliance, ni naissance, ni distinctions: le hasard seul, aveugle et farouche divinité, préside au cercle, et y décide souverainement; ils l'honorent tous par un silence profond, et par une attention dont ils sont partout ailleurs fort incapables; toutes les passions, comme suspendues, cèdent à une seule; le courtisan alors n'est ni doux, ni flatteur, ni complaisant, ni même dévot.[28]

Like Scudéry's description of the king's gambling party, this portrait stresses the unique force of gambling over its players, but it is quite a different kind of involvement than that conjured up for Scudéry's inattentive Aminte. La Bruyère's scene shows the tension of real gambling, created by each participant's fear of losing. The players are locked in a stressful social encounter, in which all distinctions between them are forgotten, but the exchange will result in a radical unbalancing of individual status relationships. At the Marly *fête*, by inviting the participants to gamble with his possessions, the king mediates their obsession with private gain and substitutes himself for the object of each player's desire.

The king orchestrates this lavish circulation of precious objects symbolizing the global expansion of his power, thus providing his guests with a diversion similar to a ceremonial potlatch. In primitive societies, potlatch is a form of ritual consumption distinguished from other types of ceremonial exchange by its extreme abundance, its function as a sign of power asserted by the giver over the receiver, and by the obligation it imposes on the receiver to offer an even more lavish potlatch in return.[29] The king's carefully orchestrated display of wealth to his subjects, followed by their collective consumption of it, is precisely what occurs at a potlatch ceremony, or *fête*, as Mauss calls it.[30] The Marly gambling party clearly functions, moreover, as an assertion of royal power over the players who all nonetheless ostensibly "win." The spectacle of himself as "noble loser," his possessions consumed by his subjects, gives a sacramental dimension to the king's political power.

It is obvious, however, that the *fête* at Marly does not represent simply one in a series of displays and counter-displays of wealth and ritual consumption between the king and his courtiers. What distinguishes the structure of this *fête* from a potlatch is the fact that the giver and receivers are clearly not intended to reverse roles. In fact Louis XIV's lavish displays at Versailles in the 1660's and 1670's had not only established the myth of his limitless wealth, but they also, as Jean-Marie Apostolidès has shown, confirmed the king's unique privilege to display it.[31] After Foucquet's arrest in 1664, no courtier attempted to compete with the celebrations of conspicuous consumption hosted by the king.

Scudéry's description of the gambling party is based on a real "journée galante" held by Louis XIV at Marly in the fall of 1683. As yet unfinished, the château de Marly was the latest of Louis XIV's architectural projects. The "galanterie" he orchestrated to initiate it in the fall of 1683 prefigured what Marly was to represent in the iconography of Louis XIV's palaces for years to come. He had conceived of it from the beginning as a place of escape where he would flee, with a select entourage, the burdensome ceremonial and political realities of the court.

Of the many courtiers who have left us descriptions of the *fêtes* held there, few were ever invited, for to be included in a Marly excursion was to be singled out as a member of the ultra-elite. In fact, it was in the first year of his permanent residency at Versailles that the king had

Marly built, as though Versailles, having itself been transformed from a place of escape (from the Louvre) into a more official political space, was no longer the proper site for the king's more aleatory dramatizations of limitless power.

Donneau de Visé, in his November 1683 issue of *Le Mercure galant*, describes the first Marly *fête*, reporting that the appearance of the king's collection of precious objects seemed magical: "On n'avait ouï aucun bruit; on n'avait entendu marcher personne; on n'avait rien vu apporter, ni briller aucune lumière par les portes . . . (p.288). As in Scudéry's conversation, this report views the king's innovative version of a gambling party as a manifestation of his inimitable "magnificence": "Quel autre Prince a jamais donné d'une manière aussi agréable?" (p.300). The account stresses the impact on the guests, who are repeatedly described as overwhelmed by each new display: "La surprise de ceux qui étaient entrés dans les trois premières chambres, ayant toujours augmentée, ils demeurèrent quelque temps muets d'étonnement en entrant dans la dernière" (p.294). Both descriptions marvel at the pleasure the king seems to take in seeing his wealth consumed, but Scudéry's Clindor also seems to take a similar pleasure in simply enumerating these riches. Unlike the *Mercure galant* description, Scudéry's indulges in a lengthy detailing of all the objects that had been displayed; her speakers seem to match the king's "penchant naturel à la libéralité" with their own self-indulgent verbalization of it (*Mercure galant* p.302).

Scudéry's speakers enumerate and itemize to create a kind of feast of words that is displayed and consumed in the act of conversation. Like the modified gambling party at Marly, all of Scudéry's conversations construct social encounters where the words are circulated, admired, and displayed, though never fixed in a regular pattern of exchange. In her system, the value of conversation depends precisely on the sense that the speakers have an unlimited supply of words at their disposal. No topic is ever exhausted, nor can the supply of subjects run out at the court of a king "qui nous donne tous les jours de nouveaux sujets d'admiration . . ." (*EM* I, 188).

How to Repay Louis XIV

While his guests were firmly placed in the role of receivers of the king's beneficence, while they never turned the tables on their host in the ritual potlatch reversal, they had nonetheless contracted a debt to him by receiving his gifts. As Apostolidès has explained the psychology of the guest-host relationship at Louis XIV's court, this debt was perceived as enormous but unpayable: "En acceptant le don irréversible du prince, les courtisans contractent une dette à l'égard de l'état . . . ils se trouvent pris entre la nécessité de se libérer de la dette et l'impossibilité de rendre au même niveau" (p.106–7). In Scudéry's description, as we have seen, the guests learn early on that the objects they will be gambling have no exchange value. They are to be appreciated first as tokens of the royal expansion of political power. Then, once the collection is dispersed and each guest has claimed an object, either meaning changes; they are to be kept as "souvenirs," not only of the evening's pleasure, but of the king's largesse: "les plus petites bagatelles qu'on y a gagnés doivent être conservées avec plaisir; et si on ne les a pas reçues de la propre main du roi, on les doit en général à sa volonté, et à la libéralité de son coeur" (p.500).

In the social dynamic of the real *fêtes* at Versailles, the counter-gift that is most obviously expected of the courtiers is their utter submission to royal power.[32] Certain individuals, however, have another means of "repaying" the king for his gifts. Seventeenth-century rhetorical theory gives a privileged place to the *éloge* or *louange*, since under an absolutist regime flattery became a mode of expression that was unlikely to be censored. In his study of rhetoric and absolutist ideology under Louis XIV, Louis Marin has analyzed the psychological interdependence of king and courtier in the construction of political myth. Reading André Félibien's descriptions of the Versailles *divertissements*, Marin notes the close interconnection of military victories and royal *fêtes:* "Les divertissements . . . représentent les guerres dans le temps des paix qui les interrompent, comme les guerres sont les fêtes du prince dans un autre champ et sur une autre scène."[33] In Marin's analysis, the Versailles *fêtes* were illusionistic counterparts to political realities, in which the king constructed a mythical relationship with his subjects based on a deification of himself. This strategy is confirmed and echoed by his courtiers in the rhetoric of flattery: ". . . le roi se donne à consommer come corps symbolique à ses sujects et . . . ceux-ci le constituent tel par les discours qu'ils lui adressent" (p.115).

The book of conversations in which "De l'ennui sans sujet" appears functions, in a sense, as a text offered to the king in exchange for a gift he had accorded its author. In 1683 Mademoiselle de Scudéry had been

granted a royal pension, and while most of her previous works had
been dedicated to illustrious women, all of the books published after
1683 were dedicated to Louis XIV. The opening piece in *Conversations
nouvelles* is entitled "Conversation de la magnificence et de la magnanimité." Like "De l'ennui sans sujet," it was composed for the new collection, and deals with interactive problems that did not concern the
speakers in Scudéry's earlier conversations. One of the speakers, Philémon, has returned to Paris after a ten-month absence, and he marvels
at the changes that have occurred at the court. Discussion of these nov-
elties focuses on ceremonial, specifically the new daily ritual of the
king's *appartement*. After a detailed description of the hall of mirrors
and adjoining rooms, the group praises "la libéralité, la magnificence et
la magnanimité du roi" (p.53). What distinguishes *magnificence* as it is
displayed at Versailles from other forms of *libéralité* is that it has no
utilitarian function: "la magnificence consiste souvent à ne rien épargner pour les choses qui ne sont pas d'une necessité absolue, et un
excellent homme a dit autrefois qu'une grand dépense faite à propos
pour le plaisir d'un seul jour est plus magnifique que si elle était pour
plusieurs années" (pp.55–56).

The consumption enacted at Versailles is self-contained. As in a
potlatch ritual, on this single occasion the host and his guests are
bonded together by a gratuitous destruction of wealth. The act of liberal spending—*magnificence*—is considered related to the political virtue of *magnanimité*, or justice, and both are seen to be part of the new
ritualization of all aspects of court life. The act of giving more than
what is expected of you, of making a lavish gesture that ostentatiously
goes beyond the demands of utility, is a "grande qualité", and, one of
the speakers is careful to add, can be found in both women and men,
although women do not have as many occasions to exhibit it (p.63).

If there is any occasion when women do have the opportunity to   P + authority
display this particular quality it is in conversation. The women in
Scudéry's conversations are constantly praised for their ability to judge
as a wise monarch would, and the discussions are often set up as mock
courts, with one woman, usually the hostess, asked to give the group
her pronouncement on a topic. Inevitably, though, the speaker who is
asked to do this will refuse to assume such an authoritative role, and
instead will simply put the conversation in motion, encouraging the
apparently limitless loquacity of her friends until the conversation

seems to come to a natural end. The role of these central figures in the conversations is very much like the role played by the king in Scudéry's description of the Marly *fête*, except that the conspicuous spending of words that occurs in a conversation is not finally transformed into a tribute to one speaker.

But in Scudéry's last conversations the figure of Louis XIV totally dominates the social encounters, as a transcendent model for all forms of interaction. In "De la politesse" her characters conclude that perfect sociability is made possible by the existence in an absolute monarchy of "un premier modèle": "la source de la politesse étant le désir de plaire . . . ce désir doit être plus vif dans un état monarchique que dans une république, parce que les grâces dependant d'un seul, le désir de lui plaire rend capable de plaire à tous . . ." (*CN* I, p.181). The speakers contrast this situation to a republic, where they say the effort to please is dissipated: "le désir de plaire à tous, ou du moins à un grand nombre, fait qu'on ne plaît quelquefois à personne" (p.184). In "De la magnificence et de la magnanimité," the speakers tell Philémon that the new focus on the court and the quasi-mythical presence of the king places all interaction that occurs there on a higher plane. Marveling at his companions' descriptions, and at their claim that the king's personal virtues exert a transcendent power over all aspects of social life, Philémon asks what place *conversation* has in the *appartement* ritual. Parthénie replies: "On l'y trouve comme un autre quand on veut, on se tire à part, on s'assied et l'on parle deux ou trois ensemble: on y est donc en conversation comme par tout ailleurs, excepté qu'on n'y parle que de choses qui plaisent, et qui divertissent, personne ne s'avisant de parler en ce lieu-là de choses tristes et fâcheuses . . ." (p.43).

Thus the myth of Louis XIV as "le parfait modèle" envelops those in his presence. And as "le parfait magnanime," the king ostensibly *gives* perfection to the flow of conversation: "la libéralité du roi s'étend jusqu'à donner de l'esprit à ceux qui ont l'honneur d'être dans ses plaisirs" (p.45). Having achieved a state of perfection, the social existence of this select circle surrounding Louis XIV is static. Not only is it impossible for the courtiers to reciprocate, but the king cannot outdo himself either: ". . . le roi a surpassé tous ses prédécesseurs, et tous ceux des autres rois. Mails il ne pourra jamais se surpasser lui-même . . ." (p.118).

In the last volume of Scudéry's conversations, the first to be published by the *Imprimerie Royale*, flattery of Louis XIV is the centerpiece of even the most unlikely topics. "De la modestie," written on the occasion of the victory of the royal troops at Namur, praises the perfect modesty of a conquering hero. In "Des fleurs et des fruits," everyone marvels at the royal gardens and at the miracle the king has achieved by cultivating plants out of season, creating "plusieurs climats en un seul jardin . . ." (p.156). Such heavy doses of adulation can disrupt the smooth flow of conversation, even among Scudéry's supremely well-adjusted speakers. In "De l'expérience" she gathers a group of friends of different ages, and the talk turns to the past. The old woman in the group (Scudéry herself was 85 when the book was published), complains of the "incivilité" of youth, who have no appreciation for the past. Two of the younger members of the group begin to debate whether any moment but the present is worth talking about. Anacrise says she loves to hear old stories about the habitués of the *chambre bleue:* "J'écoute avec plaisir ce qu'était l'Hôtel de Rambouillet où tout ce qu'il y avait de grand, de brave, de savant, de galant, de poli, et de vertueux se trouvait." Célinte objects that nothing could be as engaging as the life of the monarch under whom they are now living: "ce que fait *Louis le Grand* m'occupe si agréablement et j'en ai l'esprit si rempli, qui je ne m'informe point de ce qui s'est fait avant lui . . . " (*EM*,p.129).

Pushed to its logical conclusion, the idea that one is living in utopia naturally leads to a kind of narcissism, and, even more threatening to the pleasures of conversation, it leads to a univocal adulation of the perfect monarch. To do him justice, says one speaker in the conversation on "les désirs," one would have to enumerate all his achievements, but "ce ne serait plus une conversation, ce serait une belle et grand Histoire" (p.215).

Is it ever possible, then, to verbally repay the king for his favor while still respecting the requirements of a good conversation? In the piece that closes her last volume, Scudéry seems to be attempting to do just that. "De la reconnaissance" is her gift to Louis XIV, which purports to settle her debt to him without losing control of her own share of their interaction. In it, she narrates the wild fantasy of a writer trying to figure out how to repay royal *magnificence*. The speakers initially take up a discussion similar to one from *Clélie*, which Scudéry had reprinted in her first volume of conversations.[34] The company is discussing ingratitude, only here they are doing so at the secluded residence of a disaffected courtier, who has abandoned "le monde," he says, because "je n'ai jamais trouvé que de l'ingratitude en tous ceux que j'ai obligés" (*EM*, p.410).

True gratitude, or *reconnaissance*, however, is hard to recognize and as hard to demonstrate. Most people, it seems, observe a mechanical system of trading favors that suggests the marketplace. This kind of rigid exchange cannot express true gratitude:

> . . . Ceux qui comptent si juste les services qu'ils rendent en échange de ceux qu'ils ont reçus, n'ont pas une noble reconnaissance, et comme les personnes véritablement généreuses, ne comptent jamais les services qu'ils rendent pour ceux qu'ils valent, à plus forte raison ceux qui servent par reconnaissance ne doivent pas s'amuser à peser leurs services . . .   (p.414).

While it is true that "tout bienfait . . . nous demande une reconnaissance proportionée à lui," Scudéry maintains that instead of insisting on observing a strict balance of one service in exchange for another of equal value, one should follow a different rule: "le règle la plus juste est de vouloir toujours surpasser ceux dont nous acceptons les bons offices . . ."   (p.421–22).

But obviously this rule, which is the principle of potlatch, cannot be observed when one has to decide how to thank the king. On this problem, Periandre says he has an anonymous manuscript he would like to share with the others. Its author has received a "grâce" from an important personnage: "selon toutes les apparences c'a été pour le Cardinal de Richelieu ou pour le Cardinal de Mazarin; ou enfin pour quelque grand homme . . . " (p.422–23). The text recounts a vision of a conversation with Apollo that the author had had one night when trying to think of how to "rendre à un grand héros un petit remerciement pour un grand bienfait" (p.424). Those with absolute power never have to experience this problem: "Vous autres Dieux immortels, vous ne savez ce que c'est de recevoir un bienfait sans le pouvoir rendre" (p.425). Apollo responds by observing that a writer can always reciprocate with flattery: "Ne sais-tu pas qu'en louant un héros on le remercie, et que quelque grand et quelque puissant qu'il sont, il a moins de biens à donner qu'on ne lui peut donner de louanges?" (p.425).

But the hero in question has refused in advance to accept praise as a counter-gift. "Le héros dont il s'agit, et qui mérite de si grandes louanges, ne les aime point du tout: it me le dit l'autre jour de sa propre bouche . . ." (p.426). This, Apollo agrees, poses a difficult but not insurmountable problem: he tells the writer that they need to travel "à la source oú tu choisiras comme il te plaira" (p.426). Suddenly the narrator is transported to another world, which Apollo announces is "(le) monde des fictions, ou des inventions" (p.427). This world, infinitely larger than the one they have left, is, like the other, divided into regions, in each of which the narrator observes allegorical representations of a virtue or rhetorical "ornement" ("hyperbole," "prosopopée," "anachronismes," "prophéties").

It is in the land of "bienfaits," which Apollo says borders the land of "reconnaissance" (p.430), that the writer sees a parade of figures representing different "remerciements." Apollo identifies each type: "remerciements de refus, de bienséance, intéressés ambitieux," and finally "sincères," which of course are the ones the writer needs to use. They are reticent in the presence of the person they are thanking, but elsewhere they ceaselessly proclaim their benefactor's glories: "ils le remercient à toutes les heures du jour sans qu'il le sache, soit en particulier, soit en public" (p.436).

The listeners in the conversation immediately respond to this anonymous tale by remarking that it might well have happened to someone who had received a "bienfait" from Louis XIV, and they proceed to enact the mechanism of the "remerciment sincère" by detailing the king's virtues, and finally concluding that this king left nothing to be desired by his subjects: ". . . plus j'y fais de reflexion, plus je crois qu'on ne peut lui désirer que d'être toujours ce qu'il est" (p.442).

This final conversation of Scudéry's collection flamboyantly displays the double rhetorical function of enumeration in her idealized verbal encounters. The dream story within the conversation enacts the lesson it purports to teach, by bombarding the listeners with a vision of limitless riches, all described as reified forms of talk to be applied to the task of repaying the king. Within the conversation itself, the dream is a display comparable to the Marly *fête*, and the parade of things it is made up of is played into the conversation's economy like the chips at a gambling table.

Thus in Scudéry's system, not only the outer display of manners [central thesis] and etiquette, but also the concept of all sociable communication is intimately connected with the political and mythical relationship between the king and his subjects. For her, ideal conversation, as it is enacted within the wider context of aristocratic life under Louis XIV, is a protected, utopian economy of words, where, like the gambling party at Marly, nothing is really risked. This, at least, is the pretense; it is the form she gives to her dialogues, as her conversants repeatedly privilege form over substance and promote a use of language which is, as Stanton remarks, "unproductive, gratuitous, esthetic."[35] Yet at the same time the internal structure of these encounters is fundamentally linked to the wider world within which they take place. Goffman's comment on ths relationship in contemporary society is even more applicable to Scudéry's world: "We fence our encounters in with gates; the very means by which we hold off a part of reality can be the means by which we can bear introducing it" (p.78).

Teaching Conversation at Saint-Cyr

Between 1686 and 1691, Scudéry's conversation collections were used as textbooks in Madame de Maintenon's experimental school for young noblewomen. The establishment of a state funded, secular institution for children of poor noble families was a sign of the new dependency of nobles on the crown that Louis XIV wished to foster; it was one way in which a new generation of aristocrats could be socialized under the watchful eye of the state. Madame de Maintenon, in her letters to Louis XIV asking for the establishment of the school, blends moral and political arguments for reforming the nobility. Society's elites have an obligation to set an example for the lower classes, and the state-sponsored education of future aristocratic mothers will not only help to instill the nobility with virtues beneficial to the crown, but it will also tie them more closely to the king "by a new link of gratitude."[36]

Documents on the founding of Saint-Cyr attest to Maintenon's close involvement with every decision having to do with the organization of the school. No task was too small for her attention. She personally selected all the books that were to be used, and her criteria were very restrictive, as reading was not one of the most important exercises in her curriculum.[37] The fact that she initially included Scudéry's books of conversations on her extremely limited list indicates that she considered them important tools for teaching young women how to think and, more importantly, how to talk.[38]

But the kind of sociability that her pupils learned from these conversations was not, in the end, what Maintenon wanted taught at Saint-Cyr. In 1691 she instituted radical reforms at the school, claiming that it had become nothing more than a fashionable salon where courtiers came and went freely. Activities that she had intended to be edifying exercises, such as the production of *Esther*, had become public spectacles. A letter to the "maîtresse des classes" outlines the failure of her initial ideas:

> N'ayant point vu ce qui seul peut faire un fondement solide, j'ai voulu que les filles eussent de l'esprit, qu'on elevât leur coeur, qu'on formât leur raison; j'ai réussi à ce dessein: elles ont de l'esprit, et s'en servent contre nous; elles ont le coeur élevé, et sont plus fières et plus hautaines qu'il ne conviendrait de l'être aux plus grandes princesses; à parler même selon le monde, nous avons formé leur raison, et fait des discoureuses, présomptueuses, curieuses, hardies   (*Extraits*, p.13).

Most importantly, in a school where she had wanted to teach domestic virtues, there was far too much indulgence in the pleasures of talk:

> Tout à Saint-Cyr se tourne en discours; on y parle souvent de la simplicité, on cherche à la bien définir, à la bien comprendre, à discerner ce qui est simple et ce qui ne l'est pas, puis dans la pratique on se divertit à dire: "par simplicité, je prends la meilleure place; par simplicité, je vais me louer" . . . En verité, c'est se jouer de tout, et tourner en raillerie ce qu'il y a de plus sérieux"   (*Extraits*, p.14).

Scudéry's books were taken off the reading list, and replaced with a new collection of conversations written by Maintenon herself, which presented a system of interaction that was very different from Scudéry's. Maintenon's conversations were designed to be memorized, and acted out as scenes by the students before a small group of spectators, often including the king. These little scenes were rehearsals for life "outside," and frequently derived from social scenarios that the young women would be likely to encounter in the future. Like Scudéry's, they each have a title indicating a subject, but Maintenon's are short, spare,

[margin annotation: Maintenon's Conversations]

and tightly organized around the topic. The pedagogical motive is obvious: there is always a more informed authority figure who states her point of view at the outset, while objections or questions brought up by the other girls serve essentially as an opportunity for the principal speaker to clarify her position. The dangers to moral rectitude of living in polite society are ceaselessly examined, as in the conversation "Sur la réputation":

> *Placide:*   C'est un martyre de vivre dans le monde, s'il est tel que vous le dépeignez. Quoi! toujours douter de ce qu'on dit, toujours craindre qu'on ne veuille nous tromper et nous perdre!
>
> *Valérie:*   Heureux en effet ceux qui en sont retirés! Mais tous ne peuvent vivre dans la retraite, il faut se conduire au milieu des méchants avec la crainte et les précautions de ceux qui marchent au bord des précipices.[39]

Verbal restraint and even silent assent should be the rule in most social encounters, in order to avoid the risk of embarassment and ridicule. Everywhere the authoritative speakers tell the others that in most conversations, it is best to talk as little as possible:

> Vous serez bientôt tournée en ridicule, si vous parlez; car quelque esprit naturel que vous puissiez avoir, vous ignorez mille choses . . . n'est-il pas raisonnable d'écouter avant que de parler, et tâcher de discerner ce qu'on dit et les personnes les plus estimées? Votre expérience vous fera voir que ce ne sont pas les grandes parleuses   (*Extraits*, pp.246–47).

This is a far cry from the lesson Saint-Cyr pensioners would have deduced from their first readings on conversation. Scudéry's speakers live out an interactive fantasy, where embarrassment and other forms of what Goffman calls "alienation from interaction" do not exist.[40] The borders of her world are politely but firmly closed to any people or ideas that would inhibit the collectively produced ambiance necessary for ideal sociability. Maintenon's speakers, on the other hand, learn to mistrust the free play of clever conversation, which is seen as a waste of words and a threat to one's good reputation. Like the speakers in other conduct books written in the 1690's, Maintenon's young women are warned that wordly conversation can be a cheap disguise, too easily acquired by ambitious people "qui n'ont que l'écorce de la politesse."[41]

In making her initial choice of pedagogical materials to be used at Saint-Cyr, Maintenon apparently found no reason to object to Scudéry's conversations as a means of teaching aristocratic girls how to talk. But by 1691 she saw clearly that the vision of sociability presented in these works was based on principles that were fundamentally opposed to the virtues she wanted to instill. "La politesse du siècle," she writes her teachers, is our enemy.

For Scudéry's speakers, the concepts of work, family, practicality, and utility seem hardly to exist. They cannot even begin a conversation until they are in a space that seems to magically suspend them outside of reality, within which they can carefully select the few elements of the outside world that they will let in. Ideal conversation is conducted according to its own "économie du babil," in which the value of speech is reestablished with each new encounter, a value that is realizable only in the pleasurable and free circulation of words.[42] Verbal excess is as crucial to Scudéry's conversations as excess wealth was to Louis XIV's festive displays of power. There is no place in her system of *politesse* for the abrupt breaks in communication brought about by a tit-for-tat exchange of prudent remarks. Nor is there a place for the kind of authority figure who dominates Madame de Maintenon's model conversations. In Scudéry's system, the pleasure of talk derives precisely from a collective effort to create the illusion of a world where hierarchy does not exist. The king himself is seen as a kind of indulgent god who sets the game of sociability in motion. Maintenon's discarding of Scudéry's books reflects a new concept of elite interaction, which now has as its primary purpose the responsibility to serve as an example to outsiders. And the outside world is very present in these conversations, even in its most mundane manifestations. The speakers are taught how to deal with servants, how to talk to peasants, and the precise social standing of a "notaire" compared to a "procureur," "avocat," or "conseiller." They are warned of a growing disorder in the social hierarchy, and of their responsibility to set the example for others by showing respect for traditional ranks.[43]

The king, of course, is the ultimate figure of temporal authority in these dialogues, but he is described as a real person and is compared to other monarchs of his own time.[44] The achievements of his reign are praised, but not in mythical or heroic terms. Instead the speakers propagandize for specific administrative practices: the purpose of the *taille*, or Colbert's new fiscal policies.[45] Louis XIV was, moreover, a real presence in these conversations as a spectator at their performances.

The model conversations taught to the pupils of Saint-Cyr take place in the world, and they presuppose no separate reality of the sort that is so essential to salon conversation. The mark of authenticity for Scudéry's model conversations is precisely the closure that is so carefully established at the outset. Maintenon demands a new kind of authenticity from her speakers, which they can guarantee only by a utilitarian approach to speech, a simple style, and a practical reserve of expression. There are new threats, too, to this image of sociability: whereas in Scudéry's conversations everything depends on the proper set-up and the equal status of the speakers, Maintenon's speakers are constantly reminded that the shelter of the school is fragile and temporary. They are being prepared for exposure to the outside world, and they are made aware that their social interaction outside will be constantly spied upon, overheard, imitated, and judged.

In fact, it is precisely this special exposure to the outside that is the mark of their privilege, while it is the ease with which they can hide from the gaze of outsiders that distinguishes Scudéry's social groups. The boundaries of Scudéry's social encounters are secure—the speakers all look calmly at the carefully groomed world around them, but those who are excluded cannot see into their shady retreats.

Maintenon's suspicion of "la politesse du siècle" echoes the tone of conduct manuals written toward the end of the seventeenth century, which tended to recommend a healthy "méfiance" for social survival. She would have her aristocratic pupils be doubly aware of the dangers of being too open in conversation, because they are more exposed than others to the scrutiny of spectators. By memorizing and performing their lessons in front of others, her speakers are being prepared for their roles in the outside world. Everywhere, her speakers remind each other of the public exposure for which they must prepare themselves; there is never that sense of security that is the prerequisite for Scudéry's social encounters. It is not only the powerful, critical authority figure—the king or the teacher—who watches and listens, but also the rest of society, those of lower social rank for whom Maintenon's young impoverished nobles are supposed to be models.

The career of Scudéry's conversation books traces an important historical shift in standards of sociability that occurred in the last decades of the seventeenth century. When she decided to publish a collection of conversations removed from the context of her novels, she made them more accessible to a broader audience, including readers who might not care for her lengthy heroic narratives. Her anthologies also responded to the new taste for shorter, fragmentable texts that could easily pass from written to spoken form, that could be freely borrowed and imitated in the verbal marketplace of court and salons. "How-to" texts that could teach ambitious readers the art of polite interaction were much in demand. Madame de Maintenon's use of Scudéry's volumes indicates to what extent they were considered plausible pedagocical tools. With her subsequent rejection of the books and of the verbal excess that they encouraged, she was attempting to promote a new image of proper interaction in society, stressing economy, restraint, and a systematic suspicion of other speakers.

But the dialectical format of Maintenon's model conversations also gives expression to her young pupil's protests against this ideology of self-restraint. Where, they repeatedly seem to be asking, is the pleasure in this kind of talk? It is one thing to observe the rules of good judgment in one's conduct, but should conversation really be so carefully ordered? "Je comprends qu'on pense et qu'on juge sur ce qu'on a à faire, mais la conversation serait bien pesante et bien ennuyeuse, si on étudiait tout ce qu'on dit" (*Extraits*, p.245). What can this new notion of conversation offer to replace the pleasures of "vivacité," "esprit," "divertissement?"[46] The answer to these questions is not really found in Maintenon's text, for her model speakers reply only obliquely, by evoking the specter of public disapproval that threatens overly talkative women. The questioner is advised simply to learn how not to speak, and to distinguish herself by being one of the few ladies in a conversation who "talks little, listens much, and never annoys" (*Extraits*, p.247).

Maintenon's conversation book resembles others published at the end of the century in that it argues against a system of sociability which has become nothing but a "politesse purement extérieure."[47] But her book remains on the level of a reaction against Scudéry's model; unlike other authors of model conversations, Maintenon refuses to promote the new pleasures of "natural" or sincere speech "founded on true sentiments." She advises avoiding at all costs the vulnerable position that sincerity requires, and warns against the pleasures of self-expression that can lead to a verbal euphoria as dangerous to her moral program as the collective solipsism of Scudéry's encounters. But these pleasures were to have a strong appeal to a generation of aristocrats who, like the Saint-Cyr pensioners, had to realize that their elite status as members of a privileged group was no longer secure. As a rhetorical principle, sincere expression was to become a new means of distinguishing oneself in conversation. In the next chapter we will look at how one commentator on social relations, a nobleman exiled from Louis XIV's court, experimented with these changing norms of conversational rhetoric in an effort to regain prestige and credibility.

NOTES

1. Tallemant des Réaux, *Historiettes* (Paris: Gallimard, 1960), II, p.689.

2. Cited in Georges Mongrédien, *Madeleine de Scudéry et son salon* (Paris: Tallandier, 1946), p.157.

3. The history of the reception of Scudéry's works after her death is summarized in Nicole Aronson, *Mademoiselle de Scudéry* (Boston: Twayne, 1978), p.151–55. In his introduction to the only modern edition of the conversations, Phillip J. Wolfe also gives a very useful historical survey of their publication and reader reception. See *Choix de Conversations de Mademoiselle de Scudéry* (Ravenna: Longo Editore, 1977), pp. 7–23.

4. *La Société française au XVIIe siècle d'après 'Le Grand Cyrus'* (Paris: Perrin, 1905), p.2

5. *Causeries du lundi* (Paris: Garnier Frères, 1927), IV, pp.128–37.

6. Maurice Magendie, *La Politesse mondaine et les théories de l'honnêteté* (Paris: F. Alcan, 1925), p. 635.

7. Mario Bonfantini, preface to Santa Celoria, ed., *Le Grand Cyrus, Clélie: épisodes choisis avec le resumé des deux romans* (Turin: Giappichelli, 1973), p.vii.

8. The five books of conversations are: *Conversations sur divers sujets* (Paris: Louis Billaine, 1680); *Conversations nouvelles sur divers sujets* (Paris: Claude Barbin, 1684); *La Morale du monde ou Conversations* (Paris: Pierre Mortier, 1686); *Nouvelles conversations de morale* (Paris: Veuve de Sebastien Mabre, 1686); and *Entretiens de morale* (Paris: Jean Anisson, 1693).

9. *Correspondence* (Paris: Gallimard, 1974–78), III, p.27.

10. Magendie, p. 635.

11. *Les Romans de Mademoiselle de Scudéry* (Genève: Droz, 1983), p.245.

12. Antoine Gombauld, chevalier de Méré, *Oeuvres complètes* (Paris: F. Roches, 1930), I, p.51.

13. Domna Stanton, *The Aristocrat as Art* (New York: Columbia University Press, 1980), p. 81.

14. See Carolyn Lougee, *Le Paradis des Femmes: Women, Salons and Social Stratification in Seventeenth-Century France* (Princeton, N.J.: Princeton University Press, 1976), pp. 3–7.

15. Somaize, in his portrait of Scudéry as "Sophie," declares that she drew into her circle the best intellects of the period:

Sophie l'emporte sur toutes celles de son sexe à l'égard de l'esprit, de la facilité d'écrire en vers et en prose, et de toutes les connaissances, qui rendent un esprit accompli, et n'en voit point ou peu parmi les hommes les plus habiles qui ne la regardent comme une digne rivale . . . pour les alcôvistes, on ne les peut conter que par le nombre de ceux qui la connaissent, sa douceur et son esprit attirant chez elle la plus grande et la plus illustre partie de ceux qui écrivent. *Dictionnaire des Prétieuses* (Paris: Jannet, 1856), I, pp.214–15.

16. *Conversations sur divers sujets*, I, pp. 2–3. Future references to this work will appear within the text as *C*, and the titles of Scudéry's other volumes of conversations will be similarly abbreviated.

17. "Sociability," in *On Individuality and Social Forms* (Chicago: University of Chicago Press, 1971), pp.138–39.

18. Goffman, "Fun in Games," in *Encounters* (New York: Bobbs-Merrill, 1961), p. 33.

19. "Alienation from Interaction," in *Interaction Ritual* (New York: Pantheon, 1967), p. 113–14

20. "La majorité des conversations, axées autour d'un sujet déterminé, se déroule selon un scénario immuable, qui est comme une espèce de cérémonial que se doivent d'observer les participants . . ." *Les Romans*, pp.277–78.

21. While almost all the conversational settings have very similar features, Scudéry never resorts to a formulaic phrase to simply invoke the obligatory backdrop. When she chooses to describe it at all she gives a detailed picture, and though the settings are always familiar they are never identical. Phillip Wolfe remarks that, compared to the conventional frames of classical dialogue, even as it was practiced by seventeenth-century *mondain* writers, Scudéry's settings are remarkably varied. See *Dialogue et Société*, unpublished dissertation, Princeton, 1974, p.134.

22. Until recently, critics have not studied the conversations as integral works, and have assumed that they all were excerpted from Scudéry's earlier novels. Phillip Wolfe first noted that historical details in some of the conversations would indicate that they were written later (*Choix de Conversations*, p.17). This is in fact true of most of the conversations in the two books published in 1688 and 1693. More detailed and systematic textual comparisons (computer-aided, I should think, considering the thousands of pages in her novels) would be required to determine exactly how much she borrowed from her earlier writings.

23. *Pensées* (Paris: Mercure de France, 1976), p.96.

24. "Alienation from Interaction," p.134.

25. *Pensées*, p.97.

26. Roger Caillois, *Man, Play, and Games* (New York: Schocken Books, 1979), p.18; and Erving Goffman, *Interaction Ritual*, p. 192.

27. Ralph Albanese shows how the "psycho-economic crisis" of the last thirty years of Louis XIV's reign is represented in the theater of the period, in "The Dynamics of Money in Post-Molièresque Comedy," *Stanford French Review* VII (Spring 1983), pp.73–89.

28. *Les Caractères* (Paris: Garnier, 1962), p.200.

29. Marcel Mauss, *Oeuvres* (Paris: Minuit, 1969), III, 29. Mauss was the first to argue that the potlatch structure was a cross-cultural phenomenon existing, in various modified forms, in many societies outside the North American Indian culture in which it was originally studied.

30. "Le chef donne un potlatch quand il construit une maison, érige un emblème, rassemble une confrérie, etc. La fête, c'est le potlatch" (*Oeuvres*, III, 32).

31. "De l'opposition entre rareté dans le royaume et surabondance à la cour naît le mythe de la surpuissance du roi: seul le prince peut se permettre de telles dépenses de préstige." *Le Roi-machine* (Paris: Minuit, 1981), p.102.

32. Apostolidès says that this is the *only* response open to Louis XIV's courtiers (p.107). Based on its ideological content, flattery can be seen simply as a display of passive submission, but I see it more as a way for the individual subject to assume an active role in the whole process of image-making. This is what Scudéry tries to make of flattery, using it to hold up her end of an interaction with the king.

33. *Le Portrait du roi* (Paris: Editions de Minuit, 1981), p. 115.

34. "De l'oisiveté et de l'ingratitude," *C*, II, pp.385–450.

35. Stanton, p.140.

36. Cited in Lougee, p. 198.

37. "Ne les accoutumez pas à une grande diversité de lectures; sept ou huit livres qui sont en usage dans votre maison suffiraient pour toute leur vie, si elles ne lisaient que pour s'édifier . . . la curiosité est dangereuse et insatiable." O. Gréard, *Madame de Maintenon: Extraits de ses lettres, avis, entretiens, conversations sur l'éducation* (Paris, 1884), p.19.

38. Scudéry had this function in mind when she prepared her 1688 and 1691 collections, and many of the conversations from these last two volumes had not been previously published in her novels, as we have seen. *Nouvelles conversations de morale* includes a "Description de Saint-Cyr."

39. Maintenon, *Conversations* (Paris, 1828), pp.425–27.

40. "Embarrassment and Social Organization," *Interaction Ritual*, pp. 97–112.

41. See Chapter 1 above, p. 38.

42. In his analysis of *La Prétieuse ou le mystère des ruelles*, André Pessel uses the term "économie du babil" to describe Pure's idea of *précieux* conversation. He sees in Pure's descriptions of salon interaction an insistence on the principle of reciprocity. The salon is "un lieu d'évaluation," where words take on meaning by being "played." "La plus grande incivilité serait de vouloir recevoir sans donner, d'être muet, . . . le plaisir de la conversation est un modèle de rencontre sans échange." See "De la conversation chez les précieuses," *Communications* 30 (1979), p.20.

43. "Effectivement on ne voit personne à sa place; chacun veut être aussi grand que l'autre: le gentilhomme égal au seigneur; le seigneur veut être prince; le prince veut être aussi grand prince que ceux qui sont au dessus de lui, et ainsi de suite" (*Extraits*, p.229).

44. ". . . la plus grand maison que l'on connaisse est celle de Bourbon, qui nous gouverne présentement" (*Extraits*, p. 234).

45. "Sur les discours populaires," (*Extraits*).

46. "Comment peut-on être divertissant et montrer son esprit quand on ne dit mot? Ce jugement ne s'oppose-t-il pas à la vivacité de l'esprit et ne rend-il pas le commerce trop sérieux?" (p.245–46).

47. Morvan de Bellegarde, *Réflexions sur la politesse des moeurs, avec des maximes pour la société civile* (Amsterdam: Henri Desbordes, 1699), p. 4.

« 3 »

History, Social Identity, and Talk: The Writings of Bussy-Rabutin

In contemporary portraits of Roger de Rabutin, Comte de Bussy, we read that he was at once the most haughty of aristocrats and the most obsequious of courtiers. After vaunting the qualities that made him superior, writes Saint-Simon, he would display "une hauteur qui fait souvenir de ses pauvres d'Espagne qui, en tendant la main vous disent superbement: 'Seigneur cavalier, faites-nous du bien.'"[1] Such incongruities of behavior were surely not uncommon at the Versailles court, but, in the long list of aristocratic exiles during the reign of Louis XIV, Bussy-Rabutin does stand out as having been particularly tenacious in his efforts to regain royal favor. The very qualities that turned the king against him—an excessive fondness for gossip and a penchant for provocative wit—may have also sustained him in his repeated attempts to obtain a pardon and return to Paris. His dogged efforts over nearly twenty years of exile to somehow remain connected with the social world of Paris and Versailles, could only have come from a person not easily discouraged by the ridicule of his peers or the indifference of his superiors.

Prior to his exile in 1666, Bussy-Rabutin's literary reputation was based on his familiarity with illustrious if not always reputable personages. A vociferous commentator on the definition of *honnêteté*, Bussy-Rabutin's single most important goal had always been to secure a place in the world of *honnêtes gens*. His strategy for personal promotion, which he outlines in the opening sentences of his memoirs, had always been based on the importance of sociability, conversation, and talk. "Aussitôt que j'entrai dans le monde, he writes "ma première et ma plus forte inclination fut de devenir honnête homme, et de parvenir aux grands honneurs de la guerre. Pour cet effet j'essayais autant qu'il me fût possible d'avoir commerce avec les honnêtes gens."[2] He became known in salon society for his witty contributions to conversation, and for his written pieces that grew out of social gatherings. All of his writings before *Histoire amoureuse des Gaules* are of this sort—maxims, elegant and effete translations from latin poets, a satirical imitation of Scudéry's "carte du tendre" which he calls "carte du pays de braquerie." People made salon games out of his writings; they were passed around, laughed over, gossiped about, thoroughly digested by society life, and then put aside. By the time he wrote the book that was to get him arrested, Bussy-Rabutin was already well recognized for both his writing and his conversational art, which were always interdependent. But the scandal that his *Histoire amoureuse des Gaules* created suddenly called into question the claim of any writing—and particularly the writing of a "médisant de qualité," as Sainte-Beuve calls Bussy,[3]—to a circulation as limited and protected as that of a conversation.

*   *   *

A collection of satirical anecdotes written to amuse a few friends at the expense of a few others, the manuscript of *Histoire amoureuse des Gaules* was eventually copied, without the author's permission, when he agreed to leave it with a friend for the exceptionally long period of two days. This was in 1665; by 1666 the book (or possibly an altered version of it) had been presented to the king. That year Bussy was imprisoned in the Bastille, and in 1667 he was exiled to his country estate. Although he had always been good at predicting the rise and fall of reputations, his own disgrace left him both indignant and uncomprehending. His correspondence and memoirs, written over the next twenty-five years, record his tireless efforts to regain the social position he had lost, and his attempts to avoid the worst fate of a courtly aristocrat: to be both excluded and forgotten.

It is clear that Bussy-Rabutin prided himself in his mastery of the game of sociability, and that he thought of himself as the consummate "honnête homme." The fact that he was both a libertine and a satirist did not belie this self-image; for him, his skill at ridiculing courtly display was proof that he was particularly adept at the very behavior he wanted to unmask. While his "carte du pays de Braquerie" was a mocking portrait of precious debates over love and gallantry, it was addressed to the same public as Scudéry's "carte du tendre," and like her map it was intended to amuse small private gatherings of people "in the know." *Histoire amoureuse des Gaules* was composed in the same spirit. Even though it is full of stories illustrating the degradation of conventional norms of courtly behavior—stories of betrayal, violated promises, and avarice—it is clearly addressed to an audience that subscribes to a conservative view of proper social relations, an audience of privileged insiders who deplore the invasion of the world of gallantry by the spirit of middle-class merchandising. His book was written as a kind of gossipy satire to amuse and gratify members of the elite who felt their status threatened by the successful social climbing of those of lower rank.

Bussy-Rabutin's outrage when he was thrown in the Bastille for having authored *Histoire amoureuse des Gaules* was motivated not only by a sense of personal betrayal, but by his conviction that this "imprudence" was simply a private matter, in no way justifying a public humiliation. His book, he argued, could not be expected to be properly understood by outsiders, and he had never intended that it circulate beyond a small circle of friends. To be arrested for having written slanderous stories about members of the court was for him an invasion of his privacy. It was unheard of, he writes, to consider such an act a crime: "Quand on fera réflexion sur cet événement," he writes, "on trouvera qu'il est inouï qu'on ait jamais arrêté un homme de qualité, qui a bien servi et longtemps à la guerre et qui est pourvu d'une grande charge, pour avoir écrit (par manière de divertissement et sans dessein que cela devînt public) les amours de deux dames que tout le monde savait, et sur la simple accusation, sans preuves, d'avoir écrit contre le

roi et contre la reine mère"(*M* II, 221–22). He had played by the traditional rules of aristocratic conduct to assure his family an honorable
place in history, only to find that the game had changed. At his inter-
rogation, the first questions put to him establish his privileged position
at court without reference to his military record, and then suggest that
his book was a gross betrayal of that privilege, almost as though he had
acted as a spy. ("S'il n'est pas vrai qu'étant d'ordinaire près du roi et à
la cour il s'est mêlé d'écrire et de composer plusieurs histoires en manière de romans de ce qui s'y passait, n'épargnant personne?" *M* II,
455). Bussy responds that he wrote the book on his own property, away
from the court ("à la campagne, à Bussy, en une de ses maisons"
(p.455), reiterating his contention that the whole affair was a personal
matter over which by all rights he should have had exclusive control.

Bussy's indignation over his arrest and exile might seem naïve,
given the fact that the exile and imprisonment of nobles was not an
unfamiliar spectacle for his generation. The days of the Fronde had
resulted in numerous reversals of fortune; Retz, Condé, Lauzun, Lon-
gueville, and La Rochefoucauld had all provided the world with the
drama of their falls from royal favor. But the crimes of most of these
exiles were political, while Bussy was sent to the Bastille for having
displeased the king with a collection of narratives written for the enter-
tainment of his friends. In all of his arguments outlining his defense,
Bussy insists on the fact that his book was a private piece of writing,
and therefore the result of "plus d'imprudence que de malice."[4] The
only fault he acknowledges was having left his manuscript in the hands
of another long enough for it to be copied and eventually distorted by
his enemies.

Yet while Bussy claimed in his own defense that his book was of no
concern to the state, in the eyes of the law such an argument was difficult to uphold. The legal distinctions between public and private
were undergoing radical revisions. Gossip, or *médisance*, which had
been a standard part of the verbal repertoire of the "bel esprit," was
becoming an increasingly dangerous business. In 1666, the year of Bussy's arrest, Colbert was busy establishing an elaborate system of state
control over writers that was to require every printed work to pass
before royal censors. What Bussy-Rabutin insisted was a "private" joke
became, in the eyes of the king, slander against the state. Malicious
gossip, even when it was not written, was suddenly a matter which

could be brought before a judge by the injured party. Speaking ill of others was an art that now had to be practiced with more delicacy than most people were used to exercising.[5]

Bussy-Rabutin could not know that Colbert's impressive machinery of censorship, which would remain in place until the end of the ancien régime, was being designed and set in motion the same year that he was confined in the Bastille. Censorship under this new system was broadly applied, and was to be enforced by a legal structure modeled on the public administration of ancient Rome. In 1665 Louis XIV announced his program to reform the judicial system, give more authority to royal judges, and reduce seigneurial rights. After Colbert convened the first *Conseil de Police* in 1666, an official network of spies was charged with a new *surveillance des moeurs*. Members of the nobility were included and in fact specially targeted in this new program of moral reform. An important component of the surveillance of public morality was a census, begun in 1666, of all noble families, who were required to prove the legitimacy of their titles. The new office of *lieutenant général de police*, created in 1667 and given to Nicolas La Reynie, marked the beginning of institutionalized control over areas of public life that had never before been subject to state regulation.[6]

Of the five decades of Louis XIV's personal reign, the 1660's saw the most intensive state effort to impress upon French society and the governments of all the European powers the image of Louis XIV *Imperator*, heir to the glory of the Roman empire. Every major state institution introduced at this time was ceremoniously presented as part of a massive rebirth of the Roman state, made possible by the appearance of a new French Caesar. Crucial to this new image of the state was the court society surrounding the king. Life in the presence of "Louis-Auguste" was supposed to present a spectacle of moral as well as aesthetic grandeur. Writers and artists were expected to assist in strengthening the links between myth and history that were necessary to generate political power from the symbol of the "sun king." Comparisons of Louis XIV with Augustus Caesar were extended to whole sequences of events in the chronologies of the two lives, as though the modern ruler was a reincarnation of the greatest of Roman emperors. In 1663 a book by Puget de la Serre detailed the comparison: *L'Histoire d'Auguste et le parallèle de cet illustre monarque avec notre grand roi Louis XIV.*[7]

Unfortunately for Bussy-Rabutin, his ironic "history" not only presented a vision of a French society whose past grandeur was fading, but his model from classical times was *The Satiricon*, a chronicle of decadent Roman society under the most infamous of the Roman emperors. Petronius wrote about Rome in the time of Nero, and his gossipy anecdotes were much admired by Bussy-Rabutin and many of his friends in libertine circles. He quite consciously modeled his own work after Petronius, and even included in *Histoire amoureuse des Gaules* a lengthy passage translated directly from *The Satiricon*.[8]

The book's title calls further attention to its subversive function, to its being a chronicle of erotic conquests instead of a conventional history of military expansion. This type of "histoire" purports to uncover what is *not* documented by official history; its whole purpose is to bring private affairs into a more public domain, however small. Bussy's readers eagerly read the book as a barely disguised secret history, whose purpose was to reveal scandalous, hidden truths about real people. Ultimately, this was how Louis XIV was to read the manuscript. The exploits of Bussy's aristocratic characters are decidedly not conducted according to the chivalric codes of a warrior nobility. Instead, the lovers in his book use the strategies of middle-class merchants bargaining over a contract. In a sense, Bussy was imprisoned for writing an anti-heroic historical portrait of Louis XIV's court at precisely the moment when the state was undertaking the task of casting all aspects of courtly life in a heroic mold.

In choosing as his classical model a writer who satirized the pretentions to grandeur of the Roman aristocracy, Bussy was obviously not going to ingratiate himself with the royal censors. And by insisting that his text was simply a private joke, he only made his position more difficult, for to him, the most important issue at stake in his arrest was his claim to control over the circulation of his writing. He saw his book as an extension of his own conversational presence, and argued that it should have been allowed to circulate freely in a confined world of his own choosing.

All of the modern commentaries on the book recognize, without agreeing on what genre it belongs to, that it is a satire of the idealized portraiture that would have been familiar to readers of novels at the time. In the preface to his edition, Adam states that it is a "roman satirique" adhering to the already well-defined norms of that genre modeled after Petronius (pp. 16–17). César Rouben considers the work to be a more innovative blending of fiction and document, a satire of the heroic novel's glorification of aristocratic sentiment presented as a real document of current court intrigues. Marie-Thérèse Hipp reads it as an *histoire* more than a *roman*, and likens it to other accounts that purport to reveal the scandalous reality behind the heroic representations of noble living. René Démoris calls the book a collection of "mémoires au présent" that tested the limits placed by elite society on accounts of their own degradation.[9]

But this text originally functioned as part of a social interaction; Bussy's own hedging about what genre it belongs to must be considered in conjunction with his protests that it was simply a private joke, for it was written as a kind of gossipy conversation that the author is having with readers "in the know." *Histoire amoureuse des Gaules* illustrates one way in which the functions of literature and conversation can be interconnected.

Patricia Spacks has written about the different uses of gossip in literature and in real interactions. Gossip can function as a kind of "social currency," a resource for acquiring status and social success. It can also be used as "power," a more important function perhaps, but one which is much more difficult for the individual to control.[10] Significantly gossip also moves quickly from one function to another when it is circulated beyond its original, restricted audience, as in some forms of journalistic gossip. When Bussy-Rabutin protested against calling his text slanderous, he was trying to keep it in the realm of gossip as social currency. But it was getting difficult to claim such control over *médisance*, even when it occurred in private conversations. And written forms of gossip, as Louis XIV and his ministers well understood, had great potential to function as power, and were both more dangerous and more easily manipulated by others than their spoken equivalent.

In the first years of his imprisonment and exile, however, Bussy seems to have been unable to believe that he would not soon be pardoned for the "bagatelles" that had caused his disgrace (*M* II,262). He was forced to sell his military *charge* while he was imprisoned, but was subsequently released and allowed to reside on his family property in Burgundy, a form of exclusion which he chose to view as a sign that he would not long be in disfavor. Arriving at his château, he concerned himself with preparing to lead the life of a country gentleman, to savor a kind of freedom in his exile: "Je commençai alors à sentir véritablement la douceur de ma liberté, et je fis venir sept ou huit sortes d'artisans pour l'embellissement de ma maison. C'étaient les seuls plaisirs que je pusse avoir à la campagne: car il n'y a rien que je n'aimasse mieux faire que d'aller à la chasse." (*M* II,296).

The banished aristocrat was familiar to seventeenth-century readers as both a literary and historical figure. Exile to one's country estate evoked the *topos* of the rejected courtier or lover who finds wisdom and peace in a pastoral retreat from the world. The memoir, blending history and private fantasy, is the genre traditionally expressing this point of view. Prominent exiles such as Retz and Girardot de Nozeroy published memoirs during their lifetimes, basing their use of the convention on classical models as well as on the modern inflection of the theme provided by Montaigne.[11] In his memoirs and letters, Bussy-Rabutin sometimes echoes these voices of resigned *exilés*, who have gained spiritual and moral strength from observing the "world" at a distance: "Je fais des réflexions sur la folie des hommes de se tant tourmenter pour des établissements qui durent si peu." (II,49). But more often, he proposes an image of himself as a shrewd interpreter of the most minute details of courtly life, whose *in absentia* status merely means that he must be consulted in writing rather than in person.

Memoirs as Conversation

The typical seventeenth-century *mémorialiste* professes to find in exile an existence ideally suited to that retrospective reflection needed to produce a text. Bussy-Rabutin's autobiographical writing project, begun in prison, voices some of the classic motives of the *mémorialiste*, the most important being to record his role in history and protect his family name. He is undertaking this project, he says, because of a misfortune, which he fears will cause his life to be misrepresented to posterity: ". . . les malheurs qui me sont arrivés ayant rendu ma vie plus considérable, j'ai fait dessein de l'écrire; et l'oisiveté de ma prison m'a donné lieu de l'entreprendre." (*M* I,3). But in 1666, writing from the Bastille and hoping for an early reprieve, he does not wish to assume a resigned pose; on the contrary, he is writing his memoirs in an effort to document his case. In fact, most of the material making up this story of his life is written by others, inserted in Bussy's narratives to substantiate his own version of events. His project is a kind of legal dossier, and suggests the judicial sense of *mémoire* that was often present in seventeenth-century usage.[12]

At the same time, in his initial explanation of why he is compiling these memoirs, we can see that he views himself as an historian because of the fact that his documented life will contribute to a larger ensemble of material that will ultimately constitute the history of his time. Like so many other seventeenth-century aristocrats, Bussy viewed himself as an actor in the making of history, and consequently it was incumbent on him to document his own life.[13] Indeed, it is clear that long before his imprisonment he had begun collecting evidence for his own personal archives. "Lorsque mon père me mena à l'armée," he tells us, "j'écrivis mes campagnes pour me faire mieux retenir les choses qui s'y passaient. J'ai continué jusqu'à présent d'en user ainsi; et sans autre vue que de m'amuser, j'ai même écrit mes moindres occupations" (*M* I,3). He is meticulously aware of any descriptions of himself that have circulated in other memoirs. When an account conflicts with his own version, he takes care to point out to his readers that his is the truthful one, as in a description of a battle: "C'est dans ce passage dont le duc de La Rochefoucauld parle dans ses mémoires avec peu de sincérité . . . Et voulant faire voir la hardiesse de ce passage, il semble qu'il veuille en quelque façon blâmer ma vigilance" (*M* I, 263).

Bussy repeatedly calls attention to the ways in which his memoirs differ from others, in both the accuracy and tone with which he presents facts. We will be struck, he tells us at the outset, by the sincerity of his accounts: "On s'étonnera peut-être de ma sincerité, et en effet, il ne se voit point de mémoires où l'on parle de soi comme l'on parle d'autrui: les plus honnêtes gens qui en ont fait ont tû leurs mauvaises actions . . ." (*M* I, 16). But in evoking this principle of honesty and even confession (". . . je la pourrais appeler ma confession générale, si je ne disais quelquefois du bien de moi comme du mal . . ." (*M* I, 4), Bussy stops well short of assuming another classic pose of the *mémorialiste*, that of a banished courtier engaged in a "méditation sur la vanité des choses, la fuite du temps et la mort."[14] His vaunted honesty has a decidedly worldly objective, as he openly states: ". . . j'ai un amour naturel pour la vérité . . . cela doit obliger les gens de qui je dis la vérité de se faire justice" (*M* I, 16–17).

Bussy's primary motive for compiling his memoirs is to rehabilitate his own public image and counter the attacks of his detractors. For him, though, this cannot be a solitary process. As a veteran participant in the making and breaking of reputations, Bussy understood that his own depended on the talk of others. La Rochefoucauld's maxim suggests the predicament of banishment: "On n'oublie jamais mieux les choses que quand on s'est lassé d'en parler."[15] If the exile's transgression may be forgotten when people tire of talking of *it*, so might he forever lose his place in *le beau monde* when people tire of talking of *him*. Others fallen from grace tended to retreat behind a mask of resignation and philosophical speculation, but Bussy responded to his fate by tirelessly trying to reconnect with the world he had lost. All of his writing seems to have been produced with an eye to the effect it would have on the small, elite society whose attention he was trying to recapture. Even when he is ostensibly addressing a single person, he cannot prevent himself from remarking on how his letter might appear to others.

Once removed from the Paris scene, Bussy was to have little control over either his sources or his audience. In all of his works we are aware that he wants to play the role of a sharp conversationalist and a good gossip. It was even more important to keep people conversing *with* him, and this was no small task, particularly since the qualities for which he was most admired—his witty and malicious conversation and his ability to unmask the daily show of courtly interaction—would seem to require his physical presence. His memoirs had to be an interactive performance, even when the spectators were no longer visible.

The system that Bussy finally hits upon is a blend of memoirs and letters, with an increasing number of texts by other writers added to his own accounts until the narrative is conducted more through letters addressed *to* him and to others *about* him, than through his own voice. He restages his past rather than narrating it; his life story is constituted by a collection of social interactions—epistolary exchanges, letters from Mazarin and Louis XIII testifying to his loyalty during the Fronde, maxims and other written records of his contributions to verbal "jeux de société."

The section of this memoir-dossier covering Bussy-Rabutin's life up until his imprisonment was first published by his family in 1696, three years after his death, and titled his "memoirs." Bussy himself had also included, under the rubric "memoirs," a vast letter correspondence begun after his release from prison. It was his editor, and not Bussy, who imposed a conventional closure on the memoirs by publishing only the narrative of his life preceding his disgrace. The rest, we are told in the editor's *avertissement*, is not history, and thus not worth including: "on a jugé à propos d'en retrancher tout ce que M. le Comte de Bussy a écrit depuis son exil jusqu'à sa mort, parce qu'ayant passé presque tout ce temps-là chez lui à la campagne, on n'a rien trouvé parmi ses papiers qu'on ait crû devoir joindre à des évènements historiques" (*M* I, 2). Subsequent publications of the memoirs have followed the lead of the early editors, and have treated the nearly three thousand letters and connecting commentary (written between Bussy's exile in 1666 and his death in 1693) as a separate text. The most recent editor, Ludovic La-lanne, published *Mémoires* and *Correspondance* between 1857 and 1859. He explains his decision to separate the two parts of Bussy's autobio-graphical text in a footnote to his edition of the *Mémoires*, noting that the messages exchanged after 1666 had a different purpose, and cannot properly be called memoirs: "Les *Mémoires* proprement dits s'arrêtent en effet au moment de la disgrâce de Bussy. La suite, bien que portant aussi sur les manuscrits le titre de *Mémoires*, contient presque unique-ment la correspondance . . . que Bussy depuis son exil entretint avec sa famille et ses amis" (*M* I, 2).

For Bussy, though, the writing project begun in prison simply took another turn when he found himself in exile. The "histoire de moi . . . véritable et particularisée" (*M* I,4), becomes, once he is exiled, a means of retaining his place in the world. The author eventually comes to see the manuscript as naturally split from the moment of his exile into two sections, one in which his voice dominates, and another in which he is only one voice among many. In a letter to Brulart written in 1691 he describes the manuscript of his letter collection as follows: "Il est tout différent du premier. C'est une histoire écrite en lettres; et je crois qu'elle fera un jour plus d'honneur à Sa Majesté que l'autre: car dans la première c'est moi qui parle, et c'est tout le monde dans celle-ci" (V, 233). Unlike his subsequent editors, Bussy saw his memoirs and cor-respondence as an ongoing project, unified by his purpose in making it a *history*, not only his private story but a history of the reign. In the second part of this work, he proposes to use the voices of his corre-spondents to authenticate his self-appointed role as historian. His his-tory will be a record of conversations within a select group of people who are qualified to comment on the major events of their time because they have participated in them.

The possibility of maintaining regular communication with his circle in Paris suggests the novelty of continuing the project of documenting his life, even while eliding his own voice except as it participates in exchanges with others. The originality of his new project lies in the multiplicity of voices it engages to construct an epistolary collection that is both a personal "histoire" and a public history to "honor" the king. For Bussy, exile need not mean exclusion from future history. Finding that it will be possible to maintain a regular schedule of letter exchanges between Paris and Burgundy, he immediately enlists his absent friends in a project that will allow him to retain a verbal presence among them. The collectively produced text that results will ultimately serve, as he clearly plans from the beginning, to guarantee that his place in history is not forgotten.

Refashioning a World

As he begins his correspondence, Bussy's stated objective is to recreate the social circle from which he has been exiled. "Un homme de bon sens se fait un Paris partout," he writes in 1669, several months after he is first forced to retire to his provincial estate (I, 189). With each new epistolary contact he asks his correspondent for a portrait, "car je vous veux avoir dans mon cabinet aussi bien que dans mon coeur" (I,252). The growing number of letters, with the accompanying portraits of each correspondent, are seen as substitutes for their writers; by surrounding himself with these texts and images, Bussy symbolically maintains his place within his social circle. This circle in fact becomes even more exclusive, and his own inclusion in it more privileged, as he distinguishes the larger category of "fortunés" from the smaller, more elite group of "honnêtes gens": "Je vous assure," he writes the chevalier de Rivière, "que (vos marques d'amitié) me réjouissent plus que celles de milles personnes dont la fortune est plus brillante que la vôtre, parce que j'ai toujours préféré l'amitié des honnêtes gens à celle des gens seulement heureux" (I,306).

Over the years Bussy was to organize a clever display of portraits in four different rooms of his château, which he had redecorated and redesigned to house the collection to his satisfaction. Each represented a different aspect of the society from which he had been exiled. For the walls of the *Salle des Devises*, he commissioned paintings of the most famous châteaux of France, and hung his own portrait over the fireplace. In the *Tour Dorée*, he placed his portraits of the ladies of the court, accompanied by witty and often malicious inscriptions. In this room he also placed a portrait of himself, but as a youth of 20, while the portrait in the *Salle des Devises* was a more dignified representation of himself as an older man. In the *Salle des Belles Femmes*, he exhibited a collection that he called "les reines de la France," which in fact was a selection of portraits of the most illustrious mistresses of the Valois and Bourbon kings—Agnès Sorel, Diane de Poitiers, Madame de Montespan—and in this room he also placed a triptych featuring his wife, his cousin Madame de Sévigné, and her daughter Madame de Grignan. Finally, in the *Salon des 65 Capitaines*, Bussy placed an array of portraits of the great military leaders of France, including, of course, himself.[16]

In letters to his correspondents Bussy describes these portrait galleries as they are being built, claiming that he is creating a playful revision of social history: "Je suis bien aise que notre ami Hauterive ait trouvé ma maison de Bussy à son gré. Il y a des choses fort amusantes qu'on ne trouve point ailleurs . . . Tout cela compose quatre pièces fort ornées, et qui font un abregé d'histoire ancienne et moderne, qui est tout ce que je voudrais que mes enfants sussent sur cette matière" (II, 16). His architectural and decorative renovations gradually transformed the château into a space that symbolically rearranged the familiar social world he had left, and reestablished his own central position in it. The result was such an obvious reflection of his own view of the world that one of his guests remarked that the château had assumed the personality of its owner: "Vous ne vous contentez pas, monsieur, d'avoir de l'esprit plus qu'un autre, vous voulez même que votre maison en ait . . ." (III, 345).

As we can see in the responses Bussy solicits from his correspondents, the renovations at Bussy-le-Grand did not have their full effect until they were seen and admired by others. Bussy gives his friends only enough information about what he is doing to tantalize them, urging them to come and see for themselves. The strategy works, and by the end of his life Bussy had not only succeeded in making sure he was not forgotten by the society he had left long before, he had also been able to continuously draw members of the "cercle heureux" to his place of exile.[17]

"I love to build," Bussy writes when asked for a description of his life in exile. The project of rebuilding his château was but one part of the design for continuing his social existence,[18] with his letter correspondence being the most consuming of these projects. Taken as a whole, his collection of letters is constructed as one element in an exchange between Bussy and some future reader; in return for this mass of descriptive commentary and documentary evidence, his public will be asked to grant him a recognition that had been denied him during his lifetime. The precise terms of this trade, however, shift within the letter correspondence as Bussy focuses on different addressees. Taken in their chronological order, his letters change from an early set toward the primary readers, his correspondents, to a focus on a more vague, implied reader, "la postérité," in the later letters. Transcending this double image of the reader, or rather occupying the position of an omnipotent observer whose power exceeds that of the other two groups of readers, is the king, whose reply Bussy constantly solicits but never receives.

Beginning with the first letters written after his exile, Bussy lays the groundwork for his letter collection with a number of reciprocal pacts. In these early messages Bussy's main concern is to reestablish lost contact with Paris society. To do this he must give his own letters an appeal that will engage his readers' interest. He proposes to his correspondents that they provide him the raw material for his replies; in exchange for news, he will provide commentary. To Madame de Montmorency he says: "Mandez-moi des nouvelles, Madame, et moi qui ai du loisir de reste j'en ferai les commentaires" (I,93). In her reply she writes: "J'accepte le parti que vous m'offrez de vous mander des nouvelles et de recevoir de vous des raisonnements. Je me trouve bien heureuse que vous m'ayez choisie pour faire un tel parti" (I,94–95).

His readers in turn circulate the letters he sends them, helping to increase the number of his correspondents. For this growing audience Bussy is careful to express gratitude, comparing himself favorably in this respect to other exiles: "Je ne suis pas comme l'Abbé Fouquet, qui malgré toutes les honnêtetés qu'on lui peut faire, veut toujours être offensé" (I,19).

Gradually his correspondents begin to solicit his comments and praise his astute predictions concerning political events and personal reversals of fortune. They assure him that his absence from the court, rather than impairing his understanding of daily events there, has improved it. Distance has given him increased lucidity and calm, as Madame de Scudéry writes in 1677: "Par la lumière de votre esprit vous savez mieux les nouvelles du monde que nous ne les savons sur ce que nous disent les gens qui voient les choses de plus près" (III,365–66).

During the first years of exile, as Bussy gradually expands his epistolary contacts along with his collection of portraits, we can see in his letters a stronger attention to maintaining a perfect balance of exchange than we see in later letters. Most of these messages include specific references to and reminders of time passed since the last contact, as well as complaints and recriminations over the negligence of certain friends. The early letters repeatedly urge their addressees to respond promptly to each message, and point by point, Bussy requests, so as to maintain "une plus grande netteté" (I,437). It is essential for the readers of these early letters to become active participants in the ongoing production of messages, and to communicate as partners equal to Bussy's epistolary *oeuvre*. In a letter to Madame de Scudéry written in 1671, Bussy remarks that he likes writing to her because she adequately *appreciates* his effort: "Voulez-vous savoir ce qui me fait écrire des lettres qui vous plaisent? C'est que je sais que vous en connaissez le prix, et je vous avoue que cela m'anime" (I,417).

His correspondents, for their part, contribute to Bussy's vision of an exclusive society recreated through letters by eliciting services from him which they claim cannot be found elsewhere. Madame Bossuet forwards to Bussy love letters addressed to her, and he composes responses to them for her to copy (II,46). Other correspondents send regular reports of political events with requests for Bussy's commentary, claiming that his "reading" of the news is worth more than any other. Thus Bussy can assure that his voice will be reintroduced into the social circles from which he has been exiled, and that his self-styled role of court commentator will be maintained by his correspondents, who will read his letters aloud or appropriate them into their own written messages to others.[19]

The process of reconstructing the ambiance of elite society through the transposition of conversation into letters and of physical presences into a gallery of portraits nevertheless was bound to sharpen Bussy's awareness of the vast difference between speech and writing. In shifting from conversation to letters, Bussy had already abandoned the possibility of participating in a truly reciprocal system of interaction, that is, in the kind of spontaneous, creative balancing act for which the perfect courtier strives in his conversation. As we have seen, discussions of the distinction between conversation and letter writing in conduct literature suggest that an equivalence of the two modes is possible, but Bussy lays out his messages in such an orderly fashion that it seems he is much more inclined to view letters as a kind of palpable currency, each one having a specific worth in the economy of his correspondence. It is the precise exchange value of the messages he sends and receives, and of the correspondence as a whole, that changes for him over time.

During the early period of his exile Bussy carefully metes out words to his readers with the care of someone who is determined to maintain the high value of his investments. His commentary on court events is provided to readers only after a clear trade has been agreed upon. Some of Madame de Scudéry's letters to him barter for a reading of his memoirs and promise to provide him with a new contact in return: "Au nom de Dieu, monsieur, montrez-moi cet ouvrage; fiez-vous en à ma parole, on n'en fera précisément que ce que vous voudrez. En récompense, je vous promets d'obliger notre ami à vous montrer ce qu'il écrit de la cour, qui assurément vous plaira beaucoup: car, comme vous savez, il écrit bien" (I,326).

In establishing his epistolary contacts and arranging an ongoing structure of communication, Bussy seems to be using as his model the old role he used to play while he was still present in Paris society. From his provincial estate he strives to maintain his function as the acerbic reader of sentiment and politics, and in return for this continuous metacommentary his correspondents provide him with regular reports, much as they did before his exile. The subject matter of most of these exchanges written during the first few years of exile is limited to news and speculation about the immediate future, almost as though by focusing on the present he can more thoroughly dwell in it, and thus retain his insider's place in society.

As it becomes increasingly obvious that his term of exile may be long, and as his letter collection grows, Bussy begins to view his writing in a different light. The accumulation of messages exchanged with friends at the court takes shape as an *oeuvre*, an integrated text to be read as a whole. The primary function of the correspondence no longer seems to be only to maintain contact and retain a place in conversational circles; it now operates as an ongoing project of the author. Bussy begins to view his letters as a collection of thoughts on the history from which he is being excluded. Writing to one correspondent who has praised his epistolary skills, he says, "Puisque vous aimez ce qui vient de moi, je vous ferai voir les réflexions que j'ai faites pendant sept ans d'exil sur toutes les nouvelles que l'on m'a mandées" (II,297). The collection of letters now begins to take on a different shape in the eyes of its author and of his correspondents. Bussy now regards his work as a master work with which he can try to regain favor with the king.

From this new perspective the correspondence continues to operate according to rules of exchange, only now the terms are different; having recruited a number of correspondents to recreate a continuous dialogue, Bussy now applies all of these voices to a proposed trade with the king. He presents these epistolary voices as a monument to the age of civility during which Louis XIV reigns. In return, of course, he seeks an end to his exile.

This shift in perspective involves Bussy's more explicit recognition of his own position as an outsider. No longer primarily concerned with resituating himself inside the circle of sociability, Bussy now not only recognizes his distanced position from society, but also tries to make of this distance a privileged viewpoint. At a distance from events, he is able to judge them more coolly; not being embroiled in daily court politics he is better able to analyze their intricacies. His correspondents echo this new image of a wise, exiled courtier. Rapin writes in 1677: " . . . faites-nous la grâce de nous écrire quelquefois et de nous mander vos pensées sur tout ce qui se passe, de ces réflexions qui valent mieux que tout ce que nous entendons ici . . ." (III,430).

Once he has decided to emphasize rather than gloss over his own exclusion, however, Bussy is confronted with other communication problems. For as long as he was using his correspondence primarily as a vehicle for retaining his insider's status, as long as he was essentially interested simply in "keeping in touch," his own motives were not subject to question. To be sociable is simply to sustain the chain of communication, to keep discourse going, and if everyone is pretending to be equal the question of truth and sincerity is not an issue. What is at stake is simply the establishment of an equal system of give and take, to which Bussy carefully attends in his instructions to correspondents, asking them to respond point by point and to each of his letters.

But having decided to apply his collection of letters to a bargain with the king, to present Louis XIV with these letters as testimony of his own loyalty, Bussy must now find other means to establish his credibility. He had already foreseen this problem in a letter to Rapin written in 1674: "C'est une suite des malheurs de ceux qui sont dans la mauvaise fortune de ne pouvoir guère donner de témoignages d'amitié qui ne soient suspects" (II,337).

As an exile offering his letter correspondence as a gift to the king, and hoping for a pardon in return, Bussy's sincerity is suspect. The whole question of his sincerity is aggravated by his personal misfortune and by the resulting insertion of self-interest into his communication with others. Fearing that his memoirs had appeared too self-serving, Bussy presents his letter correspondence to the king as a more objective testimony to his usefulness. His interlocutors all echo his own conviction that he will be pardoned. Unable to disguise the obvious role of self-interest in all of this, Bussy decides instead to proclaim it and thus claim for himself a unique ingenuousness—his text is open, he says, he can hide nothing from the king. Writing to congratulate a friend on his return to favor Bussy remarks on the luck that this augurs for him: "J'ai appris avec grande joie votre retour auprès d'un maître aussi aimable que le nôtre, et que vous aimez autant que vous faites. Je vous avouerai aussi, avec ma sincérité ordinaire, qu'il y entre un peu de mon intérêt, et que j'espère que vous pourrez quelquefois faire souvenir sa Majesté de moi" (II,222).

These letters addressed to specific correspondents, while clearly appealing to the king as the ideal reader, demand only to be read; a favor has been granted when the king simply agrees to look at them. That the king deigns to receive his letters, Bussy writes in 1680, is a *grâce* not usually accorded courtiers out of favor" (V,72).[20]

Gradually, however, as it becomes increasingly apparent that his exile is not likely to be ended, Bussy shifts his rhetorical stance once again. This change in tone occurs after an episode in 1682 when he is granted an audience with the king only to have his banishment renewed. The king, far from being pleased with the manuscripts of Bussy's *Mémoires* and *Correspondance*, found in them instead further evidence of the *médisance* that had gotten their author into trouble in the first place (V,397). From this point on it is clear that Bussy has shifted his idea of a reader for his work to a broader, more impersonal public, "la postérité," and it is to this reader that he will now appeal for justice.

Bussy's disappointment, after seventeen years of strategic manoeuvering to put an end to his exile, was bitter, and all the more so because he had apparently so misjudged his reader's response to his work. In response to earlier warnings from friends that to show the *Mémoires* and *Correspondance* to Louis XIV might be damaging, Bussy had scoffed that the king would appreciate his honesty and truthfulness: "c'est le devoir de l'historien et du faiseur de mémoires de dire la vérité des gens dont ils parlent . . ." The king, he claimed, had read his writings "comme un ami particulier" (V,231–32).

Neither the long string of formal petitions to the king, which had been circulated openly and admired by all but their primary addressee as models of courtly writing, nor the "real" correspondence which Bussy packaged and offered Louis XIV as a chronicle of his reign, had won him the slightest reprieve. On the contrary, it appeared that his vaunted directness and honesty had only sealed his fate more securely. Bussy reacts with anger to this predicament, and in the last years of his life his mask of civility has worn thin. In a letter to François de La Chaise in 1686, he explicitly itemizes what is owed to him, and concludes: "Je ne vous ai point encore parlé si nettement que je fais aujourd'hui, mon R.P., parce que je sais avec quelle délicatesse il faut parler de ses droits quand on en a fait parler à son maître, et que de peur de lui déplaire il faut appeler grâce tout ce qu'on lui demande, quoique souvent ce soit une pure justice. Mais enfin l'extrémité où je suis me force d'appeler les choses par leur noms . . ." (VI,5).

For *grâce* he will now turn only to God. The devotional rhetoric of the courtier is gone; Bussy will no longer use it to refer to worldly power. In 1694, upon learning that the king had said of him that he had done nothing his whole life but "tear people to pieces," Bussy had made an unusually lengthy entry in his letter manuscript, explaining to his future readers how he reacted to this news: "Je ne doutai pas à cette conversation qu'on ne m'eût rendu de nouveau de mauvais offices auprès du roi, que je vis bien qui en était aussi susceptible qu'autrefois, et je me retournai à Dieu, que je connus bien qui ne voulait pas encore me donner du repos" (V, 397). The only worldly recognition for which he now hopes will come from posterity. This is his new ideal reader, who will recognize the universal, human qualities of his predicament and grant him his due. Such a reward will only be given in recompense for a truthful account of his life and of the wrongs done to him. Thus the standards of truth and sincerity assume monumental proportions; if he cannot convince posterity of this he will have gained nothing.

Bussy's more fortunate correspondents are not all so eager to participate in this project which is not likely to benefit them. "J'ai peur," writes Madame de Montmorency in 1687, "que vous ne gardiez mes lettres, et je ne me soucie point de réjouir la postérité" (VI,22). Bussy responds wryly:

> Voici donc un renouvellement de commerce Madame, véritablement conditionnel, je le veux bien. Vous ne me ferez réponse que quand vous serez en bonne humeur et vous prendrez bien garde que les nouvelles que vous me manderez ne fâchent personne, de peur que la postérité ne sache que vous disiez à vos amis ce que tout le monde disait. Pour les louanges du roi et les nouvelles avantageuses aux particuliers, vous ne me les tairez pas   (VI,25).

Bussy's own praise of the king had not stopped when he abandoned hope of a return to favor, but the rhetoric of flattery in his letters to Louis XIV had changed over the years. Although these messages were never answered, Bussy continued to send them regularly, at least once a year, until his death. Read and admired by his contemporaries as models of supplicatory prose, the letters to the king were widely circulated during his lifetime, and are excellent examples of highly self-conscious rhetorical display, combining both artistic and pragmatic purposes. These letters regularly propose new roles that Bussy hopes will permit him to be readmitted to court society. Since they are written at longer intervals than his other letters, and, more importantly, since they are not part of a correspondence, but are discrete, unreciprocated messages, these letters are also the most self-contained of Bussy's collection.[21] The variety of tones and attitudes that Bussy tries out in these texts offers interesting evidence of how the seventeenth-century rhetoric of courtesy and supplication could be manipulated as a means of coping with the personal experience of social and political change.

Letters to Louis XIV

In his earliest letters to the king Bussy tries to play the role of the resigned *infortuné*, accepting that he somehow has displeased his sovereign, but mustering the courage to ask that he be allowed to prove his loyalty by serving in a military campaign:

> . . . je m'adresse directement à Votre Majesté, Sire, pour la supplier avec toutes les soumissions imaginables de me permettre d'aller chercher la mort pour son service. J'ai été jusqu'ici trop malheureux pour oser désormais rien attendre de la fortune, et je ne suis pas assez visionnaire pour en rien espérer, je ne me relâcherai jamais du zèle ardent que j'ai toujours eu pour la personne et pour le service de Votre Majesté . . .   (I,446).

In these first letters he meticulously avoids any explicit reference to the conditions of his punishment, or to the nature of his transgression. It is enough that he has offended the king; accordingly, he assumes the tone of a penitent, faithful soldier. Any references to his status have to do with his military profession, a traditional aristocratic privilege and an obligation which he hopes to be granted again, and expects his sons will be allowed to enjoy after him. The time he has spent in prison or in exile is reckoned in vague terms, while his devotional humility is permanent and all consuming: "Je ne songe depuis le matin jusqu'au soir qu'à lui bien faire connaître que je suis avec toute la fidelité et la passion du monde . . ." (I,448). It is not until the fourth year of his disgrace that he begins to include in his letters precise mention of the material and temporal conditions of exile, while still not challenging its justice: "J'ai été treize mois en prison, pendant lesquels j'ai été destitué de ma charge; il y a quatre ans que je suis exilé, et tout cela le plus justement du monde; cependant, Sire, je supplie très-humblement Votre Majesté de trouver bon que je la fasse souvenir de moi et qu'en même temps je lui dise que je l'ai servie vingt-sept ans avec assez d'éclat pour mériter quelques grâces . . ." (I,450).

When in 1671 he first refers more explicitly to his past transgressions, he does so with a flourish, but carefully offers an interpretation of events to place the blame for his punishment on his enemies:

> . . . je n'ai pas de peine d'avouer franchement les fautes que j'ai faites. Je dirai bien plus à Votre Majesté, Sire: la créance, que j 'ai

eue qu'un homme de qualité, qui avait de longs services à la guerre et qui aimait de tout son coeur Votre Majesté, ne pouvait manquer de réussir avec de si bons principes, m'a fait relâcher sur le reste de ma conduite et négliger de faire des amis; j'ai cru que Votre Majesté étant pour moi, je n'aurais pas à craindre de ceux qui seraient contre, et j'aurais eu raison de le croire, si j'avais été aussi heureux à vous faire connaître mes bons endroits que mes ennemis l'ont été à vous faire voir les mauvais   (II,434).

As the letters continue to paint more details of his own interpretation of his case, they also begin to describe more concretely what favors he is requesting, and what services he is offering in return. In January 1677 Bussy first alludes to his project of writing a chronicle of Louis XIV's reign, and suggests that he is better qualified to compose it than other authors:

Regardez donc mes services, Sire, avec quelque bonté. Sire, dans le temps que vous punissez mes fautes, et en attendant que Votre Majesté me les pardonne tout à fait, je continuerai de parler de vous à la posterité d'une manière qui m'obligera de m'écouter un jour préférablement à tout autre de mon siècle   (III,466).

When ten months later Louis XIV commissioned Racine and Boileau to write the official history of his reign, Bussy was outraged. "Je ne pense pas," he writes Madame de Sévigné, "que Racine et Déspreaux soient capables de bien faire l'histoire du roi" (III, 390). In her answer, Sévigné relates an incident that reveals more about their reasons for objecting to the two royal appointments. In order to write history, she seems to say, one must be equipped to participate in its making:

Le Roi leur dit, il y a quatre jours: "Je suis fâché que vous ne soyez venus à cette dernière campagne; vous auriez vu la guerre, et votre voyage n'eût pas été long." Racine lui répondit: "Sire, nous sommes deux bourgeois qui n'avons que des habits de ville; nous en commandâmes de campagne; mais les places que vous attaquiez furent plus tôt prises que nos habits ne furent faits . . ." Ah! que je connais un homme de qualité à qui j'aurais bien plutôt fait écrire mon histoire qu'à ces bourgeois-là, si j'étais son maître! C'est cela qui serait digne de la posterité![22]

The argument that someone from a noble family would be better qualified to write military history than a bourgeois writer had been accepted by French historiographers since Jean Bodin had argued it in the sixteenth century. In Bodin's conception of written history, the ideal, objective historian must have participated in political life without being dependent on his civic activities for income. Readers could not be expected to trust the critical perspective of historians who accept remuneration. History writers should be able to present the demeanor of an insider, while also maintaining a certain cool distance from the events they are chronicling.

It is easy to see how this definition might be interpreted to fit the position of the aristocratic *exilé*. The arguments given by Bussy-Rabutin and his supporters in favor of his appointment as royal historiographer show, as Orest Ranum has noted, how Bodin's definition of history could "become a part of a defensive ideology of the privileged nobility."[23] Boileau's speech to the Académie Française in 1683, six years after his appointment as royal historian, articulates the bourgeois defensive position. Thanking the Academy for its willingness to accept individuals regardless of "rank," he further suggests that his humble social status was precisely what qualified him to record, in a simple style, the exploits of his king. As Louis XIV has perceived, he says, it is necessary that

> un homme sans fard, et accusé plutôt de trop de sincerité que de flatterie, contribuât de son travail et de ses conseils à bien mettre en jour, et dans toute la naïveté du style le plus simple, la verité de ses actions, qui étant si peu vraisemblables d'elles-mêmes, ont bien plus besoin d'être fidèlement écrites que fortement exprimées.[24]

The bourgeois claim to the privilege of writing history is based precisely on the fact that the historian need only be a humble compiler, a collector of records who lays no personal, authorial claim to the body of his writing. The aristocratic notion of history, on the other hand, takes the position that the greatness of an event can only be communicated by a writer who has been born to a share in the grandeur he is describing. For the rest of his life, encouraged by support from his friends, Bussy continued to argue for his appointment as royal biographer, on the grounds that his military service qualified him. In a letter to Saint-Aignan he writes: "Outre qu'un homme de guerre n'eût pas eu besoin de consulter personne pour parler en termes du métier, il me paraît que les actions du plus grand roi du monde devaient être écrites par un de ses principaux capitaines, si lui-même, comme César, ne s'en voulait pas donner la peine" (III, 424).

But Bussy-Rabutin's qualifications to write history were lacking, even according to his own criteria. He had, in fact, already written a kind of history of the reign in his *Histoire amoureuse des Gaules*, in which society under "le roi Théodose" is portrayed as having seen better days. Money, the agent of corruption that Bussy insists disqualifies a bourgeois writer of history, appears on every page of the narrative as a substance that has destroyed the traditional dignity and purpose of aristocratic courtesy codes. His characters have learned to conduct their amorous exploits as business deals, calculating the monetary value of a conquest and exchanging love letters that read like business contracts. Aristocratic women are easily corrupted by money, and prefer a rich suitor to a noble one: "Quoiqu'elle aimât le duc de Nemours, elle aimait encore mieux les richesses . . ."(*Histoire amoureuse des Gaules*, p.105).

So in his appeals for a commissioin to write an official biography of the king, Bussy had to think of some original arguments, or at least some new ways to make old arguments. In his letters to Louis XIV he seems to put every conceivable obsequious pose to the test, in an inventive display that astonished everyone who read them, except, perhaps, the king. Bussy himself openly brags about his creative supplicatory style, especially when he thinks he has detected an approving acknowledgement from Louis XIV.[25] In 1679 he writes a letter to the king in which he changes his request. He repeats that he is already writing a history of Louis XIV's reign, but this chronicle, he now says, is the one in the form of memoirs and letters: ". . . j'écris des mémoires de ma vie dans lesquels je parle de ce que j'ai vu de Votre Majesté jusqu'à mon exil, et depuis recevant de toutes parts des lettres de mes amis dont les nouvelles les plus considérables sont les actions de Votre Majesté dans sa cour et dans ses armées . . ." (IV,335). Abandoning his idea of becoming the official royal historiographer, he proposes to give to the king his collection of letters which itself constitutes, he says, a history of the reign. All of the interlocutors in this collection are qualified to participate in this writing of history, by virtue of their roles as actors in its making. Bussy will orchestrate this flattering chorus, the accuracy of which, he says, will be all the more plausible *because* of his fall from favor. As for his own accounts of the king's exploits in the letter collection, these will be particularly interesting to posterity because of the fact that he is not being paid to write them. Therefore, he concludes, he must beg to be allowed to remain in exile![26]

This letter marks a turning point in the letters to Louis XIV, not only because of the offer of his epistolary memoirs as a gift to the king, but also because of the changed image of himself that Bussy is now trying to project. This new image is based on an expanded idea of his audience. Bussy himself makes it very clear that the king is not even his primary addressee in this letter, for the audience he is now aiming at is a broader, unnamed public who will understand his true motives and do him justice. There are at least three different readers referred to directly by Bussy at this point in the letter collection, for he inserts the letter to Louis XIV in one to Pomponne, addressing a plaintive message to the latter. Then, in a gloss addressed to his future, anonymous readers, he completely unmasks the other two messages. He writes:

> Cette lettre paraîtra si extraordinaire à la plupart du monde qui ne regardent que le dehors des affaires, que je veux dire les raisons qui me l'ont fait écrire.
>
> Premièrement, il faut qu'on sache que je ne voudrais pas avoir permission de retourner à la cour, ou seulement à Paris, si l'on ne me donnait en même temps des honneurs et du bien, . . . et quand même l'on me donnerait le bien et les honneurs que je devrais avoir, à quoi je ne vois nulle apparence, je m'en soucierais fort peu. L'âge que j'ai et les injustices qu'on m'a faites me donnent un grand mépris de tout cela; cependant je voudrais bien établir mes enfants; et c'est ce qui m'oblige de faire au roi un grand sacrifice en apparence, qui ne me coûte guère en effet . . .
>
> Si l'on examine cette lettre, on la trouvera délicate et fine, et si elle ne fait pas l'effet qu'on en devroit attendre, ce serait la faute de la fortune, sans laquelle les desseins les mieux concertés et les mieux conduits ont toujours un méchant succès   (IV, 336–37).

Clearly, twelve years of unanswered supplications have begun to weaken Bussy's hope, and the abject stance of his letters to the king and Pomponne might have been plausible to both addressees. But accompanying this change in tone in the letters to Louis XIV is a new, direct appeal to the public, a reader whose judgment will become increasingly important to him in the last years of his life. Like all public figures who write memoirs, Bussy is trying to "set the record straight" by explaining his hidden motives behind actions that will be exposed to the interpretation of the public. By circulating a collection of "memoirs" dealing with the present, Bussy is breaking with a pattern established by other memoir writers, who followed what René Démoris has called the "loi du silence qui règne sur la période louis-quatorzienne."[27] Memoirs dealing with the reign of Louis XIV were rare until after 1715. Bussy's project was even more innovative because it was epistolary, so that his was not the only voice engaged in it. His memoirs are in the form of a correspondence; his relationship to posterity is also conceived as an interactive one. He is engaging in a dialogue with a future reader whose response he is trying to condition, as he would in a conversation or a letter. The commentary that he inserts in his correspondence to explicate the letters is thus not a retrospective look at events long past, but a reflection on the present, and speculation on the future inhabited by his unknown reader.[28]

Writing to Madame de Sévigné, Bussy calls his latest letter to Louis XIV his "masterpiece," for it assures him, he feels, an ultimate victory in his quest for exoneration and the approval of his readers. By making such an obsequious offer of service to the king, and then unmasking his own rhetoric for his future readers, he feels he is bound to be exonerated by one or the other.

Bussy now argues in his letters to the king that as a courtier resigned to permanent exile, his praise will in the future be all the more readily accepted as truth. Thus he goes on asserting that, while his other services to the crown deserve some reward, he is demanding nothing in return for the history he is writing. By the end of his life Bussy is openly begging the king for money, but no longer asking him to thereby signify his forgiveness. For pardon he now looks to God, who, he says, will understand that he deserves it:

> . . . je n'ai fait pendant ma disgrâce et depuis mon retour qu'admirer, qu'adorer, et que louer Votre Majesté d'une manière qui lui fera plus d'honneur que l'histoire qui portera son nom. Je n'en ai pas usé ainsi pour que Votre Majesté le sût et qu'elle m'en récompensât: j'ai dit la verité parce que j'aime à le dire, songeant d'ailleurs que je plairais à Dieu en honorant mon roi, en l'aimant et en lui rendant justice quoi qu'il me fît du mal. Cela trouvera tôt ou tard sa récompense; si ce n'est en ce monde-ci, ce sera en l'autre   (VI,578).

Along with his letter collection, Bussy did in fact write a more conventional history, published in 1699 after his death. This *Histoire en abrégé de Louis le Grand* is an extended panegyric which today interests readers only because it was written by a writer famous for his "médisance."[28] In the preface, Bussy says that the purpose of his history was to address yet another set of readers, his children: "Je n'ai voulu parler qu'à vous, mes enfants, pour n'être pas forcé, comme le sont les historiens, de n'oser dire que les faits, et pour me laisser la liberté de faire des reflexions qui vous obligeassent à en faire . . ." (pp. 4–5). Yet in reading this prolonged gesture of praise today we are only struck by the writer's tireless flattery. Here, as in his letter correspondence, Bussy is ostensibly addressing one reader while trying to catch the attention of several others.

In the end, it was his private correspondence, rather than either of his two *histoires*, that won Bussy-Rabutin the most recognition, though not for any of the reasons he might have predicted. His hope had been that through his writing he would ultimately be vindicated by readers who would have the necessary distance from events to be able to see how he had been mistreated. For him, as for other members of his class, personal worth could only be measured by the role one played in history and the glory thus accrued to one's family. Time would show, he believed, that either political favor was restored to him or, alternatively, that Louis XIV was "ingrat." Either scenario returned him to the small, elite circle of political and social prominence that he had so unwillingly left. Even as he wrote his most unctuous letters to Louis XIV, he would project how his messages might in the future be interpreted in two very different ways, depending on how they were received by their most important reader. His letter to Madame de Sévigné in 1679 sums up his strategy:

> Je suis charmé de l'approbation que vous donnez à la lettre que j'ai écrite au roi; c'est à mon gré mon chef-d'oeuvre, et je trouve que quand Sa Majesté ne serait pas touchée de ce que je fais pour elle, son intérêt propre l'obligerait à quelque reconnaissance pour moi ou pour ma maison. Je crois que mes *Mémoires*, et particulièrement cette dernière lettre, seront à la posterité une satire contre lui s'il est ingrat; et j'ai trouvé plus sûr, plus délicat, et plus honnête de me venger ainsi des maux qu'il m'a faits, en cas qu'il ne veuille pas les réparer, que de m'emporter contre lui en injures que j'aurais de la peine à faire passer pour légitimes   (IV,401).

Yet Bussy's efforts to assure himself of a sympathetic reception by revealing his "true" motives strike modern readers as naïve and hopelessly vain. It is all too clear to us that this professed sincerity is in fact yet another ploy, and in fact Bussy does not try to claim otherwise. His decision to set his sights on a future, more objective audience did not mean that he would abandon the style of communication that he had learned in salon conversations. As he shows in his 1679 letter to the king, his idea of an open communication with posterity allows him to show off all his sociable skills—he can continue to write admirable supplicatory letters, then proceed to unmask his own letters for different audiences, until hopefully one of these images of himself will reach a sympathetic reader. The most privileged reader and the one who, according to Bussy, will see the real person that he is, is his future public, who will receive all of his different voices at once.

*   *   *

In the history of reader attitudes toward published correspondences, the reception of Bussy's letters marks an important turning point. The letters of Balzac, Pasquier, and Du Tronchet had been valued primarily as models to be imitated, while the editions of Voiture's letters invited the reader to participate, to be initiated into the world of the Rambouillet salon. Janet Altman has shown that a major shift in epistolary practices and poetics occurred at the end of the seventeenth century, marked by a return to and deepening of the personal historical consciousness that had characterized much epistolary writing of the Renaissance.[29] Bussy-Rabutin's correspondence was presented to the public as a uniquely personal, even confessional document, and his letters have since been linked to a tradition of introspective, self-revelatory writing epitomized by Rousseau's *Confessions*.[30]

But while early readers of his memoirs and letters found in them a new, more personal authorial voice, the distance between Bussy-Rabutin and Rousseau is great. Bussy's self-image is determined by his social relations, and even his vaunted openness always has a transparent rhetorical purpose. It is not surprising that future generations of readers were to look in vain for a sympathetic person behind these masks. Madame du Deffand, reading Bussy's letters in 1772, writes Walpole that she is forced to admire the frankness of his vanity, although she is certain she wouldn't have liked him:

> Cependant la vanité tout à découvert n'est pas ce que je hais le plus, on peut la repousser, la combattre; celle que je déteste est celle qui prend la voile de la modestie, et qui, avec les dehors de la politesse, force à s'y soumettre ou du moins à la souffrir: Bussy ne disait de lui que le bien qu'il en pensait . . .[31]

Bussy's appeal to posterity is not, in fact, for sympathy or affection, but rather for a recognition of the legitimacy of his claims. It was impossible for him to conceive of or desire any other kind of identity. For him, the ultimate question was not whether he would be liked, but it was whether he would be remembered in the right company. As an exile, Bussy saw two roles he could play, two types of discourse he could invoke: that of a courtier seeking new favors, or of a resigned philosopher, neither being poses that suited him well. His memoirs, as they evolved into a carefully arranged collection of letters, were his innovative solution, enabling him to recreate for himself a privileged role in history.

After the publication of Bussy's memoir-correspondence, familiar letters began to be seen more and more as vehicles of self-expression, and the experience of reading a letter as a process of personal acquaintance. But this shift in the functioning of letters as communicative acts signals a broader change in the structure of communication for the society to which Bussy belonged. The ideal of *honnêteté*, of which Bussy was an important spokesman, depends on the ability of a social milieu to maintain the convention of democratic relations, of unbroken verbal commerce among equals. As this common code became increasingly difficult to sustain, with the consolidation of central authority and the concommitant unbalancing of aristocratic fortunes, the economy of verbal exchange was bound to be disrupted. The value of communication could no longer be determined by its proper enactment according to the rules of sociability—balance, reciprocity, and a heavy emphasis on phatic communication.[32] Instead, the conditions of regular social interaction shifted toward a less stable, more individually risky series of pacts, with the recognition of the speaker's sincerity being the authenticating response solicited from the listener.[33]

In an essay on the history of the idea of individuality, Georg Simmel examines how narrow social circles allow less room than wider ones for individual identity, while giving the group as a whole a sharper consciousness of its own uniqueness. Social relations within a small, elite group are centripetal, focused on sustaining a balanced equality within the group. When social differentiation within a group alters its sense of collective identity, the original centripetal dynamic of the autonomous circle is gradually supplemented by a centrifugal model of communication, enabling individuals to form links with other groups. Consequently, "individuality in being and action generally increases to the degree that the social circle encompassing the individual expands."[34]

The works of Bussy-Rabutin provide a remarkably detailed record of the personal reactions of one man to the shifting standards of social differentiation that were occurring in his community, as the narrow elite to which he belonged expanded to include a broader range of individual members. Like other members of the old *noblesse d'épée*, he held to the traditional image of the aristocracy as a warrior class, and all of his writings testify to his immense pride in his family's history of military service to the crown. In 1634, at the age of 16, he had fought in his first campaign. At 20 he had taken over his father's regiment, and in 1654 he purchased the *charge* of "maître de camp de la cavalerie légère de France."

But in 1666 an honorable military record was not enough to keep a nobleman out of prison. Bussy's exile placed him in an outsider's position, and he was forced to behave like a bourgeois newcomer, an aspirant to political power. Under Louis XIV's new legal system, members of the nobility were often treated no differently from middle-class suitors in their appeals for favor or justice. Bussy's chronicle of the experience of separation and loss of status, followed by his attempts to reconstruct a social identity through epistolary writing, give us a valuable insight into how aristocratic codes of social conduct were adapted to suit more personal modes of interaction.

NOTES

1. Cited in Gérard-Gailly, *Bussy-Rabutin* (Paris: H. Champion, 1909), p. 113.
2. *Mémoires*, ed. Ludovic Lalanne (Paris: Marpon et Flammarion, 1857) I, p. 3. All my references are to this edition, and will be indicated in the text as *M*. I will also be referring to Lalanne's edition of the *Correspondance* (Paris: Charpentier, 1857–59).

3. "Tallement et Bussy, ou le médisant bourgeois et le médisant de qualité," in *Causeries du lundi* (Paris: Garnier, 1858), XIII, pp. 142–55.

4. *Histoire amoureuse des Gaules* (Paris: Garnier-Flammarion, 1967), p.27.

5. *Le Misanthrope*, another work produced in 1666, can be read as a kind of face-off between characters adhering to different codes of conduct regarding *médisance*. Alceste, nostalgic for a lost freedom of blunt speech, falls easily prey to his enemies, who use new legal practices to sue him for slander.

6. See Orest Ranum, *Paris in the Age of Absolutism* (New York: Wiley and Sons, 1968), pp. 272–76.

7. Jean-Marie Apostolidès discusses the multi-faceted machinery of this "mythistoire" in *Le Roi-machine* (Paris: Editions de minuit, 1981), pp.66–92.

8. The passage is found on pp. 86–87 in Adam's edition of *Histoire amoureuse des Gaules*.

9. Démoris describes this social role of a "littérature de l'immédiat" in the classical period: "Plus encore qu'à l'époque antérieure, le jeu littéraire devient jeu de société, par lequel les membres d'un groupe socio-culturel, menacé dans sa différence avec les autres groupes, se créent des signes qui leur permettent de se reconnaître les uns les autres." See René Démoris, *Le Roman à la première personne* (Paris: Armand Colin, 1975), pp.91–92; Marie-Thérèse Hipp, *Mythes et réalités: enquête sur le roman et les mémoires, 1660–1700* (Paris: Klincksieck, 1976), p.26; and C. Rouben, "Histoire et géographie galantes au grand siècle: l'*Histoire amoureuse des Gaules* et la *Carte du pays de braquerie* de Bussy-Rabutin," *XVIIe siècle* 93 (1971), pp. 55–73.

10. *Gossip* (New York: Knopf, 1985), pp. 52–64.

11. Bernard Beugnot traces the history of this theme of spiritual retreat in memoirs and other autobiographical writings of seventeenth-century France in "Morale du repos et conscience du temps," *Australian Journal of French Studies* XIII (1976), pp. 183–96.

In his letters to the king, Bussy, who was fond of imagining himself in the company of heroic precursors, may well have had Ovid in mind as a literary model. Although he does not refer to the letters to Augustus, Bussy busied himself during his exile with some very free translations from the *Heroides* and *Remedia amores*. It is generally thought that the reason for Ovid's exile was that his poetry was considered to be an attack on the emperor's new moral program.

12. See Marc Fumaroli, "Les Mémoires du XVIIe siècle au carrefour des genres," *XVIIe siècle* 94–95 (1971), p. 11.

13. Fumaroli notes that the desire to participate in recording history was an important motive of the seventeenth-century *mémorialiste:* "En attendant la venue de l'Historien idéal annoncé par le Père Rapin, il faut multiplier les témoignages, accumuler les archives, préparer les mémoires qui permettront à chacun de ne pas se présenter désarmé à l'heure du jugement" (p.12).

14. Philippe Ariès, "Pourquoi écrit-on des mémoires?" in *Les Valeurs chez les mémorialistes français du XVIIe siècle avant la Fronde* (Actes du Colloque de Strasbourg et Metz, 18–20 mai 1978, Klincksieck, 1979), p. 19.

15. *Maximes* (Paris: Garnier, 1967), p.19.

16. Today the entire château of Bussy-le-Grand is a museum. It is described by Gérard-Gailly in *Bussy-Rabutin, sa vie, ses oeuvres et ses amis* (Paris: Honoré Champion, 1909), pp. 104–15.

17. Even so, after twenty years he begins to sound a little testy, responding

to admiring descriptions of his house: "Vous me mandez, Madame, qu'on se figure ma maison comme le palais des Muses, et que sous cette idée on voudrait qu'elle fût invulnérable à toutes sortes de maux. Premièrement, Madame, les muses n'ont point de palais . . . De plus, il n'y a que les personnes que l'on puisse dire invulnérables et point les corps inanimés . . ." (VI, 288–89).

18. "Pour moi, j'aime à bâtir; j'ai deux aussi belles maisons que gentil-homme de France; et c'est moi qui les ai embellies . . . Tout cela ne suffit pourtant pas aux gens qui ont de la raison; il leur faut des beautés plus animées, il leur faut des livres, de la conversation ou des commerces de lettres. J'ai ici de tout cela" (V,540).

19. C. Rouben's study of Bussy-Rabutin pays particular attention to the literary and fictive qualities of the correspondence, noting in particular the author's gradual construction of a heroic self-image: "La *Correspondance* est l'his-toire d'un disgrâcié qui tente, par le sortilège de sa plume, de se donner la stature d'un héros." *Bussy-Rabutin épistolier* (Paris: Nizet, 1974), p.65.

20. Orest Ranum, in an article on the development of courtesy and dis-courtesy as political instruments under Louis XIII, says that the most impor-tant of these uses was simply the king's "decision to accept or to decline a salutation from a subject." "Courtesy, Absolutism, and the Rise of the French State, 1630–1660," *Journal of Modern History* 52 (1980), p. 431.

21. In Lalanne's edition most of them are removed from the main body of the correspondence and included as an appendix at the end of each volume.

22. *Lettres*, ed. Gérard-Gailly, II, pp. 386–87. For another quote see II, p. 395.

23. *Artisans of Glory: Writers and Historical Thought in Seventeenth-Century France* (Chapel Hill: University of North Carolina Press, 1980), p.301.

24. Cited in Ranum, *Artisans*, p.301.

25. Writing Madame de Sévigné, he inserts a copy of a letter he had given to the king, and excitedly describes how it had been received:

. . . dès que le roi me vit, il me dit: "Je reçois les offres que vous me faites; mais il faut attendre un autre temps où l'on soit moins occupé." Je lui ré-pondis que je serais toujours prêt, quand il lui plairait.

Lisez cette lettre et la relisez, ma chère cousine, elle vous plaira encore plus la seconde fois que la première, et je crois que vous trouverez qu'il n'y a personne en France que moi qui ait droit de parler ainsi, ou qui, s'il le peut, le puisse faire aussi noblement   (VI,410).

26. "Ce qui donnera encore beaucoup de créance à ce que j'écrirai de vous, Sire, ce sera de voir que je ne suis pas payé pour en parler, et de peur même qu'on ne croie un jour que c'était pour être rappelé que j'en disais tant de bien, je supplie Votre Majesté très humblement de me laisser ici le reste de ma vie, . . ." (IV, 336).

27. See *Le Roman*, p. 190.

28. See C. Rouben, "L'Histoire en abrégé de Louis le Grand de Bussy-Rabutin," *Revue des sciences humaines* XXXVI (1972), p.525. Rouben also points out that Bussy quite deliberately writes his "histoire" from the point of view of a witness, that is, in the present, and with the obvious purpose of pleasing the king. In his writing of history, as in his other writings, Bussy doggedly presents an image of himself as someone thoroughly engaged with the world he is describing. The seventeenth-century concept of history, and its relation-

ship to the early novel, is discussed by Erica Harth in *Ideology and Culture in Seventeenth-Century France* (Ithaca, N.Y.: Cornell University Press, 1983), pp.130–42.

29. "The Letter Book as a Literary Institution, 1539–1789: Toward a Cultural History of Published Correspondences in France," *Yale French Studies* 71 (1986), pp. 17–62.

30. See Roger Duchêne, "Le Lecteur de lettres," *Revue d'histoire littéraire de la France* 78 (1978), pp. 986–87.

31. Cited in Bussy-Rabutin, *Mémoires* II, p. 461.

32. In Roman Jakobson's model of verbal communication, the phatic function is simply "the endeavor to start and sustain communication." This function, it seems to me, would always be particularly important to communication in exclusive circles, whose members are constantly preoccupied with justifying the terms of their own inclusion. In situations where the effectiveness of exclusivity is threatened, or when an individual faces possible exclusion, the ability to remain in touch, or to "check whether the channel works," is crucial to the maintenance of social identity. See Jakobson, "Linguistics and Poetics," in *Style in Language*, ed., Sebeok, (Cambridge: MIT Press, 1960), pp.355–357.

33. The idea of sincerity as both social and aesthetic virtue is historically connected with the intensified sense of personal autonomy that developed along with the expansion of the definition of "society." Lionel Trilling, among others, discusses this history in his essay *Sincerity and Authenticity* (Cambridge: Harvard University Press, 1972).

34. *On Individuality and Social Forms* (Chicago: University of Chicago Press, 1971), pp. 252–53.

« 4 »

Sociability and Intimacy in the Letters of
Madame de Sévigné

In 1691, Madeleine de Scudéry wrote a conversation on "les désirs," in which the speakers spend most of their time talking about the desire to travel. They all agree that everyone is moving around far too much, and for no useful purpose. Even people who undertake a voyage for the best of reasons, to learn more about history, inevitably return more confused than when they left. One speaker tells the story of a friend who travelled to Greece to see the great sites of ancient culture and came back disappointed:

> à la réserve de quelques débris de marbre, de temples de dieux devenus mosquées, et de quelques inscriptions à demi-effacées et peut-être mal entendus, il n'a rapporté que des conjectures de tout ce qu'il voulait savoir . . . de sorte qu'excepté des marchands qui voyagent pour s'enrichir, et qui servent à lier toutes les nations par le commerce . . . les désirs de voyagent doivent être bornés et réglés par la raison.[1]

Travelling to distant lands is an activity suited to those engaged in keeping the wheels of commerce turning; it is not appropriate for people "of quality" who can acquire no knowledge from travelling: "sinon que votre pays vaut mieux que le leur, où l'ignorance règne, et que vous valez mieux qu'eux" (p.207). Those who have the supreme privilege of living at the court of Louis XIV, the only person on earth who desires nothing ("il est parfaitement heureux en lui-même"), have nothing to gain from indulging their own "désir de changer de place" (p.209).

Scudéry's speakers may have been making a moral principle out of political expediency at a time when everything depended on remaining in favor, and remaining in favor meant remaining at court. The group's warnings of the consequences of moving too far from the center of "the world" also extend to outsiders who wish to move closer to it, "gens de province, qui sans avoir mille des qualités qui sont propres au monde, désirent ardemment d'y être, et se ruinent pour venir se faire moquer d'eux . . . " (p.209). Too much movement in both directions was blurring the boundaries of elite culture, making closure difficult to manage. But at a time when even old aristocratic families were risking financial ruin in order to exist at court in a manner suited to their station, other pressures, many of them caused by new state institutions, were making it necessary for individuals to spend long periods away from the capital. Louis XIV's costly military campaigns (one of which Scudéry wrote her conversation on "désirs" to commemorate) regularly emptied the court of its young men, and, more indirectly, often forced their families to leave Paris in order to raise the money necessary to equip them. State control over provincial governments established under Richelieu and tightened under the administration of Louis XIV required increased travel between the provinces and the capital. By the end of the century many private financial resources were so depleted that members of the nobility had to flee to their provincial estates simply to avoid the conspicuous spending required of them at Versailles, and to try to wrest additional funds from the peasants who worked their lands.[2]

As Scudéry's conversation suggests, all of this moving around creates problems for people whose identity is tightly bound to their membership in a specific social group. Closure and stability are essential for the kind of ideal verbal interaction she envisions. And the information that fed the endless conversations of polite society could only be obtained by people who were on the spot, close to the center of power. To be well-informed was one of the surest ways of gaining access to elite circles.

Increased travel was one of the most obvious causes of the growing interest in the art of writing letters. Whether travelling in the provinces or exiled indefinitely, anyone who hoped to gain favor had to be informed of the most recent news from Paris. Printed newsletters such as the *Gazette de Hollande, Muse historique* and *Mercure galant* first appeared in the seventeenth century, but were distributed no faster than private letters. A reliable correspondent could provide at least as much information to absent courtiers as a printed pamphlet.

The seventeenth-century definition of a letter as a "conversation des absents" is much more than a banal observation, for one's social conversation and to a great extent one's social status, was shaped by the company one kept. A good correspondent, writes Scudéry, is able to pass on those "nouvelles du cabinet, qui ne se disent qu'à l'oreille, et qui ne sont bien sues que par des personnes du monde bien instruites . . ."[3] For an individual like Bussy-Rabutin, letters could be a means of maintaining a public image that was crucial to his concept of self. For elite society as a whole, letters became an important means of assuring an uninterrupted circulation of talk, even in a circle whose members were often dispersed. Letters gave written form to the verbal signals that elite culture had developed to reinforce the terms of its own exclusivity.

The most famous letter writer of the seventeenth century, Madame de Sévigné, is often described by her contemporaries as a consummately sociable person. Her skill in interacting with others, her conversation, and the charm of her speech are repeatedly evoked. Madeleine de Scudéry observes approvingly that her writing is like her talk, and Somaize remarks that she is able to draw people to her with her voice: "si son visage attire les regards, son esprit charme les oreilles, et engage tous ceux qui l'entendent ou qui lisent ce qu'elle écrit." Madame de Lafayette's portrait of her friend also emphasizes the quality of her speech ". . . (votre miroir) ne peut vous dire combien vous êtes aimable quand vous parlez, et c'est ce que je veux vous apprendre . . . Tout ce que vous dites a un tel charme, et vous sied si bien, que vos paroles attirent les ris et les grâces autour de vous . . ."[4] Even in his malicious portrait of his cousin, Bussy-Rabutin conveys an image of someone remarkable because of her special, almost magical ability to interact with others.[5] Sévigné herself writes about conversation as an activity that gives shape to reality, essential not only for the formation of minds, but also for survival.[6] "Je fais toujours des résolutions de me taire," she writes her daughter, "et je ne cesse de parler . . ." (II, 1036).

Today, it is her passionate attachment to her daughter, documented in their eighteen-year correspondence, that seems to interest Sévigné's readers the most. Scudéry's fictional representation of her friend as the sociable "Princesse Clarinte," who laughingly tells her friends "qu'elle n'a jamais été amoureuse que de sa propre gloire," contrasts sharply with the Madame de Sévigné of the twentieth-century creative imagination, an obsessed mother who would gladly die for her adult child.[7] It is, in fact, in the letters to Madame de Grignan that the originality of her writing comes through. In the vast epistolary literature of the seventeenth century, few letters between mothers and daughters are to be found. Sévigné's messages to her daughter record her personal discovery of how to express intimacy, and of how to communicate passion. In reading her correspondence one is struck by the shock of her separation from her daughter and by the continuity and undiminished energy of her attachment to her. The moment of Madame de Grignan's departure has been termed her mother's literary "birth," and we are told that before the fatal day she produced little writing worth mentioning: "rien avant ce 6 février, rien avant cette déchirure, cette découverte."[8]

For the last fifteen years, Sévigné criticism has been dominated by a discussion over her status as a literary figure. On the one hand it is argued that her art derives only from her lived experience, and that she was unconcerned with literary conventions and had no pretentions to the status of author. Other readers reply that even private letters, particularly in the seventeenth century, are written with a public in mind, and as such can be studied as literary texts.[9] This debate tends to promote a dichotomy between literature and life that obscures a more interesting issue in Madame de Sévigné's letters—what do they show about the way interaction was conducted in her society? Of course the correspondence is made up of real, written conversations; all the more reason to see what it can show us about the way communication was organized in this society where an individual's every gesture was examined, talked about, and interpreted. Moreover, the two images of Madame de Sévigné as socialite and mother, talker and writer, are not as far apart as they seem.

In Sévigné's correspondence with her daughter, there can be seen a definite narrowing of her focus, and an appreciation—even a need—of privacy and solitude that we don't read in her other letters. But even in her most lonely moments she invokes other voices against which she can measure and confirm her own. There is a community of speakers present in her most narcissistic and reflective letters. The principles of conversation and sociable interaction that she so skillfully displays in her messages to friends are modified, reexamined, and adapted to the conduct of intimacy in her letters to Madame de Grignan.

Conversation as Frame: The Trial of Foucquet

One of the most famous sequences in Madame de Sévigné's correspondence is her letters to Pomponne about the trial of Nicolas Foucquet. The Foucquet affair has often been cited as an important turning point in Louis XIV's relations with the nobility. A protégé of Mazarin, Foucquet was named *Surintendant des finances* in 1653, and by that time had acquired enough wealth to undertake the construction of a château at Vaux, engaging the services of the best artists of the time. He was a committed patron of writers and artists: La Fontaine, Molière, Corneille, and Madeleine de Scudéry were among the writers from whom he commissioned works and who benefitted from his generosity. Foucquet's arrest in 1661, engineered by Colbert, came at the beginning of what was to be a long but relentless campaign to shift control of certain social functions from the powerful families who had traditionally performed them to new state institutions. During the two years that Foucquet waited to go to trial, the royal Academy of Arts was reorganized to take strong control over artistic production and to assume the protective role hitherto played by private patrons.

At the time of his arrest, which followed a lavish *fête* at Vaux, Foucquet's friends and protégés recognized that he was being made a scapegoat, but could only speculate on and talk about the far-reaching political implications of his trial as the events occurred. The most interesting testimony to these conversations is to be found in Madame de

Sévigné's letters. On December 17, 1664 she writes Simon de Pomponne:

> Tout le monde s'intéresse dans cette grande affaire, on ne parle d'autre chose; on raisonne, on tire des conséquences, on compte sur ses doigts; on s'attendrit, on espère, on craint, on peste, on souhaite, on hait, on admire, on est triste, on est accablé; enfin, mon pauvre monsieur, c'est une chose extraordinaire que l'état où l'on est présentement   (I, 76).

Foucquet's disgrace threatened both Sévigné and Pomponne personally. Pomponne was exiled during the trial under suspicion of having conspired to draw Foucquet closer to Jansenist circles. Sévigné had sought favors from Foucquet in the past, had written him letters that were confiscated when he was arrested, and had cultivated close ties with his family in the hopes that her own children would profit from the patronage of the wealthy and powerful minister. When he was first arrested in 1661, letters from her were found with others from his female acquaintances.

On first learning of this, Sévigné threw herself into the verbal fray, talking and writing to everyone she could about her innocence of any impropriety. But beyond the impact that Sévigné feared his fall could have on her own fortune, she saw the whole affair as a social drama, a political event whose significance, for the select circle surrounding Foucquet, was being discussed, examined, and generated by their constant and busy exchange of talk about it. All other events, she writes Pomponne, collapse into this one, and in their endless conversations the observers weave a texture of meanings around the daily drama to give it aesthetic and moral dimensions that they all can accept.

In a letter written to Pomponne immediately after the arrest, Sévigné establishes the basis for her subsequent role as his faithful source of news of the trial alluding to their mutual "interest" in the affair: "Il n'y a rien de plus vrai que l'amitié se rechauffe quand on est dans les mêmes intérêts; . . . j'ai les mêmes sentiments pour vous que vous avez pour moi, et qu'en un mot, je vous aime et vous estime d'une façon toute particulière" (I,50). It is essential, if these conversations and the letters reporting them are to have real value, for the participants to feel sure of their mutual interest, of their shared perspective on the events, and of their common commitment to interpreting them in the same way. Sévigné will frequently remind Pomponne that they see things the same way and that the reports she is sending are all drawn from conversations with other "gens de bien" who share their sympathies. Foucquet's trial polarized Parisian high society, his guilt was hotly debated, and it was not easy to tell from the outset what side even his friends would take.[11] Sévigné's reports serve to reaffirm the complicity of her select group as they work together to extract, from conflicting accounts, a version of events that is acceptable and gratifying to the circle as a whole. She seeks out the company of people who will not only provide her with the latest news, but who will help her interpret it. "Je viens de souper à l'hôtel de Nevers; nous avons bien causé, la maîtresse du logis et moi, sur ce chapître. Nous sommes dans les inquiétudes qu'il n'y a que vous qui puissiez comprendre . . ." (I,66).

What is important is not that all speakers make identical speculations as to the outcome of the trial, but that they all come to the conversation with a common bias and a shared assessment of the actors involved in the events they are discussing. These encounters seem to resemble what Spacks has called "serious gossip," a form of conversation in which the relationship between the speakers is more important than the facts they are discussing, their shared interpretation more crucial than the information they are promulgating.[12] For Sévigné and her interlocutors the principle of complicity is even more important, for without complicity the information she gathers and distributes is unreliable and thereby valueless. Unlike a modern-day journalist, she trusts news coming *only* from interested parties, and all the observers in her circle act to promote, through their talk, a view of events that will confirm their notions of how the principle actors—Foucquet, Colbert, the king—might be expected to behave.

The focus of all fourteen letters to Pomponne about the trial is of course Foucquet, and the figure he cuts in her accounts is the opposite of Chapelain's characterization of "ce miserable personnage" (I,54). To Sévigné, Foucquet's behavior is nothing short of heroic, a view that she says is shared by nearly everyone: "On parle fort à Paris de son admirable esprit et de sa fermeté" (I,58). She is careful to provide details of his physical bearing, his dress, his facial expressions, his gestures, and any particular information that she can glean from her principal informant d'Ormesson, or from others who have seen him.[13] She rarely transcribes what Foucquet actually says in his defense; instead, she tells Pomponne how he said it, or how his testimony was punctuated by a specific gesture—a refusal to be seated, a polite salutation, whether or not he removed his hat. These details are elaborated, while his arguments are usually summarized with a single evaluative phrase: "il a très bien répondu."[14] Her descriptions of Foucquet and of those who watch him are carefully framed for dramatic effect, and she takes obvious pleasure in having participated in the drama she narrates.

On one of Foucquet's trips from the Bastille to the Arsenal where the trial was held, Sévigné and several other ladies arrange to be able to secretly observe him. Sévigné is careful in her description to highlight the theatrical elements of the scene. The women are masked, and they position themselves in a window directly overlooking the Arsenal door. Just as the prisoner is about to enter the door, D'Artagnan stops and points to the window where the women are watching:

> En s'approchant de nous pour rentrer dans son trou, M. D'Artagnan l'a poussé, et lui a fait remarquer que nous étions là. Il nous a donc saluées, et a pris cette mine riante que vous connaissez. Je ne crois pas qu'il m'ait reconnue, mais je vous avoue que j'ai été étrangement saisie, quand je l'ai vu rentrer dans cette petite porte   (I,64).

Foucquet's gallant acknowledgment, made more theatrical by D'Artagnan's gesture which sets it up, creates a brief moment of recognition and linkage between the group of observers and the man whose story they have been incessantly contemplating and analyzing. The description is highly visual, no words are exchanged, and the onlookers are impressed by the contrast between Foucquet's laughing gesture and the dark "hole" where he is about to enter and disappear from sight.

In her letter of the previous day, Sévigné had mentioned another incident involving a group of women, in a more abject posture, hoping to receive a sign of recognition from a different idealized male figure. The women of Foucquet's family had vainly tried to attract the attention of the king as he passed by: "Le même jour le Roi ne regarda pas ces pauvres femmes qui furent se jeter à ses pieds" (I,62). The parallels in these two descriptions suggest the confrontation between royal and aristocratic authority at stake in Foucquet's trial, a confrontation which Sévigné is acutely aware of, and one to which she refers quite openly considering the fact that she fully expected her letters to be read by censors. References to the king's role in the trial are sometimes veiled (thinly) by other pieces of news, as in her letter of December 1 where she reports how the king had tricked the maréchal de Gramont into giving him an honest assessment of his efforts at writing poetry:

> Le Roi a fort ri de cette folie, et tout le monde trouve que voilà la plus cruelle petite chose que l'on puisse faire à un vieux courtisan. Pour moi, qui aime toujours à faire des réflexions, je voudrais que le Roi en fît la-dessus, et qu'il jugeât par là combien il est loin de connaître la vérité   (I,67).

And while her descriptions of the king's "grande rage" against Foucquet always deflect the blame to his malicious ministers ("Il disait l'autre jour à son lever, que Foucquet était un homme dangereux; voilà ce qu'on lui met dans la tête . . . (I,73)), they also repeatedly pit the two figures of Foucquet and Louis XIV against each other, so that what is on trial seems to be a question of deportment, of Foucquet's demeanor toward the king. The courtroom exchanges she does report almost always have to do with the prisoner's refusal or acceptance of the authority of his judges, or conversely the deference that the judges show or refuse to show to Foucquet.[15]

Her descriptions of the individual judges highlight the *politesse* of Foucquet's sympathizers and the vulgarity of those hostile to him. "Pussort faisait des mines d'improbation et de négative qui scandalisent les gens de bien. Quand M. Foucquet a eu cessé de parler, Pussort s'est levé impétueusement, et a dit: 'Dieu merci, on ne se plaindra pas qu'on ne l'ait laissé parler tout son soûl.' Que dites-vous de ces belles paroles? Ne sont-elles pas d'un fort bon juge?" (I,68). The judges who argue for Foucquet's execution are inept, even grotesque, making their arguments "pauvrement et misérablement," and with no sense of restraint: "Pussort a parlé quatre heures, mais avec tant de véhémence, tant de chaleur, tant d'emportement, tant de rage, que plusieurs juges en étaient scandalisés . . ." (I,75). D'Ormesson's opinion, on the other hand, is elegantly produced, it is "un chef-d'oeuvre . . . il y mela de l'éloquence et même de l'agrément" (I,74). And when she hears that the *Chancelier* Séguier, who was presiding over the trial and was one of Foucquet's most vehement enemies, has been making devotional visits to the convent of Sainte-Marie de Saint-Antoine, she is mystified and eager to find out the "dessous des cartes." Her correspondent's succinct reply, that Séguier's sudden devotion is "la métamorphose de Pierrot en Tartuffe," delights her, and she rushes to share it with others (I,66). [16]

In all of this attention to manner, gesture, deportment and outward signs of embarrassment or poise, there is one moment when Sévigné gives a more detailed account of the courtroom dialogue. This occurs near the end of the trial, when Foucquet has to defend himself against the most serious charge of having committed a *crime d'état*. The evidence upon which the charge is based is a document written by Foucquet, in which he had made plans and given instructions to various associates in the event of his arrest. This last day of questioning begins with the incriminating "projet" being read aloud, an irregular procedure which surprises and humiliates the accused. His defense is that the paper in question was never translated into action, and was written when he was despondent over signs that Mazarin was plotting against him. [17]

Angered by the paper's being made public, Foucquet throws the accusation of *crime d'état* back at his interrogator, who had participated in the Fronde. He explicitly turns the courtroom discussion to the question of his questioner's personal loyalty to Louis XIV: "Monsieur, dans tous les temps, et même au péril de ma vie, je n'ai jamais abandonné la personne du Roi; et dans ce temps-là vous étiez, monsieur, le chef du conseil de ses ennemis, et vos proches donnaient passage à l'armée qui était contre lui." Foucquet's statement hit the mark, writes Sévigné, adding that while it was somewhat out of control, that was excusable, for he was caught unawares when Séguier read his words aloud in public:

> Monsieur le Chancelier a senti ce coup; mais notre pauvre ami était échauffé, et n'était pas tout à fait le maître de son émotion . . . Enfin cette interrogation a duré deux heures, où Monsieur Foucquet a très bien dit, mais avec chaleur et colère, parce que la lecture de ce projet l'avait extraordinairement touché"   (I,69).

Obviously this little scene generated an unusual amount of discussion amongst Foucquet's friends, because Sévigné's next letter gives Pomponne a *revised* version of it based on five days of further conversations. Since last writing him she has heard other reports, she says, and her original source has "better remembered" how the scene went.

She is eager to keep her correspondent informed and involved in the exchanges as they unfold, so she stresses to him that her corrected account is the latest, authoritative one. In this new version, Foucquet makes a more direct attack on Séguier's methods. His crude tactics, he says, consist in simply trying to embarrass and humiliate the accused in public. But in this new version of Foucquet's responses Sévigné's "pauvre ami" does not lose his heroic composure, and he takes control of the scene by "explaining" to the court what a real "crime d'état" is:

> Cependant je veux rajuster la dernière journée de l'interrogatoire sur le crime d'Etat. Je vous l'avais mandé comme on me l'avait dit, mais la même personne s'en est mieux souvenue, et me l'a redit ainsi. Tout le monde en a été instruit par plusieurs juges. Après que M. Foucquet eut dit que le seul effet qu'on pouvait tirer du projet, c'était de lui avoir donné la confusion de l'entendre, Monsieur le Chancelier lui dit: "Vous ne pouvez pas dire que ce ne soit là un crime d'Etat." "Je supplie ces messieurs," dit-il se tournant vers les juges, "de trouver bon que j'explique ce que c'est qu'un crime d'Etat; ce n'est pas qu'ils ne soient plus habiles que moi, mais j'ai eu plus de loisir qu'eux pour l'examiner. Un crime d'Etat, c'est quand on est dans une charge principale, qu'on a le secret du prince, et que tout d'un coup on se met à la tête du conseil de ses ennemis, qu'on engage toute sa famille dans les mêmes intérêts, qu'on fait ouvrir les portes des villes dont on est gouverneur à l'armée des ennemis, et qu'on les ferme à son véritable maître, qu'on porte dans le parti tous les secrets de l'Etat: voilà, messieurs, ce qui s'appelle un crime d'Etat." Monsieur le Chancelier ne savait où se mettre, et tous les juges avaient fort envie de rire. Voilà au vrai comme la chose se passa. Vous m'avouerez au'il n'y a rien de plus spirituel, de plus délicat, et même de plus plaisant. Toute la France a su et admiré cette réponse. Ensuite il se défendit en détail, et dit ce que je vous ai mandé. J'aurais eu sur le coeur que vous n'eussiez point su cet endroit comme il est. Notre cher ami y aurait beaucoup perdu   (I, 71–72).

Foucquet's speech is literally rewritten here, and it is much improved. We are given no new details of his argument, but his manner of presenting it has been polished and refined. In the second version he is controlled, even witty; he does not resort to a direct personal attack on Séguier, but mockingly pretends to be giving a respectful clarification to dramatize the relative insignificance of his transgression. The judges smile, and "all of France" applauds. The definitive version of the scene has been produced collectively by this audience, in fact. Sévigné writes her correspondent, not that she wants him to know how it really *was*, but how it presently *is* in the conversations that he has been missing ("J'aurais eu sur le coeur que vous n'eussiez point su cet endroit comme il *est*.").

Sévigné's letters on the Foucquet trial, as carefully constructed extensions of her daily exchanges with others, demonstrate the creative power of conversation, and its function in her world as a means of presenting reality in a way that is acceptable to all of her interlocutors. Spacks, in her study of gossip, has written about the creative power of verbal exchange, and to a certain extent Sévigné's letters enact the functions of gossip as outlined by Spacks—they show her incessant conversations as power, as concealment, and as social currency (pp. 53–55). But Spacks's commentary on the aesthetic function of gossip begins with the eighteenth century, when "idle talk" became a marketable item through the burgeoning production of scandal sheets and novels. In the closed world of elite culture in seventeenth-century France, the force of conversational exchange is much more intense. The printed newsletter, which first appeared in the seventeenth century, in its beginnings functioned essentially as an extension of private dialogue. These early examples of journalism all took the form of familiar letters, suggesting that they enjoyed a complicitous relationship with their readers, comparable to that of a private conversation. In Madame de Sévigné's social milieu, conversation not only enabled individual observers to collectively interpret a publicly known event, it also actually revised and framed the event for a public that was constituted by an endless chain of speakers.

But his allies' elegant adjustments of Foucquet's behavior during the trial did not prevent Colbert's appointees from framing Foucquet in quite another sense. The verbal energy of his social circle may have saved him from execution, but they did not save him from imprisonment and early death. In her letters to Pomponne Sévigné indicates that she hopes all of this talk, properly conducted, will have an effect on the outcome of the trial. This obviously worried Foucquet's enemies at court, for eventually Sévigné's informant d'Ormesson was pressured into breaking off contact with her.[18] When she no longer is able to get reports from d'Ormesson, her conversations with others become an exercise in mutual consolation, a way of confirming the collective survival of the group.[19]

Other allies of Foucquet may have been more troubled by the helpless closure of their discourse. One of the most flamboyant texts written in Foucquet's defense was by Paul Pellisson, who had been arrested with him. He wrote an impassioned and much admired plea to Louis XIV, and also circulated elegiac verse on the disgrace of his patron. An anonymous pamphlet against Foucquet mocked the ineffectual and narcissistic eloquence of these efforts. "Le malheur du surintendant," the author writes, "ne sert qu'à faire paraître la gentilesse de votre esprit. On vous blâme . . . de composer des élégies fort inutiles pour le soulagement d'un malheureux qui languit, pendant que vous vous divertissez sur le Parnasse pour votre propre réputation."[20] In his subsequent appeals, Pellisson restricted his arguments to an analysis of the legal issues. He was ultimately restored to favor and named royal historiographer.

Talking in the Garden

Modern readers of Sévigné's letters have been struck by the contrast of her enormous verbal output with such a radically restricted frame of reference. Virginia Woolf remarks on the illusion of vastness created by her epistolary conversations, the suggestion of an entire world existing within a confined social milieu: "As the fourteen volumes so spaciously unfold their story of twenty years it seems that this world is large enough to enclose everything . . . the voices mingle; they are all talking together in the garden in 1678. But what was happening outside?[21] In fact, an important purpose of Sévigné's correspondence with her scattered group of friends is to secure the territory of the group, to define what it means to exist in this "garden," a process that involves a careful exclusion of all that is "outside." Particularly in her letters addressed to or concerning exiled friends, it is clear that the act of conversing, in speech or writing, can become a way of giving a kind of imaginative density, a more complex reality to the narrow world they all inhabit.

Bussy-Rabutin and Foucquet were among several of Sévigné's oldest friends to be disgraced or exiled. Retz, Guitaut, and Pomponne all

figure in her correspondence as banished heros, retaining only epistolary ties with the court, which she calls "un bon pays pour oublier les
malheureux." In her letters to Bussy, the "insider" tone of salon gatherings often becomes conspiratorial. She relates conversations in which
individual lives had been rearranged, in which political events had been
talked out of existence:

> J'étais l'autre jour dans un lieu où l'on taillait en plein drap. On
> ouvrait les prisons, on faisait revenir les exilés, on remettait plu-
> sieurs choses à leur places, et on en était plusieurs aussi de celles
> qui y sont. Vous ne fûtes pas oublié dans ce remue-ménage, et l'on
> parla de vous dignement. Voilà tout ce qu'une lettre vous en peut
> apprendre   (II, 645).

This kind of talk is more than playful, as her last sentence suggests.
Social gossip and speculation always hover close to political conspiracy,
at least in the eyes of potential censors and other "outsiders" who might
overhear a conversation or intercept a letter. To a certain extent, Sévigné's ability to absorb the most sweeping political events into her
narrow frame of reference, which only a few readers are expected to
appreciate, is a skill that she develops in response to the threat of censorship. Euphemism, irony, secret codes and elliptical phrases are some
of the rhetorical practices she and her correspondents use to evade the
understanding of an unwanted reader. In the letters to Provence, Madame de Montespan is called Quanto or Quantova: "On dit que l'on
sent la chair fraîche dans le pays de Quanto." In later letters to her
daughter, when hope for a liberal gift from the king is wearing thin,
she barely veils her frustration with irony: "Le roi fait des liberalités
immenses. En vérité, il ne faut point se désespérer: quoiqu'on ne soit
pas son valet de chambre, il peut arriver qu'en faisant sa cour on se
trouvera sous ce qu'il jette"(II, 793–94).

More commonly, though, and in contrast to the letters of her cousin
Bussy, Sévigné's letters to friends unwillingly absent from court have a
consolatory, retrospective tone. These letters seek both to sustain old
contacts and create new connections to compensate for other, broken
ones. The experience of one friend is linked to that of others, and
points out analogous experiences until a kind of improved mirror image
of the court is suggested by this new circle of exiles. After the disgrace
of Pomponne she writes to her daughter: "Je n'oublierai rien pour leur

confirmer la bonne opinion qu'ils ont de l'amitié et de l'estime que j'ai pour eux; elle est augmentée par leurs malheurs; je suis assez persuadée, ma fille, que le nôtre a contribué à leur disgrâce. Jetez les yeux sur tous nos amis, et vous trouverez vos réflexions fort justes" (II, 767).

As in her descriptions of Foucquet, the exiles become heros, and are placed in the company of grand figures from history or legend. When Retz is forced to "retire" in 1675, Madame de Sévigné transforms his voyage to his country estate into a heroic spectacle, while also comparing his exile to Madame de Grignan's recent return to Provence after a visit to the capital. "Notre bon cardinal est dans sa solitude. Son départ m'a donnée de la tristesse et m'a fait souvenir du vôtre" (I,744). Retz's decision to leave Paris becomes a spiritual act of self-abnegation. He receives the acclaim of a saint along the way: "Il a été reçu à Saint-Michel avec des transports de joie; tout le peuple était à genoux . . . ," and in his own messages to her he corroborates this image of ascetic retreat: "Il me mande qu'il se trouve fort bien dans son désert, qu'il le regarde sans effroi et qu'il espère que la grâce de Dieu y soutiendra sa faiblesse" (II, 3).

Conversations surrounding Retz's departure in 1675 collaborate to stage the event as a freely chosen exercise in humility.[22] The frugal measures forced on him by creditors are reported as signs of his new temperance, while he is described as reluctantly retaining a few essential possessions: "Il gardera son équipage de chevaux et de carosses, car il ne peut plus avoir la modestie d'un pénitent à cet égard-là, comme dit la princesse d'Harcourt. Il m'écrit souvent de petits billets, qui me sont bien chers, et me parle toujours de vous. Ecrivez-lui . . ." (II, 6). She also reports some less generous comments on this spectacle, all the while being careful to frame them with her own interpretation. La Rochefoucauld's portrait of Retz is one of these, which Sévigné includes in a letter to her daughter. The portrait claims to penetrate the heroic image that everyone else was applauding: "Il a plus emprunté de ses amis qu'un particulier ne pouvait espérer de leur pouvoir rendre; . . . la retraite qu'il vient de faire est la plus éclatante et la plus fausse action de sa vie; c'est un sacrifice qu'il a fait à son orgueil, sous prétexte de dévotion. Il quitte la cour, où il ne peut s'attacher, et il s'éloigne du monde qui s'éloigne de lui" (I, 737).

Sévigné introduces La Rochefoucauld's version of events by saying that he did not want it to be shown to Retz or others, and she remarks that it serves as a kind of antidote to the excessive praise that has been circulating: "On est si lassé de louanges en face qu'il y a du ragoût à pouvoir être assuré que l'on n'a point songé à faire plaisir, et que voilà ce qu'on dit quand on dit la pure vérité toute nue, toute naïve" (I,737). Yet she herself opts for the more laudatory version of Retz's motives in subsequent letters. It is as though everyone is putting into play a portrait which can then be examined by the others as they in turn offer their own, until eventually the group settles on one they can collectively approve.

La Rochefoucauld's portrait may be "la pure vérité toute nue," but as such it is less valuable as social currency than other versions. His "naked" portrait of Retz has the effect of stripping conversation of its best material. It is not only unflattering to both Retz and his entourage, but it encourages, in this group of Retz's friends, a cynical view of events which is difficult to expand upon or even share. Its author specifies, even, that the portrait is not to be shown either to Retz or to anyone outside the group where it was initially presented. Sévigné offers it to her daughter to contemplate in private, and with that its value is spent.

Three months after Retz's departure Madame de Sévigné left Paris for her country estate in Brittany. The descriptions of her new surroundings echo her evocations of Retz's new solitude. In fact, this voyage and many subsequent ones were, like Retz's trip, occasioned by personal financial problems. Prolonged stays away from the court were frugal measures taken by many members of the nobility who did not have easy access to the royal purse. On her trip to Les Rochers in 1675, Sévigné reminds her daughter that the route she is taking is the same one taken by Retz in 1654, when Renaud de Sévigné had aided his escape from the Nantes prison: "J'arrivai ici à neuf heures du soir, au pied de ce grand château que vous connaissez, au même endroit où se sauva notre Cardinal" (II, 104). Temporarily cut off from her sources of news in Paris, she turns to reconstructing the events of her past and blends these nostalgic reminiscences with reminders of her daughter's former presence: "C'est un de mes tristes amusements de penser à la différence de l'année passée et de celle-ci. Quelle joie de vous rencontrer et de vous parler à toute heure . . . Rien ne m'échappe de ces heureux jours que les jours même qui sont échappés" (II, 158). She occupies herself with reading a history of the heroic Fronde years, in which she and her friends figure: "Je m'amuse les soirs à lire *L'His-toire de la prison et de la liberté de Monsieur le Prince*; on y parle sans cesse de notre Cardinal. Il me semble que je n'ai que dix-huit ans. Je me souviens de tout" (II, 173).

The pastoral environment of Les Rochers seems to foster this more solipsistic vision, and creates a particular kind of frame for her letters written from Brittany.[23] Writing from her provincial estate where she is cut off from conversations with her daughter or others who have entree into her social world, she constructs a different kind of conver-sation, and engages literary as well as real, remembered voices in her epistolary dialogue with Madame de Grignan.[24] The common ground for these conversations includes books they both have read as much as people they both know. Texts and fictional characters become part of a system of references confirming their shared, exclusive culture.[25] In his study of *préciosité*, Roger Lathuillère has remarked that the rarified mi-lieu of the salons made pastoral novels into "a vast manual of savoir-vivre."[26] *L'Astrée* and other similar works generated a multitude of diversions for an indolent nobility, and influenced the literature pro-duced by salon culture.[27]

For Sévigné, too, certain books become guides to living, but more importantly they assume a kind of human reality, and she returns to reading them much as she would return to a conversation. Favorite characters and phrases are focal points to which she often refers to help her orchestrate the description of an experience. Her allusions to *L'As-trée* give fictional roles to the real people in her anecdotes, as when she compares a friend to a particular character from the novel, or when the society at Vichy reminds her of the group of "bergers de L'Astrée et le Lignon."

In her letters to her daughter written from Les Rochers, Sévigné often suggests that the company of books and written dialogue has re-placed other sociable contacts, and in her epistolary conversations fic-tional people and places constitute a common frame of reference. She embellishes descriptions of her woods with literary allusions and real incidents with comparisons to episodes from pastoral romance:

> Pour l'arbre bienheureux qui vous sauva la vie, je serais tentée d'y faire bâtir une chapelle. Il me parait plus grand, plus fier, et plus élevé que les autres; il a raison, puisqu'il vous a sauvée. Du moins

je lui dirai la stance de Médor, dans l'Arioste, quand il souhaite tant de bonheur et tant de paix à cet antre qui lui avait fait tant de plaisir. Pour nos sentences, elles ne sont point défigurées; je les visite souvent. Elles sont même augmentées, et deux arbres voisins disent quelquefois les deux contraires, par exemple: "La lontanza ogni gran piaga salda" et "Piaga d'amor non si sana mai"   (II, 137–38).

Sévigné shared an enthusiasm for Tasso, Guarini, and other Italian poets with many of her contemporaries. Several of the Versailles *fêtes* of the 1660's were organized around ballet spectacles based on episodes from Ariosto and Tasso, and an appreciation of Italian literature and language was an important element of salon culture.[28] What is particularly interesting to see in Sévigné's letters, though, is the extent to which she integrates these favored readings into her manner of communicating with others and describing her world.

In the passage quoted above, "la stance de Médor" alludes to an episode from *Orlando furioso* in the garden of love. In this idyllic setting removed from the ongoing story, the lovers Medoro and Angelica write amorous inscriptions on the trees; Madame de Sévigné and her daughter had imitated this fictional incident by carving Italian phrases into the trees at Les Rochers. In her letter, Sévigné reminds her daughter of these inscriptions and reports that they have delighted her friends: "Il y a cinq ou six citations dans cette contrariété. La bonne princesse était ravie . . ." But the contradictory inscriptions also echo a dialogue between the two women who had carved them, by articulating a difference between mother and daughter that Madame de Sévigné will anxiously reiterate in a letter written a few days later: "Je ne sais pourquoi vous dites que l'absence dérange toutes les amitiés: Je trouve qu'elle ne fait point d'autre mal que de faire souffrir. J'ignore entièrement les délices de l'inconstance . . ." (II, 149).

By using fictive voices to communicate her own sentiments, Sévigné calls upon a literary frame to make a private anxiety into a more playful spectacle, and one which is less threatening once it is neatly situated as part of the decor of her garden. The opposing maxims are placed side by side within a peaceful, circumscribed world. The literary voices, familiar to all who read the inscriptions, both authenticate and diminish the intensity of the private story behind them.

Sévigné uses the Italian language in her letters much as she uses references to her favorite fictional characters—as a sign of complicity with her correspondent, and as a way of deflecting the personal force of emotions. In Sévigné's letters, Italian quotes proliferate at moments when she seems to feel most cut off from her milieu, when she is alone, or feels alone, and wants to reconnect with a person or people from whom she feels separated. Italian phrases and references to works in Italian are the most frequent in the letters immediately following Sévigné's separations from her daughter.[29] During her first visit to Les Rochers without her daughter, in 1671, reading Tasso becomes a form of social interaction: "Nous lisons fort ici. La Mousse m'a priée qu'il pût lire Le Tasse avec moi. Je le sais fort bien parce que je l'ai très bien appris; cela me divertit" (I, 276). But solitary reading of letters or of favorite books is preferable to most company: "Nous sommes dans une parfaite solitude et je m'en trouve bien . . . je crains le bruit qu'on va faire en ce pays. On dit que Madame de Chaulnes arrive aujourd'hui. Je l'irai voir demain . . . Mais j'aimerais bien mieux être dans la *Capucine*, ou à lire Le Tasse . . ." (I, 229). Receiving her daughter's letters in the outdoor pavillion she calls "La Capucine," or taking Tasso's epic into her wooded garden, she ritualizes her reading activity and stages it against a sentimental background of secret hiding places and nostalgic promenades.

During a visit to Les Rochers in 1675 Sévigné is again attracted to the same readings, and especially to Tasso and Ariosto. The intransigence of her assimilation of episodes from *Gerusalemme liberata* and *Orlando furioso* to her own experience is revealed in the incongruity of many of the literary associations she makes during this period. Reading the history of the crusades makes her want to reread Tasso's epic; her daughter's aggressive confidence in the arrangement of a business affair is compared to Rinaldo's courage in traversing the illusory perils of an enchanted wood (II, 37; II, 104). In rereading the description of Clorinda's death, she remarks that the return to a familiar text such as this in no way reduces its interest for her, although it seems that her daughter does not share her enthusiasm: "Nous relûmes la mort de Clorinde. Ma bonne, ne dites point: *je le sais par coeur*, relisez-la et voyez comme tout ce combat et ce baptême est conduit; finissez à "Ahi vista! ahi conoscenza . . ."" (II, 166). A walk in the woods reminds her of a woodland scene in *Orlando furioso*, and even her daughter's letters at their best are compared to Ariosto's epic:

> Ne vous retenez point quand votre plum veut parler de Provence;
> ce sont mes affaires. Mais ne la retenez sur rien, car elle est admi-
> rable quand elle a la bride sur le cou. Elle est comme l'Arioste: on
> aime ce qui finit et ce qui commence; le sujet que vous prenez
> console de celui que vous quittez, et tout est agréable   (II, 194).

In her later letters, Sévigné's framing of personal experiences with
references to Tasso and Ariosto has a kind of obstinacy, and conveys
her nostalgia for a cultural milieu that no longer exists as it was. Her
taste for the Italian epics continues despite their greatly diminished
stature in the eyes of Boileau and other official critics.[30] In one letter
she quotes Boileau's unfavorable characterization of Tasso while maintaining her own liking for him: "Je crois, ma fille, que je serais fort de
votre avis sur le poème épique: le *clinquant* du Tasse m'a charmée" (II,
499). Many of the most frequently cited episodes from Tasso and Ariosto in her letters are precisely those which were most vigorously dis-
credited by the classical academicians. Clorinda and Bradamante
fascinated Madame de Sévigné, while theoreticians such as Le Moyne,
Mambrun and Rapin sharply criticized these female warrior figures.
Ariosto and Tasso's use of the fantastic in their epics was judged excessive by the academicians, while Madame de Sévigné continues to construct many of her private fantasies and pastoral games around
allusions to the enchanted forests, mythical creatures, and palaces of
illusion found in *Orlando furioso*, *Gerusalemme liberata*, and *L'Aminta*.[31]

As her correspondence evolves, Madame de Sévigné reveals a growing awareness that this literary role-playing is part of her nostalgic attachment to a past time. In a letter written from Livry in 1679 she
assimilates remembrances of Madame de Grignan, her rereadings of
familiar books, and her penchant for thinking of the past:

> Je m'en vais être avec moi et avec votre cher et douleureux souvenir
> . . . Je relis toutes vos lettres . . . Je lis mes anciens livres; je ne sais
> rien de nouveau qui me tente: un peu de Tasse, un peu des *Essais de
> Morale* . . . Je travaille à finir cette chaise qui est commencée en
> l'année 1674. Je pense continuellement à vous . . . Je vous écris; je
> relis vos lettres . . . je retourne sur le passé; je regrette les antipa-
> thies et les morts"   (II, 689–92).

There is a sense, too, that she can no longer count on the collabo-
rative sympathy of a group to sustain the same fictional constructs that

for her have been so important to sociable interaction. With the worsening of her family's financial situation and the decreasing likelihood of the Grignan's recall to Paris, Madame de Sévigné's nostalgia for a lost, better time becomes more somber. One period of financial crisis, in the spring of 1680, follows upon three unhappy events—the deaths of Retz, La Rochefoucauld, and Foucquet. Retz's sudden demise exacerbates Madame de Grignan's problems, as she had hoped for an inheritance from him. Further complicating matters is Charles de Sévigné's reckless spending, which forced him in June to sell the trees from an old family property. His mother describes a visit to this country estate near Nantes in a letter to Madame de Grignan, comparing the Buron wood to an enchanted forest from Tasso's epic:

> Je fus hier au Buron; j'en revins le soir. Je pensai pleurer en voyant la dégradation de cette terre. Il y avait les plus vieux bois du monde; mon fils, dans son dernier voyage, lui a donné les derniers coups de cognée. Il a encore voulu vendre un petit bouquet qui faisait une assez grande beauté; tout cela est pitoyable. Il en a rapporté quatre cents pistoles, dont il n'eut pas un sou un mois après. Il est impossible de comprendre ce qu'il fait ni ce que son voyage de Bretagne lui a coûté, où il était comme un gueux car il avait renvoyé ses laquais et son cocher à Paris; il n'y avait que le seul Larmechin dans cette ville, où il fut deux mois. Il trouve invention de dépenser sans paraître, de perdre sans jouer et de payer sans s'aquitter. Toujours un soif et un abîme de je ne sais pas quoi, car il n'a aucune fantaisie, mais sa main est un creuset qui fond l'argent. Ma bonne, il faut que vous essuyiez tout ceci. Toutes ces dryades affligées que je vis hier, tous ces vieux sylvains qui ne savent plus où se retirer, tous ces anciens bois, ces chouettes qui, dans cette obscurité, annonçaient par leurs funestes cris les malheurs de tous les hommes, tout cela me fit hier des plaintes qui me touchèrent sensiblement le coeur. Et que sait-on même si plusieurs de ces vieux chênes n'ont point parlé, comme celui où était Clorinde? Ce lieu était un *luogo d'incanto*, s'il en fut jamais. J'en revins donc toute triste; le souper que me donna le premier président et sa femme ne fut point capable de me réjouir   (II, 949).

Charles's thirst for money and the impending financial collapse of the Grignan family were familiar scenarios to many nobles at the end of the century, who, like Madame de Sévigné, were watching their fortunes disappear. The destruction of the Buron wood, forced by what Sévigné sees as baffling, modern circumstances, defaces the landscape of a more ancient, aristocratic enclave. With one violent act a forest, which for her was an enchanted resource for the play of conversations, is transformed into hard currency. And the apparent worthlessness of the money acquired by Charles de Sévigné in this transaction is a mystery his mother cannot fathom. Like the outmoded text informing her imaginative perception of the Buron wood, the place itself is devalued by modern times.

The Conduct of Intimacy

Sévigné's readers have always thought that her letters to her daughter were in a class apart from the rest of her correspondence. In the letters to Madame de Grignan the voice of Sévigné "la femme spirituelle" takes on new aspects. Madame de Grignan's departure seems to mark a split in her mother's correspondence, a change in style that reflects the personal crisis that this separation brought about. Madame de Grignan's departure for Provence effectively exiled her from the privileged society into which her mother had so carefully introduced her. Her husband's royal appointment as governor of Provence was a position that they were to spend the rest of their lives seeking to be relieved of. They were never to be compensated for the huge expenditures required by the post of provincial governor, expenses that were only occasionally offset by "gifts" from the king.

Madame de Sévigné assumed the responsibility of representing the Grignan family at Versailles and in the Paris salons, and her letters were highly prized for the news they brought of both places. Printed news journals were only beginning to be extensively distributed in 1671, the year that Madame de Grignan first left Paris. Sévigné found herself competing with other sources to keep her daughter well informed and to give her own letters value in the eyes of their reader. To her own descriptions she frequently adds a popular gazette describing the same event: "Voilà, ma chère bonne, de quoi subsister longtemps dan les conversations publiques. Vous aurez outre cela la feuille de l'abbé Bigorre" (II, 467).

In the early years of her correspondence with her daughter, Sévigné sees the worth of her letters increasing in proportion to her proximity to these "insider" conversations. As in her other correspondence, news is the element that gives her letters to Provence their social currency. She warns her daughter when she is about to leave Paris: "Tout le fagotage de bagatelles que je vous mandais va être réduit à rien, et si vous m'aimez, vous feriez fort bien de ne pas ouvrir mes lettres . . . Hélas, que vous vais-je dire du milieu de mes bois?" (I,256) She will discover that, through letters, she can not only retain her proximity to the news and gossip of Paris, but she can also construct a new social world invoking voices from her past and from her books to share with her correspondent.

But in her more sentimental letters to her daughter she discovers new motives for verbal communication. Madame de Grignan becomes the central event in these texts, a figure around which all other experience seems to crystallize: ". . . vous m'êtes toutes choses, et tout tourne autour de vous, sans vous approcher, ni sans me distraire" (I,613). Communication with her daughter becomes predicated on Sévigné's isolation from other social contacts. The prerequisite for meaningful conversation in her other letters—the fact that she is well-connected with a larger circle of speakers—is reversed. Instead, she now tries to establish that she is not "distracted" by others, that her whole social world is occupied by one other person only. In the more sentimental letters to Madame de Grignan, Sévigné develops a new set of private rituals to set up the space of their exchange and define its terms. These rituals, far from being aimed at assuring her reader of her well-placed position in other conversations, instead assure her that she is safely removed from that world; she has sacrificed it to the superior pleasure of her daughter's company: "Je suis aujourd'hui toute seule sans ma chambre, par l'excès de ma mauvaise humeur. Je suis lasse de tout; je me suis fait un plaisir de dîner ici, et je m'en fais un de vous écrire hors de propos . . ." (I, 173).

The pleasures of intimacy that Sévigné discovers in her correspondence with her daughter are all the more appealing to her as she becomes disenchanted with her conversations with less worthy listeners. As her family's links to courtly society weaken, Sévigné becomes more involved in the routines organizing her epistolary contacts, more attracted to a life ordered around the regular arrivals of a courier. As she shifts her verbal energy to the correspondence with her daughter, she finds that the arrival of a letter from Grignan can transform solitude into a world of sympathetic voices:

J'aime passionnément vos lettres d'Avignon, ma chère bonne. Je les lis et les relis. Elles réjouissent mon imagination et le silence de nos

> bois. Il me semble que j'y suis; je prends part à votre triomphe, je cause, j'entretiens votre compagnie, que je trouve d'un mérite et d'une noblesse que j'honore; . . .   (III,620).

Interaction with her daughter can be a means of escaping everything else; Madame de Grignan's letters enable her mother to put herself in her place, imagine herself totally in her daughter's world. This of course means that many of the conventional rituals of sociable conversation do not apply, and in fact they interfere with the kind of communication Sévigné wishes to have with her daughter. The golden rule of conversation as stated by Scudéry, La Rochefoucauld, and so many others—that every utterance must be a response, proof of the speaker's perfect awareness of the other—is reversed in Madame de Sévigné's instructions to her daughter: "Ne vous amusez point, ma chère bonne, à répondre à mes vieilles lettres; on ne s'en souvient plus. Parlez-moi de vous sans fin et sans cesse, et de tout ce qui est à Grignan . . ." (III,621).

She wants to draw everything from her daughter's letters, and she wants her daughter to write back to her as though she were writing to herself, unrestricted by the need to adjust her voice to the voice of another. In one sense, this correspondence seems to mimic conversational interaction even more closely than her other letters. She requires an even stricter tit-for-tat pattern of exchange in order to be able to continue their correspondence—if she does not receive an anticipated letter she has difficulty composing her own.[32] But at the same time the artificial nature of this requirement is highlighted, because in the *content* of her daughter's replies she demands no comparable attention to her own messages; in fact, she is often put off by her daughter's responses to her "old" news.

But in the letters to Grignan the process of communication poses larger problems, problems that are not resolved by Sévigné's inventions of new rituals for intimate interaction. From the first sentence she writes after Madame de Grignan's departure in 1671, she expresses an anxiety about the inadequacy of language to communicate her passion: "Ma douleur serait bien médiocre si je pouvais vous la dépeindre; je ne l'entreprendrai pas aussi" (I, 149).[33] In her love letters to her daughter, she experiences the unfamiliar feeling of being at a loss for words. Those that come to her pen, she says, don't seem to adequately communicate her feelings. But at the same time, she wants her voice in her letters to Grignan to have a special weight, a privately understood meaning that she also will be able to attribute to her daughter's replies: "Si mes paroles ont la même puissance que les vôtres, il ne faut pas vous en dire davantage; je suis assurée que mes vérités ont fait en vous leur effet ordinaire" (I,155).

In a sequence of letters to Madame de Grignan written in 1680, the two worlds of sociability and intimacy are presented in dramatic contrast. Writing from Rennes near the end of a meeting of the provincial estates, Sévigné complains of the endless feasting and talking. The economy of this festive occasion has demanded that both food and talk be liberally spent and consumed, but for her, the whole process has been dissipating instead of nourishing:

> Je souhaite avec une grande passion d'être hors d'ici, où l'on m'honore trop; je suis extrêmement affamée de jeûne et de silence. Je n'ai pas beaucoup d'esprit, mais il me semble que je dépense ici ce que j'en ai en pièces de quatre sols, que je jette et je dissipe en sottises, et cela ne laisse pas de me ruiner . . . ce sont des festins continuels. Ah, mon Dieu! quand pourrai-je mourrir de faim et me taire?   (II, 1040–41).

Like the unaccountable financial practices of her son Charles, polite talk is here seen as a kind of crazy economy of words. Her conversation, like her family fortune, used to have a value that was appreciated, but now she feels that both are consumed and unreciprocated. These conversations are not a free circulation of words, but a wasteful dissipation of them which can only be controlled by a retreat to a more stable system of exchange. A week later she writes from Les Rochers, "C'est à cette heure, ma fille, que je suis dans le repos de mes bois et dans cette abstinence et ce silence que j'ai tant souhaités . . ." (II, 1046).

The idea that polite society has come to demand unrewarded expenditures from its members is a strong preoccupation in the letters to her daughter. Even in her earliest letters, we find that she has created a new, private world for this part of her correspondence, situated within but apart from her old circle, which has now become the "public." What she withholds from one world she gives to the other: ". . . ce que j'épargne sur le public, il me semble que je vous le redonne . . ." (II, 314). Within this new space she sees words operating differently, and not always adequately: "Je ne sais que vous dire de mon amitié, les paroles me manquent, je les trouve trop petites" (III, 373). But the expression of love becomes for her an endless project, never fully accomplished, and forever repeated: "Nous épuisons tous les mots . . . voilà toutes les paroles employées . . . je suis à vous en un mot comme en mille . . ." (III, 1013; III, 1004). Underlying all of her efforts, and functioning as a kind of guarantor of their worth, is a mutual promise of sincerity, a word that has a special force in the letters to Grignan.

The few surviving pieces of Madame de Grignan's side of the correspondence are mostly in letters written by her mother, where she quotes and highlights her daughter's words in her own response to them. One of these letters is particularly remarkable, revealing the subtle and inextricable intertwining of sentiment and the words used to express it.

> Vous les recevez donc toujours, ma bonne . . . Ce sont vos *chères bonnes*, elles sont *nécessaires à votre repos*. Il ne tient qu'à vous de *croire que cet attachement est une dépravation*; cependant vous vous tenez *dans la possession de m'aimer de tout votre coeur, et bien plus que votre prochain, que vous n'aimez que comme vous-même. Voilà bien de quoi!* Voilà, ma chère bonne, ce que vous me dites. Si vous pensez que ces paroles passent superficiellement dans mon coeur, vous vous trompez. Je les sens vivement. Elles s'y établissent. Je me les dis et les redis, et même je prends plaisir à vous les redire, comme pour renouveler vos voeux et vos engagements. Les personnes sincères comme vous donnent un grand poids à leur paroles. Je vis donc heureuse et contente sur la foi des vôtres"   (III, 868).

Of course, the special "weight" of her daughter's words is more than enhanced by her mother's repetition of them; it is through an almost incantatory process that she comes to experience a faith in Madame de Grignan's declarations. Belief in the sincerity of each other's words requires work on the part of both speakers. Even in Sévigné's statement of faith in language the skills of sociability have not been entirely abandoned. It is only by appropriating the other's words into her own discourse that she is able to give them the force she wants them to have. It is only by examining, repeating, and revising the "paroles sincères" of her interlocutor that she is able to establish the truth of what she had observed in one of her first letters to Madame de Grignan in 1671: "Vos paroles ne servent tout au plus qu'à vous expliquer, et, dans cette noble simplicité, elles ont une force à quoi l'on ne peut résister. Voilà, ma bonne, comme vos lettres m'ont paru" (I,155).

Confidence in the truth of appearances is difficult for a writer whose verbal skills were learned in salon conversations where, as Scudéry's speakers decided, extreme sincerity has no place: "Mais si l'on portait la sincérité si loin, . . . il faudrait renoncer à la société . . ."[34] Madame de Sévigné's discovery of a new form of interaction, a new way of looking at words, was precipitated by a break with the world of sociable interaction. This break was surely not as total as some have suggested,[35] but the separation from her daughter was a personal shock that gave Madame de Sévigné new reasons to compose her written conversations; it placed demands on her verbal skills that she had not encountered before. This break was aggravated by the fall from royal favor that her daughter's move to a remote province suggested. The political misfortune of many of her aristocratic friends and her own dwindling family money served to further remove her, psychologically and physically, from the circle of insiders into which she had been so well integrated. The art of Madame de Sévigné's letters to her daughter derives directly from her own complex and unique experience, but that experience is also emblematic of the decline of aristocratic sociability as the dominant mode of interaction in seventeenth-century worldly society. Intimate conversation, based on the principle of private exchange, would come to be regarded as infinitely more satisfying than sociable conversation, based on the principle of pure reciprocity. In the next chapter we will look at how innovative forms of writing that prompted a new rhetoric of intimacy came to prove their worth in the changing literary marketplace.

NOTES

1. *Entretiens de morale* (Paris: Jean Anisson, 1693), p.208.
2. For a good summary of the financial crisis of the last years of Louis XIV's reign, see "The Price of War," in G. R. R. Treasure, *Seventeenth-Century France* (New York: Barnes and Noble, 1966), pp. 431–42.
3. *Conversations nouvelles sur divers sujets* (Paris: Barbin, 1684), II, p. 532.
4. Scudéry describes Sévigné in her portrait of *la princesse Clarinte* in *Clélie*, and Somaize's portrait is in the *Dictionnaire des précieuses*. Both are cited, with Lafayette's portrait, in the appendix to Sévigné's *Lettres*, ed. Monmerqué (Paris: Hachette, 1866).
5. "Si l'on a de l'esprit, et particulièrement de cette sorte d'esprit, qui est

enjoué, on n'a qu'à la voir, on ne perd rien avec elle: elle vous entend, elle entre juste en tout ce qui vous dites, elle vous devine, et vous mène d'ordinaire bien plus loin que vous ne pensez aller . . ." *Histoire amoureuse des Gaules* (Paris: Garnier Flammarion, 1967), p.144.

6. Her letters of advice to her daughter on the education of her young granddaughter also stress that conversation is the best form of education: "La vraie morale de son âge, c'est celle qu'on apprend dans les bonnes conversations, dans les fables, dans les histoires, par les exemples; je crois que c'est assez. Si vous lui donnez un peu de votre temps à causer avec elle, c'est assurément ce qui serait le plus utile." *Correspondance*, ed. Roger Duchêne (Paris: Gallimard, 1972–78), III, p. 810. All my citations from the correspondence are from this edition, and will be indicated in the text.

7. The most recent example is in Cynthia Ozick's novel *The Cannibal Galaxy*, in which a schoolteacher is obsessed with the resemblance of the mother of one of his students to Madame de Sévigné.

8. Jean Cordelier, *Madame de Sévigné* (Paris: Seuil, 1967), p.6.

9. See Roger Duchêne, "Réalité vécue et réussite littéraire," *RHLF* 71 (1971), pp. 177–94; Bernard Bray, "L'Epistolier et son public en France au 17e siècle," *Travaux de linguistique et de littérature* II (1973), pp. 7–17; Bernard Beugnot, "Madame de Sévigné tel qu'en elle-même enfin?", *French Forum* 5 (1980), pp. 207–17; and Louise Horowitz, "The Correspondence of Madame de Sévigné: Letters or Belles-Lettres?", *French Forum* 6 (1981), pp. 13–27.

10. See her letters to Ménage and Pomponne in 1661 (I, 49–50).

11. A letter from Chapelain to Sévigné indicates that he thought she might lean either way. He reassures her that he is talking to everyone "pour imprimer fortement l'opinion de votre pûreté," and launches into a diatribe against Foucquet's crimes as well as his reckless habit of saving letters from women, "afin que le naufrage de sa fortune emportât avec lui leur réputation" (I, 48–49).

12. *Gossip* (New York: Knopf, 1985), pp. 5–6.

13. Olivier d'Ormesson, one of the judges at the Foucquet trial, was an old acquaintance of Sévigné. His *Journal*, which is an important source of information on the case, includes many references to her and to his conversations with her during the course of the trial. Duchêne's edition of Sévigné's correspondence includes liberal quotes from d'Ormesson's account, which, compared to Sévigné's, provides much more detail on the actual arguments presented, and less on the nuances of the behavior of Foucquet and his observers.

14. "On a continué la pension des gabelles, où il a parfaitement bien répondu (I, 58)"; "Foucquet a été interrogé ce matin sur le marc d'or; il y a très bien répondu (I, 59)"; "M. Foucquet s'est fort bien tiré d'affaire (I, 63)"; "On l'a écouté; il a dit des merveilles (I, 65)"; "Il a fort bien répondu sur tout les chefs (I,66)" etc.

15. For example, in the first two letters:
"M. Foucquet a répondu que souvent on faisait des choses par autorité, que quelquefois on ne trouvait pas justes quand on y avait fait réflexion. Monsieur le Chancelier a interrompu: 'Comment! vous dites donc que le Roi abuse de sa puissance?' M. Foucquet a répondu: 'C'est vous qui le dites, Monsieur, et non pas moi'" (I, 59). "Foucquet a été interrogé ce matin sur le marc d'or; il

y a très bien répondu. Plusieurs juges l'ont salué. Monsieur le Chancelier en a fait reproche, et dit que ce n'était point la coutume . . ." (I,59).

16. For a discussion of how Sévigné's aristocratic bias against the *noblesse de robe* is revealed in her attitude toward Séguier see Marie-Odile Sweetser, "Madame de Sévigné et Saint-Simon, artistes et aristocrates: deux procès sous l'ancien régime," *Cahiers Saint-Simon* 9 (1981), pp. 35–47.

17. ". . . ce sont des pensées qui me sont venues dans le fort du déséspoir où me jetait quelquefois Monsieur le Cardinal . . ." (I,69).

18. When she reports that d'Ormesson is no longer giving her accounts of the trial, she quickly adds that they remain in contact: "Il affecte une grande réserve; il ne parle point, mais il écoute, et j'ai eu le plaisir, en lui disant adieu, de lui dire tout ce que je pense" (I,70). D'Ormesson indicates in his journal that others thought he was allowing himself to be influenced in favor of Foucquet by Sévigné and her circle: ". . . Charles avait dit que Madame de Sévigné me gouvernait en faveur de M. Foucquet contre le sentiment de mon père, et des sottises de cette force; et l'on m'avait averti du côté de la cour."Cited in Sévigné, *Correspondance*, I, p. 888.

19. "Je causai hier de toute cette affaire avec Madame du Plessis; je ne puis voir ne souffrir que les gens avec qui j'en puis parler et qui sont dans les mêmes sentiments que moi. Elle espère comme je fais, sans en savoir la raison" (I, 71).

20. *Avis sur les principaux points contenus dans les libelles pour la justification de M. Foucquet*, cited in U. V. Chatelain, *Le Surintendant Nicolas Foucquet* (Paris: Didier, 1905), p. 510.

21. "Madame de Sévigné," in *Death of the Moth* (New York: Harcourt Brace Jovanovich, 1942), p. 57.

22. There is, of course, a long literary tradition for this flattering image of an aristocrat fallen from grace. In the figures of Bussy, Retz, and Pomponne we see the "sublimation of worldly failure into a triumph of the spirit," Poggioli's definition of a courtly pastoral which flatters the disgraced patron. See "The Oaten Flute," *Harvard Library Bulletin* (1957), p. 168. In Sévigné's letters this convention is part of a common code delineating her community and later, in the letters to her daughter, facilitating the communication of intimacy.

23. "Vous êtes trop bonne de me souhaiter du monde, il ne m'en faut point, ma bonne: me voilà accoutumée à la solitude . . . C'est ce bois qui fait mes délices; il est d'une beauté surprenante . . . Je suis assez souvent dans mon cabinet, en si bonne compagnie que je dis en moi-même: 'Ce petit endroit serait digne de ma fille; elle ne mettrait pas la main sur un livre qu'elle n'en fût contente'" (II, 973).

24. Seventeenth-century aristocrats frequently invoked bucolic enclaves as ideal spaces for exclusive sociability. Mademoiselle de Montpensier's fanciful correspondence with Mademoiselle de Motteville includes lengthy descriptions of an imagined country retreat where a small circle of intimates could voluntarily ("sans être rebutées") escape from the court for the primary purpose of conversing. La Fontaine situates his dialogue "Les Amours de Psyché" in a garden where "natural" and unconstrained conversation can occur. We have seen that Scudéry's conversations often begin with a voyage of the group to a country estate or garden. See Phillipe Amiguet, *La Grande Mademoiselle . . .* (Paris: Albin Michel, 1957), p.420; and La Fontaine *Oeuvres diverses* (Paris: Gallimard, 1958), pp. 127–28.

25. In an article on the role of novels in Sévigné's culture, Duchêne discusses the playful, impersonal aspects of her frequent comparisons of real events to scenes from novels. References to episodes from *Le Grand Cyrus* or *L'Astrée* function among her friends as code words signaling the speaker's inclusion in a specific social circle. See "Signification du Romanesque chez les mondains: L'Exemple de Madame de Sévigné," *RHLF* 77 (1977), pp. 578–94.

26. Roger Lathuillère, *La Préciosité* (Genève: Droz, 1966), p.339. He examines in particular the profound influence of *L'Astrée* in the seventeenth century, pp.324–55.

27. Jacques Ehrmann's book on *L'Astrée* also focuses on its reception and shows how the characters themselves model a certain way of reading:

Les Bergers de ce monde pastorale dédaignent "la vie" dans sa grossièreté quotidienne, sa platitude. Ils ont pour rôle de dégager la vie de sa réalité, de lui donner les dimensions d'un rêve. En arrachant la vie à sa réalité ils veulent en faire un spectacle, retrouvant ainsi les aspirations de la société aristocratique qui cherchait à dresser la vie aux dimensions d'une mise-en-scène *(Un Paradis désespéré: L'Amour et l'illusion dans l'Astrée* (Paris: P.U.F., 1963), p.11.

28. Italianism in seventeenth-century French courtly culture has been studied in a collectioin of essays, *L'Italianisme en France au 17e siècle* (Torino: Società Editrice Internazionale, 1968), which includes a study of Sévigné's letters, "L'Italianisme dans les lettres de Madame de Sévigné," by Henri Baudin. See also Alexandre Ciorenscu, *L'Arioste en France* (Paris: Ed. des Presses Modernes, 1939), and Clara Friedmann, "La cultura italiana di Madame de Sévigné," *Giornale storico della letteratura italiana* 60 (1912), pp.1–72.

29. This has been demonstrated by Baudin, p.117.

30. See Friedmann, p. 115; and Ciorenscu, p. 55.

31. Ciorenscu remarks on Sévigné's continued adherance to a waning literary sensibility, calling her "une des dernières précieuses, qui vit au milieu d'un monde dans lequel elle aime se ménager des illusions et où elle voudrait parfois faire revivre les fictions de son poète favori" (p.55).

32. For more detailed discussions of the reciprocal structures Sévigné demands of this correspondence see Bernard Bray, "L'Epistolière au Miroir: Réciprocité, réponse, et rivalité dans les lettres de Madame de Sévigné à sa fille," *Marseille* 95 (1973), pp. 22–29, and Elizabeth C. Goldsmith, "Giving Weight to Words: Madame de Sévigné's Letters to her Daughter," *New York Literary Forum* 12–13 (1984), pp. 107–15.

33. Two recent studies have paid particular attention to the ways in which the letters to Grignan work out a discourse of maternal passion, an original mother's voice for which Sévigné would not have found literary models. Solange Guénoun writes that the letters to Grignan are increasingly marked by a "dialectique du brouillage," or merging of the two voices of *mondaine* and *mère passionnée*. Harriet Allentuch notes that in her letters Sévigné "achieves something altogether more impassioned than what we read in other correspondences of her day . . ." See Allentuch, "My Daughter/Myself: Emotional Roots of Madame de Sévigné's Art," *Modern Language Quarterly* 43 (1982), p.123; and Guénoun, "Correspondance et paradoxe," *Papers on French Seventeenth-Century Literature* VIII, no. 15–2 (1981), pp. 132–52.

34. *Conversations sur divers sujets* (Paris: Louis Billaine, 1680), p.369.

35. Bernard Rafalli, for example, in his introduction to an edition of the letters, talks about Sévigné's two different languages: "Son vrai langage, Madame de Sévigné ne se trouve guère que dans les lettres à sa fille à partir d'une idée de séparation qui joue chaque fois pour elle le rôle de la tasse de thé ou du fameux pavé disjoint de Proust: l'épreuve d'une distanciation et la découverte d'une conscience." Madame de Sévigné, *Lettres* (Paris: Garnier Flammarion, 1976), p. 28.

<< **5** >>

Teaching Sociability Through Literature:
The Works of Edme Boursault

In 1651, a boy of thirteen arrived in Paris from his native vil-
lage in Champagne with no financial or educational resources, but apparently with a strong will to make a place for himself in Parisian
society. Ten years later, Edme Boursault was a popular visitor to the
most exclusive salons in the Marais, was personal secretary to the
Duchess of Angoulême and had become a much admired writer of letters, gossipy anecdotes, and occasional poetry. Encouraged by his literary patron and friend Pierre Corneille, he began writing for the
theatre, and by 1675 was one of the most successful playwrights in
Paris. When he died in 1701, his plays were known throughout Eu-
rope. His popularity continued through the eighteenth century, when
Montesquieu wrote enthusiastically of Boursault's moralizing play
about courtliness: "Je me souviens que, sortant d'une pièce intitulée
Esope à la cour, j'en sortis si pénétré du désir d'être plus honnête homme,
que je ne sache jamais avoir formé une résolution plus forte . . ."[1]

Today Boursault's experimental novels continue to receive critical attention, while literary historians tend to express a certain surprise at his spectacular rise in popularity as a dramatist among his contemporaries. But this soldier's son from the provinces was entertaining the Parisian elite with his writing even before the production of his first play. He had begun his career as a writer by acting as secretary to a personnage with close ties to the royal family,[2] and his epistolary anecdotes were widely circulated. For a brief period he was commissioned by the king to produce a weekly newsletter to amuse the court with the latest gossip, and throughout his career he was to maintain his reputation as an "informed source" with close ties to the most exclusive social circles. Indeed, it is impossible to separate Boursault's literary success from his social one; his career as a writer is closely intertwined with his strategy of personal promotion at court and in the Paris salons.

Boursault's fascination with the tactics of sociable interaction is evident both in his private life and in his writing. Arriving in Paris, he seems to have followed Faret's first rule for the newcomer, to seek out friends who will be useful to you.[3] His eagerness to rise in the world of literary and personal fashion on more than one occasion got him involved on the wrong side of artistic quarrels. He is remembered today for his play *Le Portrait du peintre* attacking *L'Ecole des femmes*, which inspired Molière's devastating counter-critique. But by the end of his career Boursault had become one of the few writers of his period who was able to actually earn a living from his writing. Thus he has the unusual distinction of having successfully established himself as a writer using the traditional resources of artistic patronage, and later becoming one of the first professional writers to successfully sell his work in a new literary marketplace. Between 1683 and 1694 Boursault made more money from his plays than any other playwright before him. His comment on his success in a letter he writes to his wife suggests its novelty: "Qui serait assuré de faire deux pièces par an avec le même succès, n'aurait guère besoin d'autre emploi."[4] His most successful works, and those that retain the most interest for today's reader, are the ones dealing most explicitly with the art and politics of social interaction, with the drama of social mobility and bourgeois ambition, and with the spectacle of individual attempts to adapt prevailing codes of social conduct to the realization of private dreams.

Modern Image-Making: "Le Mercure galant"

Boursault's output as a writer is remarkably diverse; he seems to have tried his hand at every form that was in his day considered a vehicle for the writer's display of his art. His published work includes plays, letters, novels, epistolary manuals, poems, essays, a treatise for the instruction of the dauphin, and a serial news gazette. Yet linking this apparently disparate assortment of literary ventures that spanned some fifty years is a lively interest in the workings of cultural fashion, and in the shifting currents of popular taste. In Boursault's time artistic production was of course heavily influenced if not dictated by the court, with the king playing the role of chief patron and censor. But even though royal authorities exerted ultimate control over the publishing world through an increasingly strict system of *privilèges*, the demands of a reading public growing both in size and sophistication were making it impossible for literary fashion to revolve exclusively around courtly culture. Control over the book trade was tightened under Colbert, who issued a series of decrees designed to reduce the number of printers and booksellers. At the same time, during the second half of the century French books acquired an international market.[5]

Probably the most important innovation in the world of cultural production was the newspaper, or more properly, in its emergent seventeenth-century form, the *gazette*. The invention of this new method of information dissemination was to have an enormous impact on the extent to which people thought they could control their public image.[6] The concept of reputation, so crucial to the courtly definition of the *honnête homme*, and even more the *honnête femme*, would be irrevocably altered by the printed newsletter. Initially, the *gazette* seemed to be simply a written form of gossip, an invention that made it easier for more people to have access to what Faret had said were "(les) choses qui ne se peuvent apprendre que sur les lieux."[7] A seventeenth-century reporter was essentially someone who had access to gossip and, more importantly, had control over its transmission to others.

Boursault was one of these, and although his official appointment as court gazzetier was short lived, apparently due to some printed indiscretions for which he was responsible, his fascination with the medium persisted.[8] In 1679 he wrote a play called *Le Mercure galant*, based on the operations of Donneau de Visé's popular prose gazette. The central character is a young nobleman Oronte, who poses as his cousin, the editor of *Le Mercure galant*. The play stages his reactions to this new experience through a series of conversations with characters asking him, in one way or another, to tell their stories in his newspaper.

While the idea of basing a play on the process of publicity-making was completely original, in other respects the work closely resembles Molière's *Les Fâcheux*. A comparison of the two plays brings out some interesting features that show how they are satirical portraits of some of the obstacles to communication in both "cour" and "ville" society.[9] Molière's play, commissioned in 1661 for the amusement of Foucquet's guests at his famous three-day festivity at Vaux, is a *comédie-ballet* in which the central character, Eraste, finds himself beseiged by a parade of annoying narcissists who insist on addressing him at length as he impatiently tries to arrange a solitary tête-à-tête with his Orphise. These "fâcheux" all display a stubborn capacity for monologue and are utterly without the requisite trait for good conversation, the ability to listen. As a courtier with a certain degree of status, Eraste is in a position analogous to that of the king, who must suffer the perpetual clamor of underlings seeking his audience, and whose own words are often of interest only to the extent that they grant status to the listener:

> Ciel! faut-il que le rang, dont on veut tout couvrir,
> De cent sots tous les jours nous oblige à souffrir,
> Et nous fasse abaisser jusques aux complaisances,
> D'applaudir bien souvent à leurs impertinences!
> (*Les Fâcheux* I,iii)

Boursault's play, while clearly patterned after Molière's, has a much more pronounced satirical tone. Oronte, like Eraste, must suffer (in silence) while visitors incessantly arrive to demand favors of him. But much more than Eraste, Oronte does engage in conversation with his visitors, and what he reacts against is not their annoying monologues, but their appalling dialogues. The setting is the busy office of a professional writer, not the idyllic landscape of a palace garden, and Oronte's interlocutors do not simply neglect the rules of civility, they turn them upside-down. The situation at the outset suggests a kind of preposterous inversion of standard hierarchical values (as well as standard comic scenarios). The young nobleman poses as a professional editor in order to marry Cécile, whose father is determined to marry her to the author of *Le Mercure galant:* "le fils d'un duc et pair ne lui plairait pas tant."[10] He is chided by Cécile's maid for not disguising himself carefully enough:

> Cette grande perruque et ce linge et ce point
> Avec le nom d'auteur ne sympathisent point.
> J'en vois par-ci, par là; mais ils ont tous l'air mince:
> Et sous cet équipage on vous croirait un prince.
> Par là votre dessein peut être divulgué   (p. 161).

Oronte is progressively more and more amazed by the power that his visitors perceive him to have, and by the cynical manner in which he is asked to exercise it. These *fous,* as he repeatedly calls them,[11] see the power of the press as almost magical, and he is the maker of "ce beau livre/ qui n'est pas plutôt vieux qu'il redevient nouveau" (p. 162). He is asked to perform this sorcerer's trick on the record of their lives. Monsieur Michaut, grandson of an apothecary, wants a noble title: "Tout vous devient possible étant ce que vous êtes./ Vos Mercures sont pleins de nobles que vous faites . . ." (p. 152). And an embezzling tax collector, aptly named Monsieur Longuemain, asks the editor to announce his return of half the money he had stolen, and to twist the story in such a way that he will be rewarded instead of punished for his crime:

> Les fermiers généraux, voyant ma bonne foi,
> Me pourront confier quelque meilleur emploi.
> C'est ce qu'avec grand art, comme par bonté pure,
> Il faut insinuer dans le premier Mercure   (p. 165).

Throughout this dialogue Longuemain insists that he is concerned with restoring his honor; he begins his story with the assertion, "Je crois en vous, monsieur, trouver un honnête homme," and he repeatedly reminds Oronte that his motive is to be like him: "Pour vivre en honnête homme il faut avoir du bien . . ." (p. 163). By the end of the scene the words *honneur, honnête,* and *honnête homme* have been so abused by Longuemain that they can only sound incongruous in Oronte's refusal to accept a bribe: "Vour oubliez, je crois, que je suis honnête homme?" (p. 165).

In fact, forgetting that aspect of Oronte's identity seems to be precisely what Longuemain and the other *fous* have done, with a certain amount of assistance from Oronte himself, disguised as a writer interested in earning his living. And without the cloak of *honnêteté* securely fastened about him, Oronte experiences a broader range of worldly power than the courtier Eraste ever could. Both characters are asked by others to mediate contacts with the king, but in Oronte's case, the ridiculous Du Mesnil wants the king to read about him in the *Mercure*, while Eraste has to agree simply to pass on a letter written by a petitioner. As an author, Oronte is able to do more than transmit the words of others. He will write them himself, and they will be reproduced and read by a multiplicity of readers, the king being only one of them.

Thus Boursault's play gives a twist to its precursor produced eighteen years earlier, not only by refocusing the ridicule on inept middle-class imitations of courtly conduct, but by centering his circle of characters around a professional writer and the new publicity medium he controls. It is interesting that the play never stages a conventional unmasking of the disguised central character, an omission that certainly must have surprised seventeenth-century theater audiences. We never see the real editor, so that the authority invested in this figure by the other characters is never even remotely legitimized, and the power of the author remains a comic imposture to the end.[12]

Spacks has described how modern-day journalistic gossip "both imitates and debases social functions of oral gossip."[13] Boursault's play on the seventeenth-century news gazette focuses on precisely this effect of what was then a new cultural artifact. The *Mercure galant* markets reputations, imitating the power of conversation to create or destroy individual status. But journalistic gossip is both more powerful and less credible than the insider conversations it tries to reproduce. Although it reaches many people, its audience is too diverse, and its processes too subject to corruption. The authenticity of the information communicated in this kind of gossip is much more likely to be questioned. Readers may be willing to pay good money to read the personal details of the lives of public figures, but they do not accept the authority of a publisher of newsletters. The true identities of everyone involved in this interaction—the publisher, the people written to and written about—are thought to be hidden somewhere behind their social masks, and the discourse people use to create their social selves is suspect.

"*Esope à la ville*", "*Esope à la cour*"

Boursault's reputation as a writer who was exceptionally good at discerning fashionable trends and exploiting them in his own works is born out in three plays he wrote in the last ten years of his life. Two of these, *Esope à la ville* and *Esope à la cour*, were inspired by his admiration for La Fontaine's fables. Like *Le Mercure galant*, their central character is a writer whom other characters cajole, flatter, and attack because of his power and influence. In *Esope à la ville* the writer is also an infatuated bourgeois father's choice as husband for his daughter. Like Tartuffe, Esope is a moral paragon to the father figure, but unlike Molière's character, he is authentic. In successive dialogues with characters who approach him, usually for advice, he produces a fable for them to apply to their situation. In the end he wisely withdraws his claim to the young daughter of Léarque, acknowledging the virtues of her preferred suitor and his own offensive ugliness.

This didactic drama was extremely popular in its time, and drew more spectators in the *parterre* than any other seventeenth-century play. Shortly before he died, Boursault wrote a sequel to it, (published posthumously in 1701) and that took a more daring critical look at the moral emptiness of court society. Although the text of the play was published intact, it was censored for the stage, and Boursault was said to have been required to remove certain passages that reflected badly on Louis XIV.[14] *Esope à la cour* is set at the court of king Crésus, who has elevated his protégé Esope to the post of Minister of State, and who devotedly follows his advice on all matters. Esope is charged with reforming the abuses of the court, beginning with the personal flaws in the character of the king.

This king is clearly not the idealized, artificial figure usually represented in late seventeenth-century literature. He is unhappy with his relationship to his court, and with the image others have of him and its effects on the way his subjects communicate with him: ". . . le trône enfin l'emporte sur le roi . . ." (p.78). Esope's special privilege derives from his sincerity, as one courtier tells him: "Le plaisir le plus grand que vous me puissiez faire,/ C'est de m'ouvrir votre âme et de ne me rien taire" (p.111). He is a new kind of solitary, superior courtier, who understands the workings of courtly life better than any of the other actors in it, and who is valued for his uniqueness, his sincerity, his

wisdom, and his artful way of communicating it. For he does acknowledge that there is an art to being sincere, particularly when talking with
kings:

> C'est un sentier étroit qui de chaque côté
> Présente un précipice à la sincérité.
> Les rois et les flatteurs étant de même date
> Il n'est dans l'univers aucun roi qu'on ne flatte,
> Et qui dans leurs plaisirs a l'honneur d'avoir part,
> S'il reprend leurs défauts le doit faire avec art   (p. 101).

In a way, this sounds very much like Castiglione's courtier, for
whom the transcendent purpose of civility was to instruct the prince.[15]
The king asks Esope to instruct him, to make him "digne enfin d'être
ce que je suis." Esope's art, though, is not motivated by the "principle
of courtship," as Burke has termed the force behind the perfect courtier's rhetoric.[16] Far from having as his prime concern the fostering of
social cohesion, Esope argues that people must never be insincere just
to avoid unpleasantness. He has none of the traits of the sociable courtier—he is aloof, ugly and immune to embarassment, and is a former
slave whose total lack of ambition is what dignifies his new stature as
solitary truth-teller. The dramatic climax of the play comes when his
enemies—two more conventional courtiers—having convinced the
king that Esope has been secretly amassing wealth, break open a chest
whose contents he had refused to reveal, only to find that it contains
his slave's tunic.

The moralizing Esope seems to be Boursault's image of the writer
in society, who has the capacity to have tremendous influence on standards of social behavior.[17] Like the publisher in *Le Mercure galant*,
Esope has all the traditional privileges of a favored courtier but none of
the traditional qualifications. When Montesquieu observes that *Esope à
la cour* inspired him to be a better *honnête homme*, we know that the
meaning of the term has changed. Boursault's ideal courtier valorizes a
kind of interaction that Faret's *honnête homme* would have thought risky
at best, and societally destructive at worst. He observes without participating, has no fear of offending anyone, and speaks to people of all
stations. He is valuable to others because he can expose the hypocrisies
of conventional sociability codes.

Boursault's Epistolary Experiments

Le Mercure galant dramatized a new form of social publicity, and the *Esope* plays critiqued traditional courtliness, but Boursault's most innovative literary works were his epistolary narratives. Having earned his living in part as a private secretary to wealthy patrons, he decided to compile his own collection of model letters, and in 1669 published *Lettres de respect, d'obligation, et d'amour*. The book included a sequence of messages ostensibly exchanged between the writer and a young woman which, with a few additional letters interspersed reiterating the lovers' story, made up a sustained epistolary tale.

Boursault's publisher Claude Barbin, who in the same year published *Lettres portugaises*, must have recognized the special marketability of Boursault's model love letters, for in subsequent editions of the manual he agreed to publish the "Lettres de Babet" apart from the rest, and after 1709 they were published as a separate work.[18] Thus Boursault became, with the anonymous author of *Lettres portugaises*, the author of one of the first epistolary novels.[19] Yet his letter narrative, which was to be widely imitated and modified into a more complex fictional genre during the eighteenth century, has strong ties to the manual form in which he had first published it. Boursault always had a strong commitment to the didactic functions of his writing. His *Lettres de Babet* was conceived as an illustration of certain modes of behavior and styles of interaction, and the problems of teaching and learning sociability are central to the organization of his tale.

Lettres de Babet tells the story of a merchant's daughter and her literarily inclined lover: it details their first encounter, their flirtation and courtship, and finally the rupture of their relationship by Babet's father, who tries to force her to marry a wealthy provincial landowner. Unlike *Lettres portugaises*, Boursault's story is rich in details of daily social encounters. While the heroine in *Lettres portugaises* is cut off from her worldly existence and writing from the void left by her lover's departure, Babet leads a full social life, and her letters are dotted with anecdotes recounting her exchanges with members of her social circle. Literary historians have traditionally viewed these two novels as prototypes of two forms of the epistolary novel as it was to develop in the eighteenth century: the univocal series of letters by a single author, and the more complex polyphonic narrative made up of messages by two or more correspondents.[20] *Lettres de Babet* and *Lettres portugaises* also mark a turning point in fictional representations of love relationships.[21]

But if we consider these two pivotal works in relation to the genre of the letter manual out of which they grew, they may be seen as parallel experiments in the representation of codified interaction. Mariane's story in *Lettres portugaises* begins with conventional seclusion, and Babet's ends with it, but each narrative deals with the consequences of failed communicative pacts. Both stories play out certain interactive problems addressed in seventeenth-century conduct literature.[22] Boursault's story in particular seems to explore the codes of acceptable interaction as they are observed, challenged, modified, and rejected by Babet in her dialogues with her often mystified suitor.

Babet's Metaphors of Exchange

Two recent commentaries on the place of Boursault's novel in literary history make strikingly different observations on the novel's principal character. Jean-Michel Pelous notes that Babet was one of the first fictional heroines to illustrate the new idealization of innocent love, a figure that contrasted with the accomplished "mondaine" who treats sentiment as a game and derives pleasure from mastering its rules. He argues that *Lettres portugaises* and *Lettres de Babet* both illustrate the increasing "uncertainties of gallant ideology" by presenting readers with female characters whose principal virtues are spontaneity, authenticity, naïveté, and simplicity. Babet is, moreover, a middle-class heroine who was nonetheless much admired by her aristocratic readers: "Les aventures d'une petite bourgeoise parisienne font les délices d'une grande dame; c'est le nouveau privilège de la naïveté" (p. 294).

In his essay on Boursault and the letter novel tradition, Arnaldo Pizzorusso sees in Babet no such departure from the conventional image of sophisticated desirability. For him she is, in fact, a "coquette précieuse" who delights in toying with her lover, "qui n'accorde à son amant aucune faveur inconciliable avec la décence."[23] He observes that the lovers conduct themselves in the traditional manner of *précieux* courtship, engaging in playful discussions of the impossibility of constancy, the "war" between the sexes, the impropriety of jealousy, and the failure of others to properly play the game of sociability. The story itself Pizzorusso places squarely in a comic tradition: a lively and cultivated daughter refuses to marry the rich provincial boor chosen for her, her lover and her sympathetic brother conspire to help persuade her father to go along with her choice. The stubborn father refuses and the story ends, predictably, with an explosive confrontation that Pizzorusso terms "une scène de comédie, presque de roman comique" (p.532). He dismisses Babet's confinement to a convent as an "epilogue," and fails to mention at all her subsequent death, of which the author informs us in his preface, and which, as we shall see, is crucial to his decision to publish Babet's letters in the first place.

These conflicting readings of Babet in fact apply to different moments in Babet's discourse. She tries on a number of social roles and in her letters to her lover explores different modes of interaction and self-representation. The role of *coquette* is indeed one of these, and it dominates the beginning of her correspondence. But the patterns of the beginning of their correspondence start to break down, and Babet tries a more direct approach to communication. The playful, balanced exchanges of the early letters give way to a rhetoric of personal revelation.

*   *   *

Babet's first letter is a reprimand. Her correspondent had for three days failed to keep his promise to visit her. His reply, that he has been avoiding her for fear of being "conquered" by the sight of her, sets off a series of conventional gallant preliminaries: she delights in her power and challenges him to battle (letter 3), he declares himself her prisoner and begs for small mercies from his captor (letter 4), she recognizes that he is an "honnête homme" and asserts her own virtue as an "honnête fille" (letter 5). Having thus established the terms of their relationship, they agree to meet at a performance of one of his plays, and in the next letter her suitor makes a "serious" declaration, announces he is breaking with her rival, and asks that Babet "repay" him with a similar gesture:

> Vours savez, Babet, que l'amour n'est jamais dignement payé, à moins qu'il ne soit payé par l'amour même; je ne demande pas que vous en ayez autant que moi, puisque je n'ai pas le pouvoir d'en faire naître comme vous; mais vous m'en donnez tant, que quand je vous en rendrai un peu, je ne laisserai pas d'en avoir encore assez. Examinez un peu votre coeur, avant que de vous emparer du mien:

demandez-lui s'il est d'humeur à prendre par reconnaissance de ce
que je prends de vous par inclination   (pp. 118–19).

Thus Babet's lover proposes the sort of reciprocal commitment typically found in the baroque novel, using the playful gallant vocabulary
that Madeleine de Scudéry had made famous in her *Carte du Tendre*.
But in her reply, Babet assumes a new tone which seems to reject the
carefully balanced relationship that the two of them had been setting
up: "Si jusqu'ici je n'ai répondu qu'en jouant aux grâces que vous me
faisiez, c'est que j'ai cru que ce n'était qu'un jeu. Je vous ai rendu des
civilités, parce que je vous en dois; je vous ai estimé parce que vous le
méritez; . . ." (p. 120). For her part, she refuses to bargain and at the
end of the letter declares herself openly: "je crois m'être assez expli-
quée, pour ne pas avoir besoin de vous dire que je serai ravie que vous
soyez à moi toute votre vie, comme je veux être toute la mienne, à
vous" (p. 120).

While Babet's declaration marks a break in the rhetorical pattern of
the letter dialogue, it also precipitates a shift in the temporal structure.
For although none of the letters is dated, we have a sense that a larger
amount of time has passed between these two letters than between any
of the first nine. Letter 10 begins with a plea to Babet to return to Paris
from Bagnolet, her family's country retreat, and to secretly meet
"comme dernièrement," (p. 122), although this is the first mention of
any secret meetings. Thereafter the balanced pattern of exchange that
was established in the beginning is abandoned completely. With the
exception of the initiatory letter, all of Babet's messages up to letter 15
are labeled "réponses," and they fulfill the requirements of the "lettre
de réponse" as defined by epistolary manuals. They are letters whose
primary function is reactive; the writer of a "lettre de réponse" orga-
nizes the message in reply to specific matters raised in an earlier letter
from the addressee.[24] Thus Boursault's headings on the first 15 letters
emphasize the balanced quality of the correspondence up to this point:
"à Babet, réponse de Babet, à Babet, réponse de Babet," etc. Moreover,
almost all of Babet's letters labeled *réponse* are in the first part of the
correspondence.[25]

Both Babet and her lover continue to invoke the conventional tropes
of gallantry throughout their correspondence, but Babet's letters increasingly stretch and twist some of the metaphorical claims made in

her lover's discourse. He writes that he is sure to recognize her at a masked ball, for "la grâce qui vous est si naturelle, et que personne n'a que vous, ne manquera pas de me sauter d'abord aux yeux" (p.126). In her response she gleefully reveals that she had attended the ball and, unrecognized, had observed him all evening. She had been disguised as Scaramouche: "Quoique je fusse fort près de vous, je cachai si bien la grâce qui m'est si naturelle, et que personne n'a que moi; que vous ne me reconnûtes pas" (p.127).

Unlike Babet, her lover is quite comfortable with the confusion of fiction and reality, and the elaborate artifices that the discourse of gallantry regularly impose on conversation. He views his own roles of artist and lover as not simply compatible, but mutually sustaining. He is reluctant to share his most recent play with her until their relationship is more advanced, not out of modesty, but because he is sure that the "scenes" the two of them will create together will provide him with better material for his writing:

> laisse-moi m'accoutumer au plaisir qu'il y a d'aimer une fille si aimable, afin que je puisse ressentir ce qu'il est nécessaire que j'exprime . . . faisons des scènes si passionnées, qu'il n'y ait qu'à les coudre à mon ouvrage pour ne plus avoir lieu de douter de son succès. Je t'aime pour le moins aussi tendrement que le duc de Guise aimait la princesse de Montpensier; aime-moi aussi fortement que la princesse de Montpensier aimait le duc de Guise . . .   (p.123).

Babet's lover invites her to join the company of other illustrious couples, both fictional and real, and to learn how to communicate intimacy by imitating the best models.

Babet, meanwhile, is developing a different notion of how to express her sentiments. She is willing to compare herself to the figures of fiction only to point out the incongruity of such parallels. This kind of imitation, for her, would be inauthentic, even though she is troubled by the idea that she really should be able to sound more like an illustrious model of gallant behavior. When her lover invites her to attend the new production of Corneille's *Attila* she refuses, saying that she would only be made to feel to what extent her own behavior is unlike that of the princess in the play: "Loin de prendre du plaisir à voir la scène dont tu fais tant de cas, la princesse qui ne se peut résoudre à dire *j'aime* me reprocherait que je te l'ai dit trop tôt . . ." (p.145). Instead, she proposes that they rendez-vous at a gambling party, where she is about to indulge in her favorite pastime. To watching actors "jouer de sérieux," she says she prefers taking real risks, "jouer à la bête."

Babet is lucky at this game. She seems to have a knack for it shared by none of her friends, least of all her lover who always loses money. Her luck at gambling is most dramatically illustrated at a gathering she describes in letter 33, just before we are to learn of her father's marriage plans for her. Babet excitedly recounts her success amidst the losses suffered by everyone else: ". . . j'ai gagné deux cent je ne sais combien de livres, qui sont à ton très humble service, mon cher. Si jamais nous ne sommes mariés ensemble, quand tu iras jouer d'un côté, j'irai vitement jouer de l'autre, afin de regagner ce que tu perdras . . . Il n'y a que moi qui ai été heureuse, et j'espère l'être bien davantage, quand malgré toute la terre il me sera permis de dire que je suis . . . A toi" (p.149).

Babet's stories about salon gambling are interesting as an illustration of the popularity of this pastime in the social circles of the Marais. But gambling is also a rich metaphor for the dynamic of sociability, and gambling scenes are often crucial representations of power relationships in seventeenth-century literature.[26] Unlike Madeleine de Scudéry's idealized gamblers,[27] Babet is interested in real risk-taking. She does not hesitate to express her pleasure at winning money. In fact, she has a very bourgeois facility for obtaining it, a talent not shared by her artistic suitor. But winning at gambling does require taking risks against heavy odds, as her description of herself as the only lucky winner in letter 33 emphasizes. Planning to marry her lover is a similarly uncertain proposition that seems realizable only "malgré toute la terre," and even their regular communications are potentially dangerous exchanges, particularly for Babet. In her letters, spending and acquiring money becomes a metaphor for her efforts to plan out her relationship with her lover in her own way, which usually involves going against the prevailing codes of behavior prescribed for her by others.

In the beginning of their letter dialogue, the lovers use the metaphor of money exchange to establish the equality of their relationship. In a style typical of gallant discourse they offer favors and demand others in return. As we have seen, Babet is more hesitant than her lover to found their relationship on the principle of reciprocal payment, but she enters into the game adding a proviso that her favors will be freely given, not committed in advance in exchange for his. In his first letter to her, Babet's suitor had asked that she return a medallion called a "joie," a coin that he had left with her, and the question of how this coin will be returned to him becomes the playful subject of their first messages. Babet holds it as an enticement for him to visit but will not promise that she will return it: ". . . je vous déclare dès à présent que vous n'aurez point la joie que vous dites avoir laissé chez nous, à moins que vous ne la veniez quérir vous-même; et quand même vous y viendriez, il n'est pas sûr que vous la remportiez toute, si je n'ai la bonté de vous la rendre généreusement . . ." (p.113). And when her correspondent tells her he has so much love that he wants to give some to her in order to be loved in return, she puts an end to their bartering:

> Je vous défends de me rendre de l'amour que je vous ai donné . . . J'aime mieux que vous gardiez pour vous le présent que vous me promettez, que de me le faire. Quand vous aurez autant d'amour que je vous en souhaite, je vous en déroberai si j'en ai besoin. Bonjour. Brûlez ma lettre quand vous l'aurez lue, et ne manquez pas de me venir voir après dîner . . .   (p.120).

Thus in her own declaration of love Babet shifts from the playful rhetoric of *précieux* conversation to a new posture of openness and honesty, in which she criticizes coquettish behavior and unmasks her own earlier responses:

> La colère qui font éclater la plupart de celles à qui l'on apprend ce que vous m'apprenez, est ridicule ou feinte. Qui nous aime nous honore . . . toutes les fois que vous m'avez pressée de vous dire si je voulais vous aimer, quoique jamais je ne vous aie répondu "oui," si je n'avais pas eu envie de le faire, il m'eût été aisé de vous répondre "non"   (p.120).

Concommittant with her first departure from the "game," as she puts it, is her request to "burn this letter," a demand whose nonfulfillment ultimately makes possible the publication of their story.

Just as she insists on taking her own idiosyncratic approach to expressing her feelings, Babet takes an unconventional approach to the process of spending money. She becomes increasingly aware of the var-

ious ways that money controls her life, a fact most dramatically illustrated by her father's refusal to allow her to marry her impoverished
suitor. Babet's luck and fascination with gambling seem to hold out the
hope, however remote, of a sudden reversal of fortune for the couple.
The letters reporting on gatherings with friends to "jouer à la bête" are
all in the middle phase of the correspondence, after the two have begun
meeting secretly but before she is betrothed to another. Once the lovers
are confronted with this most imposing obstacle (first revealed in letter
38), Babet seems to lose interest in gambling, and she turns to some
less playful uses of money to regain the upper hand in the conflict with
her father.

In the last ten letters of the story Babet, consulting with her lover,
embarks on two real business propositions that she has arranged in an
effort to reestablish control over her resources. The first of these is
recorded in letters 41–42. Babet's miserly uncle has just died and she,
irritated at having to waste time away from her friends pretending to
grieve, decides to buy a piece of furniture from his estate, a "lit de
garçon," for her suitor. She takes evident pleasure in getting the best
price for it, as well as in stealing smaller items without being noticed.
Her correspondent playfully encourages her to make a profit from the
exchange, rather than sell him the bed at exactly the price she paid for
it: "Il n'est pas juste que tu avances ton argent pour rien. Cela serait
bien, vraiment, que le premier marché que tu aies peut-être fait de ta
vie ne te profitât de quoi que ce soit, et qu'un lit, qui est de tous les
meubles celui sur quoi tu peux gagner le plus, ne te rapportât pas l'in-
terêt de ton argent . . ." (p.159). Indeed Babet's way of doing business
turns out to be too unguarded for her own good. While she may have
learned to take what she wants and disguise her pilfering from others,
when she has to openly enter into market exchanges she leaves herself
vulnerable. At the end of the story, forced by her father to face the
unwanted suitor who demands her final consent to marry him, she
decides to write him a letter proposing a financial statement. This message she sends via her lover, whom she asks also to dissuade Launay
from his project at all costs: "Si tu ne gagnes rien par la douceur, me-
nace; il n'importe de quelle façon tu m'arraches à lui, pour être . . . à
toi" (p.168).

Babet anticipates the miserly Launay's resentment over having
spent money to no avail in courting her, and offers to pay him off:

> Comme il n'est pas juste que vous ayez fait l'amour à vos dépens,
> et que j'aie eue l'honneur de vous voir sans qu'il m'en coûte quel-
> quechose, il ne tiendra qu'à vous que nous ne nous accomodions
> par moitié touchant les frais de vos voyages: vous paierez ceux que
> vous avez faits à venir, parce que je ne vous ai pas mandé; et je
> paierai ceux que vous ferez à vous en retourner, parce que je vous
> en prie   (p. 170).

In making him this offer and openly telling him she cannot love him,
she says that she is exhibiting a sincerity for which he should be grateful: "Vous devez m'être obligé de ma sincerité, comme je vous le suis
de votre amour, et me savoir autant de gré de la dépense que je vous
sauve, que je vous en sais de celle que vous avez faite" (p.170).

But this bold attempt to take direct control of her own affairs is a
dramatic failure, and in the final letter we learn of the disastrous consequences of the lovers' last gamble to save the situation by revealing
their true intentions. Babet, who of the two had the most to lose, had
expressed confidence in this final tactic, but in his last letter her correspondent is uncertain and fearful, predicting the end of their liaison.
Her final attempt to resolve the situation by openly buying her own
way out of it outrages both her father and her proposed spouse, and
even her lover is appalled by her daring intervention. "Je ménagerai si
bien les choses," she writes him, "que je ne ferai rien contre ce que je
lui dois, ni contre ce que je t'ai promis" (p.167). But in his last letter
he has already given up, and he reminds her of her true powerlessness.

> Ton père a sur toi tout le pouvoir qu'il y veut prendre, et jusqu'ici,
> si j'ose dire, ton obéissance a prévenu ses commandements:
> Quoique l'époux qu'il te veut donner soit indigne d'un bonheur si
> grand, sa prévention lui fait trouver des raisons dans ce qu'il fait,
> qu'à peine oseras-tu combattre; et quand tu les combattrais, il n'est
> pas sûr que tu en triomphes   (p. 169).

And the story ends very abruptly indeed, with Babet announcing
her exile to a convent and ending the final letter with a sworn promise
to spend her life there. As we have learned from the preface, her final
words "je n'en sortirai de ma vie que pour être à toi" (p.171), predict
her death. Babet's story is the tale of a failed gallantry, which from her
point of view is also a failure to take control of a process of exchange.
After successfully managing the terms of interaction in her letter dialogues, she suddenly finds that she herself is the object being marketed.

There are many lessons that can be drawn from this sequence of letters originally published in Boursault's manual. The two lovers' debates over what kind of form to give their expressions of sentiment offer a catalogue of conversational styles to their readers. Babet's deviation from the conventional norms is clearly being promoted here; it charms her correspondent, and the editor's preface further praises her sincere, natural style. But her direct approach to verbal as well as monetary interaction puts her in a dangerous, "winner-take-all" position. By choosing to abandon coquetry and respond honestly to her lover's letters, she increases the danger to herself of her letters being read by anyone else. She throws away the rhetorical masks that could protect her, as the précieuse Célimène does in the famous scene in *Le Misanthrope*. *Lettres de Babet* already incorporates two important "lessons" that subsequent epistolary novels were to develop; namely, that the purest form of communication is sincere, unguarded expression, and that this kind of interaction is incompatible with sociability. It can only survive in private.

Boursault's preface to *Lettres de Babet* tells another story—the story of its publication—while proposing a reading of the narrative as well as a justification of the editor's purpose in printing it. Anticipating that the reader may be dubious about the authenticity of Babet's letters, he points out the difference in style between Babet's messages and his own, noting that such "esprit" in the writing of a woman is exceptional, but certainly not impossible:

> quoique dans le sexe dont elle était on rencontre infiniment de l'esprit, on y trouve toutefois si peu de plumes qui aient la même délicatesse, que quand un siècle en produit une ou deux, on crie miracle; et comme on n'est pas obligé d'avoir de la foi pour tous les miracles qui arrivent, je laisse la liberté à tous ceux qui ne voudront pas me croire, de croire tout ce qu'il leur plaira   (p. 107).

The assurance of a letter collection's authenticity will become, in the eighteenth century, part of a formulaic argument in epistolary novel prefaces. The other part of the formula is the author's justification of his motive in publishing the letters, which in Boursault's preface is by far the most important question. If he is willing to drop the issue of authenticity with the comment that his readers can "believe what they will," he is more defensive when it comes to his own honor. There are those who will disapprove of his decision to "expose to public censure letters that were meant for myself alone" (p.108). What justifies him, he says, is the fact that Babet is dead: "Loin de m'imaginer faire le moindre tort à une personne que j'ai aussi honnêtement que passionnément aimée, j'ai cru qu'elle morte, il était de mon devoir de faire mes efforts pour tâcher d'en faire vivre ce que c'eût été dommage de laisser mourir . . ." (p.108). And it is this fact, too, that should shield her from any condemnation of her conduct: "Si je croyais qu'il y eût des âmes assez basses pour oser attaquer la conduite d'une fille qui n'est plus, je ferais l'éloge de celle dont je parle . . ." (p.108).

While Boursault takes such care to explain his honorable motives for publishing his lover's letters, he nonetheless writes in the same preface that he regrets being unable to publish all of them because he has been handing them out to other people, and they are no longer in his possession. "(Je) les ai prêtées," he writes, "à tant de personnes, et ces personnes-là les ont prêtées à tant d'autres, que si je recouvrais ce qu'elles en ont égaré . . . il y aurait de quoi faire un second volume" (p.108). This distinction between commercial publication and a more selective public reading of private letters seems unconvincing today, but Boursault's contemporaries might have found it plausible. Nonetheless, it is a distinction based on social arrangements that were breaking down. It assumes the existence of a safely closed circle of readers who share the same culture and who are clearly separated from the large anonymous public. An expanding and increasingly voracious reading public was helping to weaken these old barriers. Women writers, in particular, were recognizing that the increasing reader interest in love letters by women was creating a market demand that posed a serious threat to a system of private circulation over which they had some control.[28] The purest form of sincere expression was thought to be an authentic love letter, and authentic love letters were precisely the sort of writing that was most dangerous for a woman to circulate.

"Treize lettres": A Manual of Female Passion

In 1697 Boursault produced another epistolary narrative, and again he introduced it as part of a letter collection. Like his first collection, *Lettres nouvelles* includes a sequence of letters that tell a sentimental story. But both the book as a whole and the epistolary tale it contains are organized differently from the ones he had published nearly thirty years earlier. Like many of the letter collections being produced at the end of the century, *Lettres nouvelles* does not propose categories of letters according to subject or occasion, but simply presents the texts as examples of a single author's writing.[29] The "treize lettres amoureuses d'une dame à un cavalier" that form the epistolary love story are appended to the rest of the collection, not integrated with the others as Babet's initially had been.[30]

In his initial preface, which is in the form of a letter to the lady who had sent him the packet of letters, Boursault goes to some trouble to convince his reader of their authenticity while protecting the author's anonymity. We learn that his addressee had said they were written by yet another anonymous lady, whom she characterized simply as "une des plus belles personnes du monde . . ." (p.331). Boursault says he is glad to publish what she gives him, and reminds her that she has promised more. Sure enough, the second edition of *Lettres nouvelles* contained six more letters, and in his preface he announces further installments of a correspondence that totals over three hundred letters. As editor of the letters, he writes that he is simply acting as the middle-man, but he entices the reader by hinting that it may be possible to identify the anonymous author even though she takes pains to conceal her identity. His source, he suggests, seems to understand the publisher's law of supply and demand:

> Je ne sais si c'est pour les faire trouver meilleures qu'on en donne si peu à la fois; ou si l'on craint qu'en allant un peu plus loin, les intrigues ne conduisent insensiblement à la vérité . . . quelque prières que j'ai faites, il m'a été impossible d'en obtenir plus de six; qui a ce que je crois, feront assez de plaisir pour causer ensuite du chagrin de ce qu'il n'y en aura pas davantage   (pp.331–32).

The letters begin with the suggestion that they are picking up where conversation left off. "Je ne croyais pas qu'on pût rien ajouter à ce que votre honnêteté vous fit dire hier à mon sujet. Cependant je viens de recevoir une grande lettre, où il n'y a pas un mot de la conversation que nous eûmes" (p.333). This juxtaposition of conversation and letter-writing is repeated often in the thirteen letters, and always to suggest that the letters are going further, that they are the more sincere expressions of both writers' sentiments. Conversation is associated with the value of *honnêteté*, which, from the outset, the writer says is simply an obstacle to sincere expression, a technique of disguise and manipulation.

In her second letter the writer is already critiquing her lover's controlled gallantry: "La lettre que vous m'avez ce matin écrite, me paraît plus honnête que sincère" (p.337). In this context, *honnêteté* has come to signify superficiality, a characteristic of interaction that hides the true self. Her lover defends himself against her jealousy by saying that the attentions he paid to another woman were mere *honnêtetés*, a claim that becomes an occasion for his correspondent to expound on the opposition between *honnêteté* and *sincérité*, *esprit* and *coeur*: "Est-il vrai que toutes les honnêtetés que vous eûtes hier pour Mlle de . . . n'ayent été que des honnêtetés, et le coeur n'y eut-il point autant de part que l'esprit?" (p.381). When it comes to a love relationship, *honnêteté* seems to mean nothing more than "keeping up appearances." She observes that she no longer can abide by this principle in her letters, even though she may continue to observe it in person. Tempted to confront him in person rather than wait for his letter, she had been restrained by the thought of his disapproval: "la peur de perdre votre estime, m'a obligé à en prendre un peu de soin; et j'ai crû que pour toucher un honnête homme, il ne fallait point cesser de paraître honnête femme" (p.381). But since she has confessed that she loves him in her letters, this pretense has been dropped: "Je ne vous écrivais que pour vous faire paraître mon esprit; et je ne vous écris que pour vous dire ce que sent mon coeur" (pp.381–82).

Boursault makes one editorial note after the ninth letter, to alert his readers to the change in style in the messages written after the lovers have consummated their liaison, and to remind us of the planned publication of more of both types of letters: The last three letters, he writes,

> ne sont pas du même style des précédents, quoiqu'elles soient de la même personne. Les premières sont tendres et amoureuses, mais pures: et les trois suivantes sont pleins d'emportements, qui font

bien connaître le même amour, mais non pas la même vertu. Aussi
y a-t-il cent quatre-vingt-quinze lettres entre les unes et les autres;
et quand l'amour s'en mêle, en peu de temps il arrive bien des
choses"   (pp.423–24).

But his fictional female writer herself does considerable editorializing.
At every stage, she seems to step back from the act of writing to char-
acterize her own text in relation to norms of acceptable behavior and
conventional opinions on the conduct of love. The reader thus has a
very strong impression of being instructed, and that this is also a con-
scious exercise in a new style of lovers' discourse. And although we
never see the letters of the "chevalier," his mistress repeatedly compares
her own to his, usually finding his less satisfying.

She initially tries to explain why this is so by speculating on sexual
difference: ". . . je ne vous vois ni ma prévoyance, ni mes craintes: est-
ce que parce que mon sexe est plus faible que le vôtre; ou ne serait-ce
point parce que le vôtre est moins sensible que le mien?" (p.358–59).
When she finally admits her feelings in letter 5, she immediately asserts
that her lover cannot possibly reciprocate with the same intensity. "Je
vous aime au-delà de tout ce que vous pouvez vous imaginer, quelque
étendue que votre imagination puisse avoir, et je souhaite que vous ayez
autant de plaisir à l'apprendre que j'en ai à vous le dire . . ." (p.364). In
letter 7 she again classifies her own letters as characteristic of a type:

> Vous avez bien raison de ne pas avoir pris garde à tout ce que je
> vous ai mandé la nuit passée. Eh! qu'est-ce qu'une femme qui aime
> avec transport, et qui est jaloux avec excès, n'est point capable de
> dire? Ce sont deux passions trop violentes pour se plaindre avec
> modération; et plus elles sont impétueuses, plus elles vous doivent
> sembler excusables . . . Il y a de l'excès dans ce que je sens pour
> vous; eh! le moyen d'aller plus loin que l'excès!   (pp. 380–82).

Her behavior is in keeping with the role she has taken on, she is "une
femme qui aime avec transport . . . ," who claims that her feelings,
expessed in a more controlled fashion, would be inexcusable. In the
end the chevalier, threatened by his mother with being disinherited
because of his liaison, leaves on a voyage to England. In the thirteenth
letter we again read that his messages fall short of her expectation, and
that her own style of expression is superior: ". . . tes paroles me pa-
raissent trop bien arrangées pour être sincères. Mon amour s'exprime

plus naturellement que le tien: par tout où il paraît, le désordre qui l'accompagne est une preuve qu'il est véritable . . . " (p.439) As for the representation of her own passion, this can only be done if her lover recognizes that it exceeds his wildest conception: "Dis-toi, je te prie, toi-même, tout ce que mon amour imagine; et à quelque excès que tu le puisses faire aller, rends-moi assez de justice pour croire qu'il va encore plus loin" (p.440).

Thus the last of these letters ends with the writer seeming to have discovered the key components of an authentic love letter. She has taught herself what these elements are and her letters teach Boursault's readers what to look for in this kind of writing. The magic ingredient that confirms the authenticity of passion she calls "excès," a term which has meaning only in relation to a norm, and which here seems to mean always "going further" than her correspondent. The authenticating mark of her own "excess" in her style of expression is that her lover cannot ever adequately respond to it. As a standard of expression or interaction, excess also implies a social transgression, a form of behavior that consists in breaking the rules and "going too far." But by writing in a manner that is supposed to prove her lack of control over passion, the original transgression that passion represents becomes forgiveable.

*   *   *

Lettres de Babet and *Treize lettres* both illustrate how letter novels can function as pedagogical tools, teaching their readers a new rhetoric of intimate interaction: how to communicate feelings, how to test the authenticity of another's speech, how to appear sincere. These new versions of ideal interaction were by definition difficult to teach, for sincere expression was purportedly unique, inimitable, and springing directly from lived experience. The only way one might learn how to conduct intimate conversations is by overhearing them, or reading other people's letters. This tactic raises certain moral questions, which prefaces to epistolary novels quickly became very good at manipulating and obfuscating. Boursault's prefaces to *Lettres de Babet* engage in some of this, as he defends himself for having published the letters and points out the signs of their authenticity. In the preface to *Treize lettres*, though, he makes no attempt to moralize about this story of a fallen woman. Instead he tells a story of how the letters came to be published that draws further attention to the role of artifice in both the representation of passion and its exposure to public view.

The preface is in the form of a letter to the unnamed Madame***, who had provided the editor with his text. We learn that he was not the first publisher she had approached. Boursault is very hard on the publisher who had rejected the manuscript, comparing him to the *coq* of a fable who could not tell the difference between a precious stone and a piece of grain. Boursault, on the other hand, says he not only recognizes the worth of the letters, but he also wishes to place them at the beginning of his collection, against the wishes of the lady who had provided them. In his own assessment of the letters, though, Boursault says there is more artifice in them than their writer (or their writer's friend Madame***) would want readers to see:

> Je n'ai jamais vu de lettres où il y ait eu plus d'esprit et plus d'amour que dans celles que je trouvai hier dans le paquet que vous m'envoyâtes . . . mais je trouve dans ce que j'ai vu, un tour qui est moins l'ouvrage de la passion, que du jugement; et si j'étais sûr que vous ne voulussiez point avoir de rancune, je vous dirais qu'il y a plus de raison que votre sexe n'a coûtume d'en avoir. Je ne puis croire aussi que ce soit d'un homme: les hommes ont plus d'amour que les femmes, mais ils ne l'ont pas si violent . . .   (pp. 328–29).

He insinuates that this may be why the other publisher would not print the letters, thinking that readers would not accept a sincerity whose rhetorical design was not better disguised. His predecessor was foolish not to see that he had a profitable venture on his hands: "Quoiqu'il en soit, le libraire à qui vous avez montré de si tendres et de si amoureuses lettres, ne me semble pas habile de n'avoir pas su en profiter" (p. 329).

This certainly sounds like the story of Boursault's own attempts to publish the letters as a separate epistolary narrative. These efforts were apparently frustrated by what he saw as a market demand for examples of private writings that give no hint of either the role of artifice in the repesentation of passion, or the manner in which it was being made into a profitable artifact.

Boursault's letter novels, like many of his plays, present readers with counter-examples to the traditional models of courtly and gallant interaction, and promote a new aesthetic of candor and openness in both public and intimate settings. But what constitutes natural or sincere speech is still something that has to be taught in his texts, even when, as the preface to *Treize lettres* indicates, it was no longer fashionable to acknowledge the artifice underlying such ostensibly un-self-conscious discourse. Boursault's *Esope* not only makes moral arguments for sincere speech, he also teaches his admirers how it is done. Babet and the anonymous writer of the thirteen letters both point to the exemplary force of their own natural style. Oronte in *Le Mercure galant*, and Boursault himself in the prefaces to his epistolary tales demonstrate how writers can build their own reputations by convincingly arranging other people's private utterances.

Boursault's preface to *Treize lettres* is perhaps a little petulant—he decides to underscore both the rhetorical design of the letters and the editorial packaging that seems to be required to make them marketable. To score points against the publisher who had rejected the manuscript, he exposes the mechanism that is enabling him to make a profit. The "excess" that his female writer says is the feature of her writing that gives it value, could have become a source of hard currency for an astute publisher. And his letter to Madame*** draws attention to the fact that the easily marketed texts are now those that produce unreflecting, "natural" expressions of passion by effacing the more reasoned codes out of which they grew.

NOTES

1. *Oeuvres complètes* (Paris: Gallimard, 1949) I, p. 985.
2. The Duc D'Angoulême was an illegitimate son of Charles IX.
3. "La plus épineuse difficulté qui se rencontre à cet abord, est de savoir choisir un ami fidel, judicieux et experimenté, qui nous donne les bonnes adresses, et nous fasse voir un tableau des coûtumes qui s'observent, des puissances qui règnent, des cabales et des partis qui sont en crédit, des hommes qui sont estimés, des femmes qui sont honorées, des moeurs et des modes qui ont cours, et généralement de toutes les choses qui ne se peuvent apprendre que sur les lieux." *L'Honnête homme ou l'art de plaire à la cour* (Paris: P.U.F., 1925), pp. 39–40.
4. Cited in John Lough, *Writer and Public in France* (Oxford: Clarendon Press, 1978), p. 94.
5. See Lough, pp. 70–80. Robert Darnton summarizes Colbert's efforts to bring the publishing trade under state control in "Reading, Writing, and Publishing in Eighteenth-Century France," *Daedalus* 100 (Winter 1971), pp. 228–30.

6. Roger Duchêne's article on the similar social functions of the *gazette* and the familiar letter also contains useful observations on the influence of this new medium on the diffusion of aristocratic culture. See "Lettres et gazettes au XVII siècle," in his *Ecrire au temps de Madame de Sévigné* (Paris: J. Vrin, 1982), 89–102.

7. See note 3 above.

8. After the death of Loret in 1665, Boursault was briefly given the *privilège* to continue his weekly verse gazette. See the introduction to *Lettres de Babet* in *Lettres portugaises, Lettres d'une Péruvienne, et autres romans d'amour par lettres*, ed. Bray and Landy-Houillon (Paris: Flammarion, 1983), p. 102.

9. Elizabeth A. Marlow, in the only recent assessment of this play, surveys its relationship to literary precursors. See "*Le Mercure galant* de Boursault: une heureuse imitation des *Fâcheux* de Molière," *PFSCL* 16 (1982), pp. 213–32.

10. Boursault, *Théâtre choisi* (Paris: Laplace, Sanchez et Cie, 1883), p. 160. Unless otherwise indicated, further references to Boursault's plays will be to this edition.

11. For example, on pp. 185, 188, 193.

12. Nonetheless, Donneau de Visé regarded Boursault's play as slanderous, and brought suit against him, forcing him to change the title, which he obligingly did, to *La Comédie sans titre*.

13. *Gossip* (New York: Knopf, 1985), p. 66.

14. See "Avis au Lecteur," *Esope à la Cour*, in *Répertoire du Théâtre Français*, ed. Petitot (Paris: P. Didot L'Aîné, 1804), pp. 145–46.

15. As Ottaviano says in Book 4, "the end of the perfect courtier . . . is, by means of the accomplishments attributed to him by these gentlemen, so to win for himself the mind and favor of the prince he serves that he can and always will tell him the truth about all he needs to know, without fear or risk of displeasing him." *Book of the Courtier* (Baltimore: Penguin, 1967), p. 284.

16. In Burke's definition, the underlying purpose of courtly rhetoric is always to promote social cohesion: "By the 'principle of courtship' in rhetoric we mean the use of suasive devices for the transcending of social estrangement." *A Rhetoric of Motives* (Berkeley: University of California Press, 1950), p. 208.

17. Esope's explanations of his purpose in telling fables are very similar to Boursault's defense of theater in his preface to another play, *Les Mots à la mode*. He argues that art should be a means of rendering moral lessons palatable: ". . . il faut prendre l'âme par son faible, et tâcher de la conduire à la vertu par un chemin qui ne la rebute pas . . . " (*Théâtre de feu M. Boursault* (Paris: Le Breton, 1725), III, 97). Near the end of his career, in 1694, Boursault was involved in a violent quarrel with Bossuet over the latter's attack on theater. Boursault's letter to the archbishop of Paris defending Caffaro's "lettre sur les spectacles" argues that the playwright has a legitimate, even sacred moral purpose. See vol. I, 1–83. The play itself is based on François de Callières's popular book, *Les Mots à la mode* (1690), which decries the breakdown of commonly accepted norms of conversational interaction. See Chapter 1 above.

18. Bray/Landy-Houillon, eds., pp. 99–173. This is the most recent edition of *Lettres de Babet*, and the one we will be referring to here.

19. H. Porter Abbott, in his study of diary fiction, has remarked that "the year 1669 may be one of the neglected dates in the history of letter fiction,"

because it was the year that both *Lettres portugaises* and *Lettres de Babet* were published, and then "immediately imitated, pirated and travestied." *Diary Fiction: Writing as Action* (Ithaca: Cornell University Press, 1984), p.79.

20. This distinction is made in studies of the epistolary novel by Jean Rousset, *Forme et Signification*, ch.2; and most recently by Abbott, pp. 79–80. Janet Altman modifies the categories to the "kinetic" and "static" methods of narration in *Epistolarity: Approaches to a Form* (Columbus: Ohio State University Press, 1982), p. 194. Abbott remarks that the univocal *Lettres portugaises* survived only marginally in the following century, while "Boursault's work grows into the complex symphonic correspondence novels for which the eighteenth-century is noted . . ." Charles Kany also says that *Lettres de Babet* and *Lettres portugaises* initiated two different types of epistolary novels, which he calls "the frivolous" and "the psychological," in *The Beginnings of the Epistolary Novel in France, Italy, and Spain* (Berkeley: University of California Press, 1937), p.126.

21. See Jean-Michel Pelous, *Amour précieux, amour galant, 1654–1675* (Paris: Klincksieck, 1980), pp. 293–304.

22. Bernard Bray has considered the connections between these two works and earlier collections of model epistolary messages. He argues, with Deloffre and Rougeot, that Guilleragues also originally intended *Lettres portugaises* to be published as part of a manual illustrating different letter styles appropriate to love situations. After its publication, Guilleragues was apparently considered a master epistolary writer in any case for he was appointed personal secretary to Louis XIV in October 1669. Boursault's narrative, of course, was first printed as part of a collection of model letters. See Bray, *L'Art de la lettre amoureuse: des manuels aux romans* (LaHaye/Paris: Mouton, 1967) pp. 23–27, and the introduction to *Guilleragues, Lettres portugaises*, eds. Deloffre and Rougeot (Genève: Droz, 1972), pp. lx–lxx.

23. "Boursault et le roman par lettres," *RHLF* 69 (1969), p.531.

24. See Chapter 1 above.

25. Ten out of fourteen letters by Babet in the first half of the novel are "responses" while only four out of sixteen in the second half have that label.

26. See Tamara Alvarez-Detrell, *The Gambling Mania on and off the Stage in Pre-Revolutionary France* (Washington, D.C.: University Press of America, 1982).

27. See Chapter 2 above, pp.54–61.

28. Joan DeJean has shown that seventeenth-century female writers frequently viewed anonymity as a strategic self-defense against the typical betrayal of their authority once their writing was published. See "Lafayette's Ellipses: The Privileges of Anonymity," *PMLA* 99 (1984), pp.884–902.

29. Boursault clearly situates his text in a new sub-genre popularized by *Lettres portugaises* in 1661—an epistolary narrative comprised of the letters of a woman who loves too much. For a discussion of this "type portugais" as it developed in the late seventeenth century in France, see Susan Lee Carrell, *Le Soliloque de la passion féminine ou le dialogue illusoire* (Tübingen/Paris: Verlag/Place, 1982), pp. 39–72.

30. The first edition of *Lettres nouvelles de Monsieur Boursault, accompagnées de fables, de remarques, de bons mots et d'autres particularités aussi agréables qu'utiles*, published in 1697, included *Sept lettres amoureuses d'une dame à un cavalier*. In the

second edition Boursault added six more letters. A later edition, to which I will be referring (Paris: Michel-Etienne David, 1738), added *Treize Lettres Amoureuses* to the title page, an indication that Boursault's readers had, in fact, found these letters at the back more interesting than the others, as he had predicted (p.328).

Afterword

The increasingly broad spectrum of interactive situations presented in seventeenth-century writings on sociability seems to reflect a growing conviction that all communication has a place in a system of proper conduct. As both a vehicle for realizing one's social ambitions and a way of life, conversation is an activity that comes to be taken more and more seriously during the era of Louis XIV. Even earlier, in the novels of Madeleine de Scudéry, we see that she gives progressively more space to conversation, until, reading *Clélie*, we have the sense that her characters do almost nothing but talk to each other, and that action consists entirely in their verbal interaction. Letters, too, as vehicles for mitigating the effects of distance on sociable life, play a progressively more important role in each of her three novels.[1]

But the aristocratic model of conversation promoted by Scudéry is based on a premise of verbal abundance within a restricted frame of reference—a homogeneous and exclusive social circle. Within this carefully defined space conversation is one artifact of an aristocratic system of representation based on principles of resemblance and imitation as a method for enhancing individual worth. As a technique for cultivating the self, imitation works best when status systems are stable, when social closure is possible, when the verbal economy of a conversational circle is restricted, and when the value of each member's contribution is predetermined.

This kind of social interaction is fragile and easily unbalanced. Social changes that grant some individuals new rights or cause others to lose them give rise to new styles of interaction, new ways of making verbal exchange both meaningful and pleasing. Erica Harth has recently written about some seventeenth-century literary forms that challenged the aristocratic representational system by promoting a notion of an objectively verifiable truth which could be signified without recourse to the mediations of rhetoric or even artistic imitation.[2] In a sense, the epistolary novel was one of these subversive genres, for the act of letter-writing soon became emblematic of a new privatized form of interaction, adapting the patterns of sociability to a vision of the true self as unique and autonomous. In its beginnings, moreover, the letter novel emerged as a woman's discourse of passion, excessive and unreciprocated, and precisely the type of verbal performance that conventional sociability could not tolerate—the ultimate transgression for an *honnête femme*.[3]

The art of conversation will continue to be the primary rhetorical model for French epistolary novels of the eighteenth century.[4] Particularly in the earliest epistolary tales, readers are presented with a collection of letters that both tell a story and exemplify prevailing notions about proper interaction. The epistolary exchanges of Boursault's novels, like the written conversations of Scudéry's, always seem to have both a normative and a narrative function. But as the realm of sociability codes expands and lays claim to even the most intimate relationships, the utility of those norms begins to come into question. The success of the epistolary novel in the literary marketplace was not ultimately due to its use as a pedagogical tool, at least not in any obvious sense. In fact, epistolary novelists gave their readers more models of failed interactions than successful ones. The heroines of these stories have been thoroughly socialized, they are expert conversationalists and exemplary cultivated women, but in the end they use their verbal skills to strip away the appearances of *politesse* and gallant exchange and to discover in themselves a new, unique *sincérité*.

As a principle of interaction, sincerity is not without its own system of rhetorical figures. In the last years of Louis XIV, words like *franchise* and *politesse*, which seem so innocuous today, could be highly charged political terms. Montesquieu's, exuberant "Eloge à la sincérité," written shortly after the death of Louis XIV, reads like a call to arms, in which *sincérité* is paried with *vie privée* to evoke a new, utopian future age.[5] As a motive for communication, sincerity has both a history and a meta-phorical space which, unlike the airy pavillons of Scudéry's ideal con-versations, is usually behind closed doors. The design and practice of both modes of interaction can tell us a great deal about how reality is constructed and framed, about how people place themselves and each other in the world. Status, while it may be acquired, is nonetheless fabricated by those who vie for it, as Goffman writes: "A status, a position, a social place is not a material thing, to be possessed and then displayed, it is a pattern of appropriate conduct, coherent, embel-lished, and well articulated."[6] The written conversations of elite soci-ety, produced at a crucial transitional period in the history of the *ancien régime*, offer a rich textual record of personal responses to dramatic changes in a very well articulated status system. Verbal interaction, as both art and instrument, was to redefine exclusive social boundaries and traditional codes of conduct in response to a new diversity of ex-perience.

NOTES

1. See René Godenne's discussion in *Les Romans de Mademoiselle de Scudéry* (Genève: Droz, 1983), pp. 277–89; and Charles Kany's tables in *The Beginnings of the Epistolary Novel in France, Italy, and Spain* (Berkeley: University of Califor-nia Press, 1944), pp. 90–100.

2. *Ideology and Culture in Seventeenth-Century France* (Ithaca, N.Y.: Cornell University Press, 1984).

3. For a discussion of the "political challenge" historically posed by femi-nine epistolary desire in literature, see Linda Kauffman, *Discourses of Desire: Gender, Genre, and Epistolary Fictions* (Ithaca, N.Y.: Cornell University Press, 1986).

4. Janet Altman comments that the French epistolary novel is much more closely modeled on conversation and the rhetorical arts than the German or

English letter novels. See *Epistolarity: Approaches to a Form* (Columbus: Ohio State University Press, 1982), p. 194.

5. "Détestons la flatterie! Que la sincérité règne à sa place! Faisons-là descendre du Ciel, si elle a quitté la terre!" *Oeuvres complètes* (Paris: Gallimard, 1949), I, p.103.

6. *The Presentation of Self in Everyday Life* (Garden City, N.Y.: Doubleday, 1959), p.75.

Selected Bibliography

PRIMARY SOURCES

Bary, René. *L'Esprit de cour ou les conversations galantes, divisées en cent dialogues.* Bruxelles: Balthazar Vivien, 1664.

Boursault, Edme. *Lettres de Babet* in *Lettres portugaises, Lettres d'une Péruvienne, et autres romans d'amour par lettres.* eds. Bernard Bray and Isabelle Landy-Houillon. Paris: Flammarion, 1983.

———. *Lettres de respect, d'obligation et d'amour.* Paris: Girard, 1669.

———. *Lettres nouvelles de Monsieur Boursault . . . avec sept lettres amoureuses d'une dame à un cavalier.* Paris: Veuve de T. Girard, 1697.

———. *Lettres nouvelles de Monsieur Boursault . . . avec treize lettres amoureuses d'une dame à un cavalier.* Paris: Michel-Etienne David, 1738.

———. *Théâtre choisi.* Paris: Laplace, Sanchez et Cie, 1883.

Bussy, Roger de Rabutin, comte de. *Correspondance.* ed. Ludovic Lalanne. Paris: Charpentier, 1858–9.

———. *Histoire amoureuse des Gaules.* ed. Antoine Adam. Paris: Garnier-Flammarion, 1967.

———. *L'Histoire en abrégé de Louis le Grand.* Paris: Florentin et Pierre Delaulne, 1699.

———. *Mémoires.* ed. Ludovic Lalanne. Paris: Marpon et Flammarion, 1857.

Caillère, Jacques de. *La Fortune des gens de qualité et des gentilhommes particuliers, enseignant l'art de vivre à la cour. . . .* Paris: Etienne Loyson, 1661.

Callières, François de. *Des Mots à la mode.* Paris: Claude Barbin, 1690.

———. *Du Bon et du mauvais usage dans les manières de s'exprimer.* Paris: Claude Barbin, 1693.

Castiglione, Baldesar. *The Book of the Courtier.* Baltimore: Penguin, 1967.

Courtin, Antoine de. *Nouveau traité de la civilité qui se pratique en France.* Paris: H. Josset, 1671.

Des Rues, François. *Les Fleurs du bien dire.* Lyon: P. Roche, 1605.

Du Bosc, Jacques. *L'Honnête femme.* Paris: Jean Cochart, 1662.

Du Plaisir. *Sentiments sur les lettres et sur l'histoire. . . .* Genève: Droz, 1975.

Du Tronchet, Etienne. *Lettres missives et familières.* Paris: Lucas Breyer, 1568.

Faret, Nicolas. *L'Honnête homme ou l'art de plaire à la cour.* Paris: P.U.F., 1925.
Grenaille, François de. *L'Honnête fille.* Paris: Jean Paslé, 1639.
Grimarest, Jean Léonor de. *Traité sur la manière d'écrire des lettres et sur le cérémonial. . . .* Paris: J. Estienne, 1709.
Jacob, Paul. *Le Parfait secrétaire.* Paris: A. de Sommaville, 1656.
La Bruyère, Jean de. *Les Caractères.* Paris: Garnier, 1962.
La Fevrerie. "Du Style épistolaire," Extraordinaire du *Mercure galant,* juillet 1683.
La Fontaine, Jean de. *Oeuvres diverses.* Paris: Gallimard, 1958.
Lamy, Bernard. *De l'Art de parler.* Paris: André Pralard, 1676.
Lannel, Jean de. *Lettres.* Paris: T. Du Bray, 1625.
La Rochefoucauld, François, duc de. *Maximes.* Ed. J. Truchet. Paris: Garnier, 1967.
Leven, Templery de. *La Rhétorique française, très propre aux gens qui veulent apprendre à parler et à écrire avec politesse.* Paris: Martin Jouvenal, 1698.
Maintenon, Françoise d'Aubigné, marquise de. *Conversations.* Paris: Blaise, 1828.
———. *Extraits de ses lettres, avis, entretiens, conversations sur l'éducation.* ed. O. Gréard. Paris: 1884.
Méré, Antoine Gombauld, chevalier de. *Oeuvres complètes.* Paris: Editions Fernand Roches, 1930.
Milleran, René. *Le Nouveau secrétaire de la cour.* Paris: N. Le Gras, 1714.
Montesquieu, Charles Louis de. *Oeuvres complètes.* Paris: Gallimard, 1949.
Morvan de Bellegarde. *Modèles de conversations pour les personnes polies.* Paris: J. Guignard, 1697.
———. *Réflexions sur la politesse des moeurs, avec des maximes pour la société civile.* Amsterdam: Henri Desbordes, 1699.
Ortigue de Vaumorière, Pierre. *Lettres sur toutes sortes de sujets. . . .* Paris: J. Guignard, 1689.
Pascal, Blaise. *Pensées.* Paris: Mercure de France, 1976.
Pasquier, Nicolas. *Le Gentilhomme.* Paris: Jean Petit-Pas, 1611.
Puget de la Serre, Jean. *Le Secrétaire à la mode.* Amsterdam: L. Elzevier, 1663.
Pure, Michel, Abbé de. *La Précieuse ou le mystère des ruelles.* Paris: Droz, 1938.
Rénaud, André. *Manière de parler la langue française.* Lyon: Claude Rey, 1697.
Richelet, Pierre. *Les Plus belles lettres françaises. . . .* The Hague: Guillaume de Voys, 1708.
Rosset, François de. *Lettres amoureuses et morales des beaux esprits de ce temps.* Paris: S. Thiboust, 1618.
Scudéry, Madeleine de. *Conversations nouvelles sur divers sujets.* Paris: Claude Barbin, 1684.
———. *Conversations sur divers sujets.* Paris: Louis Billaine, 1680.
———. *Entretiens de morale.* Paris: Jean Anisson, 1693.
———. *La Morale du monde ou Conversations.* Paris: Pierre Mortier, 1686.
———. *Nouvelles conversations de morale.* Paris: Veuve de Sebastien Mabre, 1686.
Sévigné, Marie de Rabutin Chantal, marquise de. *Correspondance.* Paris: Gallimard, 1974–78.
———. *Lettres.* Paris: Hachette, 1866.
Somaize, Antoine Baudeau, sieur de. *Dictionnaire des prétieuses.* Paris: Jannet, 1856.

Tallemant des Reaux, Gédéon. *Les Historiettes*. Paris: Gallimard, 1960–61.
Voiture, Vincent. *Oeuvres*. Paris: Charpentier, 1855.

SECONDARY SOURCES

Abbott, H. Porter. *Diary Fiction: Writing as Action*. Ithaca, N.Y.: Cornell University Press, 1984.
Albanese, Ralph. "The Dynamics of Money in Post-Molièresque Comedy." *Stanford French Review* 6 (Spring, 1983): 73–89.
Allentuch, Harriet. "My Daughter/Myself: Emotional Roots of Madame Sévigné's Art." *Modern Language Quarterly*. 43 (1982): 121–37.
Altman, Janet Gurkin. *Epistolarity: Approaches to a Form*. Columbus: Ohio State University Press, 1982.
———. "The Letter Book as a Literary Institution 1539–1789: Toward a Cultural History of Published Correspondences in France," *Yale French Studies* 71 (1986): 17–62.
Alvarez-Detrell, Tamara. *The Gambling Mania On and Off the Stage in Pre-Revolutionary France*. Washington, D.C.: University Press of America, 1982.
Amiguet, Phillipe. *La Grande Mademoiselle*. . . . Paris: Albin Michel, 1957.
Apostolidès, Jean-Marie. *Le Roi-machine*. Paris: Minuit, 1981.
Ariès, Philippe. *L'Enfant et la vie familiale sous l'ancien régime*. Paris: Plon, 1960.
———. "Pourquoi écrit-on des mémoires?" in *Les Valeurs chez les mémorialistes français du XVIIe siècle avant la Fronde*. Actes du Colloque de Strasbourg et Metz, 18–20 mai, 1978. Paris: Klincksieck, 1979.
Aronson, Nicole. *Mademoiselle de Scudéry*. Boston: Twayne, 1978.
Auerbach, Erich. *Scenes from the Drama of European Literature*. New York: Meridian Books, 1959.
Baudin, Henri. "L'Italianisme dans les lettres de Madame de Sévigné." in *L'Italianisme en France au 17e siècle*. Torino: Società Editrice Internazionale, 1968.
Beugnot, Bernard. "Madame de Sévigné tel qu'en elle-même enfin?" *French Forum* 5 (1980): 201–17.
———. "Morale du repos et conscience du temps." *Australian Journal of French Studies* XIII (1976): 183–96.
———. "Style ou styles épistolaires?" *Revue d'histoire littéraire de la France* 78 (1978): 929–57.
Billacois, François. "La Crise de la noblesse européenne (1550–1650)." *Revue d'histoire moderne et contemporaine* 23 (1976): 258–77.
Bitton, Davis. *The French Nobility in Crisis, 1560–1640*. Stanford, Ca.: Stanford University Press, 1969.
Bonfantini, Mario. "Preface" to Santa Celoria, ed., *Le Grand Cyrus, Clélie: Episodes choisis avec le resumé des deux romans*. Turin: Giappichelli, 1973.
Bray, Bernard. *L'Art de la lettre amoureuse: des manuels aux romans*. LaHaye/Paris: Mouton, 1967.
———. "L'Epistolier et son public en France au 17e siècle." *Travaux de linguistique et de littérature* II (1973): 7–17.
———. "L'Epistolière au miroir: réciprocité, réponse, et rivalité dans les lettres

de Madame de Sévigné à sa fille." *Marseille* 95 (43 trimestre 1973): 22–29.

Burke, Kenneth. *A Rhetoric of Motives.* New York: Prentice-Hall, 1950.

Caillois, Roger. *Man, Play, and Games.* New York: Schocken Books, 1979.

Carrell, Susan Lee. *Le Soliloque de la passion féminine ou le dialogue illlusoire.* Tübingen/Paris: Verlag/Place, 1982.

Châtelain, Urbain-Victor. *Le Surintendant Nicolas Foucquet.* Paris: Didier, 1905.

Ciorenscu, Al. *L'Arioste en France.* Paris: Editions des Presses Modernes, 1939.

Cordelier, Jean. *Madame de Sévigné.* Paris: Seuil, 1967.

Cousin, Victor. *La Société française au XVIIe siècle d'après 'Le Grand Cyrus'.* Paris: Perrin, 1905.

Darnton, Robert. "Reading, Writing, and Publishing in Eighteenth-Century France" *Daedalus* 100 (Winter 1971): 214–56.

DeJean, Joan. "Lafayette's Ellipses: The Privileges of Anonymity." *Publications of the Modern Language Association* 99 (1984): 884–902.

Démoris, René. *Le Roman à la première personne.* Paris: Armand Colin, 1975.

Dens, Jean-Pierre. "L'Art de la conversation au 17e siècle." *Lettres romanes* 27 (1973): 215–24.

———. *L'Honnête homme et la critique du goût: esthétique et société au 17e siècle.* Lexington: French Forum, 1981.

Duchêne, Roger. "Le Lecteur de lettres." *Revue d'histoire littéraire de la France* 78 (1978): 977–90.

———. "Lettres et gazettes au XVIIe siècle." *Ecrire au temps de Madame de Sévigné.* Paris: J. Vrin, 1982.

———. *Madame de Sévigné et la lettre d'amour.* Paris: Bordas, 1970.

———. "Réalité vécue et réussite littéraire." *Revue d'histoire littéraire de la France* 71 (1971): 177–94.

———. "Signification du romanesque chez les mondains: l'exemple de Madame de Sévigné." *Revue d'histoire littéraire de la France* 77 (1977): 578–94.

Ehrmann, Jacques. *Un Paradis désespéré: l'amour et l'illusion dans l'Astrée.* Paris: P.U.F., 1963.

Elias, Norbert. *The Civilizing Process.* 1939, rpt. New York: Urizen Books, 1978.

———. *The Court Society.* New York: Pantheon, 1983.

Friedmann, Clara. "La cultura italiana di Madame de Sévigné." *Giornale storico della letteratura italiana* 60 (1912): 1–72.

Fumaroli, Marc. "Les Mémoires du XVIIe siècle au carrefour des genres en prose." *XVIIe siècle* 94–95 (1971): 7–37.

Gérard-Gailly, Emile. *Bussy-Rabutin, sa vie, ses oeuvres et ses amis.* Paris: Honoré Champion, 1909.

Godenne, René. *Les Romans de Mademoiselle de Scudéry.* Genève: Droz, 1983.

Goffman, Erving. *Encounters.* New York: Bobbs-Merrill, 1961.

———. *Interaction Ritual.* New York: Pantheon, 1967.

———. *The Presentation of Self in Everyday Life.* Garden City, N.Y.: Doubleday, 1959.

———. *Strategic Interaction.* Philadelphia: University of Pennsylvania Press, 1969.

Goldsmith, Elizabeth C. "Giving Weight to Words: Madame de Sévigné's Letters to her Daughter." *New York Literary Forum* 12–13 (1984): 107–15.

————. "Madame de Sévigné's Epistolary Retreat." *Esprit Créateur* 2 (1983): 70–79.

Guénoun, Solange. "Correspondance et paradoxe." *Papers in French Seventeenth-Century Literature* 15–2 (1981): 132–52.

Harth, Erica. *Ideology and Culture in Seventeenth-Century France*. Ithaca, N.Y.: Cornell University Press, 1983.

Hiller, C. F. *Edme Boursault*. Diss. Harvard University, 1934.

Hipp, Marie-Thérèse. *Mythes et réalités: enquête sur le roman et les mémoires, 1660–1700*. Paris: Klincksieck, 1976.

Horowitz, Louise. "The Correspondance of Madame de Sévigné: Letters or Belles-Lettres?" *French Forum* 6 (1981): 13–27.

————. *Love and Language: A Study of the Classical French Moralist Writers*. Columbus: Ohio State University Press, 1977.

Huppert, George. *Les Bourgeois Gentilhommes: An Essay on the Definition of Elites in Renaissance France*. Chicago: University of Chicago Press, 1977.

Jakobson, Roman. "Linguistics and Poetics." In *Style in Language*. ed. T. Sebeok, Cambridge, Ma.: MIT Press, 1960.

Kany, Charles. *The Beginnings of the Epistolary Novel in France, Italy, and Spain*. Berkeley: University of California Press, 1937.

Kauffman, Linda. *The Discourses of Desire: Gender, Genre, and Epistolary Fictions*. Ithaca, N.Y.: Cornell University Press, 1986.

Lathuillère, Roger. *La Préciosité*. Genève: Droz, 1966.

Lawrence, P. A., ed., *Georg Simmel*. Sunbury-on-Thames: Nelson, 1976.

Lievsay, John. *Stefano Guazzo and the English Renaissance*. Durham: University of North Carolina Press, 1961.

Lougee, Carolyn. *Le Paradis des Femmes: Women, Salons and Social Stratification in Seventeenth-Century France*. Princeton, N.J.: Princeton University Press, 1976.

Lough, John. *Writer and Public in France*. Oxford: Clarendon Press, 1978.

Lyons, John. "Being and Meaning: The Example of the Honnête Text." *Papers on French Seventeenth-Century Literature* 17 (1982): 153–72.

MacLean, Ian. *Woman Triumphant: Feminism in French Literature 1610–1652*. Oxford: Clarendon Press, 1977.

Magendie, Maurice. *La Politesse mondaine et les théories de l'honnêteté en France au dix-septième siècle*. 1925; rpt. Genève: Slatkine, 1970.

Marin, Louis. *Le Portrait du roi*. Paris: Editions de Minuit, 1981.

Marlow, Elizabeth. "*Le Mercure galant* de Boursault: une heureuse imitation des *Fâcheux* de Molière." *Papers on French Seventeenth-Century Literature* 16 (1982): 213–32.

Mauss, Marcel. *Oeuvres*. Paris: Minuit, 1969.

————. *The Gift*. New York: W. W. Norton, 1967.

Mongrédien, Georges. *Madeleine de Scudéry et son salon*. Paris: Tallandier, 1946.

Mousnier, Roland. *The Institutions of France Under the Absolute Monarchy, 1598–1789*. Chicago: University of Chicago Press, 1979.

Niderst, Alain. *Les Romans de Mademoiselle de Scudéry*. Genève: Droz, 1983.

Pelous, Jean-Michel. *Amour précieux, amour galant, 1654–1675*. Paris: Klincksieck, 1980.

Pessel, André. "De la Conversation chez les précieuses." *Communications* 30 (1979): 15–35.

Pizzorusso, Arnaldo. "Boursault et le roman par lettres." *Revue d'histoire littéraire de la France* 69 (1969): 525–39.

Ranum, Orest. *Artisans of Glory: Writers and Historical Thought in Seventeenth-Century France.* Chapel Hill: University of North Carolina Press, 1980.

———. "Courtesy, Absolutism, and the Rise of the French State, 1630–1660." *Journal of Modern History* 52 (1980): 426–51.

———. *Paris in the Age of Absolutism.* New York: Wiley and Sons, 1968.

Rouben, César. *Bussy-Rabutin épistolier.* Paris: Nizet, 1974.

———. "Histoire et géographie galantes au grand siècle: *L'Histoire amoureuse des Gaules* et la *Carte du pays de braquerie* de Bussy-Rabutin." *XVIIe siècle* 93 (1971): 55–73.

———. "L'Histoire en abrégé de Louis le Grand de Bussy-Rabutin." *Revue des Sciences Humaines* XXVI (1972): 525.

Sahlins, Marshall. *Stone-Age Economics.* Chicago: Aldine-Atherton, 1972.

Saint-Beuve, Charles-Augustin. "Tallement et Bussy, ou le médisant bourgeois et le médisant de qualité," in *Causeries du lundi.* Paris: Garnier, 1927, XIII, 172–88.

———. *Causeries du lundi.* Paris: Garnier, 1858.

Schalk, Ellery. *From Valor to Pedigree: Ideas of Nobility in 16th and 17th Century France.* Princeton, N.J.: Princeton University Press, 1986.

Sennett, Richard. *The Fall of Public Man.* New York: Knopf, 1977.

Simmel, Georg. *On Individuality and Social Forms.* Chicago: University of Chicago Press, 1971.

Skinner, Quentin. *The Foundations of Modern Political Thought.* Cambridge: Cambridge University Press, 1978.

Spacks, Patricia. *Gossip.* New York: Knopf, 1985.

Stanton, Domna. *The Aristocrat as Art: A Study of the honnête homme and the dandy in seventeenth- and nineteenth-century French literature.* New York: Columbia University Press, 1980.

Starobinski, Jean. "Sur la flatterie." *Nouvelle revue de la psychanalyse* 4 (1971): 131–51.

Strosetski, Christoph. *Rhétorique de la conversation: sa dimension littéraire et linguistique dans la société française du dix-septième siècle.* Paris/Seattle/Tübingen: Biblio 17 Papers on French Seventeenth-Century Literature, 1984.

Sweetser, Marie-Odile. "Madame de Sévigné et Saint-Simon, artistes et aristocrates: deux procès sous l'ancien régime." *Cahiers Saint-Simon* 9 (1981): 35–47.

Treasure, G. R. R. "The Price of War." In *Seventeenth-Century France.* New York: Barnes and Noble, 1966.

Trilling, Lionel. *Sincerity and Authenticity.* Cambridge, Ma.: Harvard University Press, 1972.

Viala, Alain. "La Genèse des formes épistolaires en français." *Revue de littérature comparée* 55 (1981): 168–83.

Whigham, Frank. *Ambition and Privilege: The Social Tropes of Elizabethan Courtesy Theory.* Palo Alto, Ca.: Stanford University Press, 1984.

————. "Interpretation at Court: Courtesy and the Performer-Audience Dialectic." *New Literary History* XIV (1983): 628–29.

Wolfe, Phillip J. ed. *Choix de Conversations de Mademoiselle de Scudéry.* Ravenna; Longo Editore, 1977.

————. *Dialogue et société.* Diss., Princeton University, 1974.

Wood, James. *The Nobility of the 'Election' of Bayeux, 1463–1666.* Princeton, N.J.: Princeton University Press, 1980.

Woolf, Virginia. "Madame de Sévigné." In *Death of the Moth.* New York: Harcourt Brace Jovanovich, 1942.

Index